THE FILMS OF
TIM BURTON

Animating Live Action in
Contemporary Hollywood

Alison McMahan

continuum

NEW YORK • LONDON

10066421

2006

The Continuum International Publishing Group Inc
80 Maiden Lane, New York, NY 10038

The Continuum International Publishing Group Ltd
The Tower Building, 11 York Road, London SE1 7NX

www.continuumbooks.com

Printed in the United States of America

Library of Congress Cataloging-in-Publication Data

McMahan, Alison.
     The films of Tim Burton : animating live action in contemporary
Hollywood / Alison McMahan.
        p.   cm.
     Includes bibliographical references and index.
     ISBN 0-8264-1566-0 (hardcover : alk. paper)—ISBN 0-8264-1567-9
(pbk. : alk. paper)
     1. Burton, Tim, 1958—Criticism and interpretation.   I. Title.
PN1998.3.B875M36   2005
791.4302′33′092—dc22
                                                            2005009872

ALSO AVAILABLE FROM CONTINUUM:

Joseph Kickasola:
The Films of Krzysztof Kieslowski

Jonathan Rayner:
The Films of Peter Weir, 2nd edition

Ximena Gallardo-C. and C. Jason Smith:
Alien Woman: The Making of Lieutenant Ellen Ripley

Rémi Fournier Lanzoni:
French Cinema: From Its Beginnings to the Present

Peter Bondanella:
Italian Cinema: From Neorealism to the Present, 3rd edition

Deborah Shaw:
Contemporary Cinema of Latin America

To Warren

Contents

Acknowledgments

I was a bit surprised in the spring of 2001 when my editor and publisher, David Barker at Continuum, who was about to publish my critical analysis of the work of the first woman filmmaker, *Alice Guy Blaché, Lost Visionary of the Cinema* (Continuum, 2002), suggested that I write a book on Tim Burton. David had heard me give a paper on special effects and thought I would be just the person for the job. I was a fan of Burton's work, but I didn't know if fandom would be enough to carry me through several years of intensive writing and research. I also wondered if it wasn't premature to write an overview of a career that is surely just reaching its midpoint.

At the time, I was teaching cinema and media studies at the University of Amsterdam, and it just so happened that several local theaters were jointly presenting a Festival of Fantasy Films, which included a retrospective of Tim Burton's feature films. It was a great opportunity to see all of his films on a big screen again. It did not take me long to decide that not only could I spend several years of my life on Burton's work, it would be fun. Furthermore, it wouldn't have the challenges that I had on my first project, which was about a silent filmmaker. It would be fairly easy to establish a complete filmography. It was easy to find almost all of his films. I would be able to study them in my own home instead of traveling to archives. Burton was born in Southern California, like me, around the same time. None of this was true of Guy Blaché's films: most of them were lost, those that existed were in archives all over the world, to which I had to travel, and though I spoke French, I found her culture of origin rather remote from mine. With Burton I looked forward to an easier experience, something more fun because it was more accessible.

At the same time, analyzing Burton's films was fraught with its own special difficulty. Since he is still alive and working, new data were coming up every day. Not that much has been written about him; with a few exceptions, most of what has been written is pure public relations. Wading through all that press, most of it not even very imaginative spin, became tiresome very quickly.

As anyone who picked up this book is already aware, Burton is a very special filmmaker. Though he works in Hollywood, his films often fall outside the contemporary Hollywood paradigm. His films are rife with tension-filled contrasts: he started out as an animator and, in a certain sense, still thinks like one, but almost all of his work as a director has been in live action. He is fond of old-fashioned special effects techniques and eschews CGI, but his films have their share of digital as well as traditional effects. He has a huge respect for actors, but what most people remember about him is his stunning sense of visual design. He is recognized around the world as a film auteur, but he is firmly entrenched in the Hollywood studio system. His career has lasted long enough that he has had to weather several marked changes in how movies are made and how the industry works, but he manages to keep expressing his own particular vision in his films, often with the same handful of people working on his production crew.

As I describe in detail in the introduction, writing about his films has led me to question the traditional academic divide between live action cinema and animation. Burton is fond of certain genres of film, such as fairy tales, horror, and fantasy (though he has also made action films, biopics, and documentaries), and often combines all of those genres in each film he makes. After closely studying his films for over a year, I finally realized that, when it came to Burton and others like him (some of whom are discussed toward the end of the book), I needed to come up with a new genre term, as the old ones have metamorphosed, recombined, and grown into something that the old names can no longer adequately describe. (I explain this new genre theory in the introduction.)

My research has especially benefited from previous work carried out by Janet K. Halfyard, Ken Hanke, Helmut Merschmann, Jim Smith and J. Clive Matthews, Mark Salisbury, Frank Thompson, and Paul A. Woods (book titles are listed in the bibliography), as well as many academic and journalistic authors too numerous to mention here, but most of whom are listed in the bibliography or in the chapter notes.

Parts of this book were given as papers at the following conferences: "The Day Hollywood Went Digital: *Jurassic Park* and the Transition from Stop-Motion and Animatronics to CGI in Hollywood," Society for Cinema and Media Studies Conference, Minneapolis, March 2003; "Will the Real Animation Please Stand Up: The Transition from Stop-Motion and Animatronics to CGI in Hollywood Films," 14th Annual Society for Animation Studies Conference, Glendale, California, September 2002; "The Animation Paradigm," 7th International Congress of Domitor, Montreal, May 2002; and "Machine (the Computer) + Cinema = Machinima," Society for Cinema Studies Conference, Denver, March 2002. I benefited greatly from the stimulating environment provided at these conferences.

I would like to thank Warren Buckland for inviting me to test out various chapters in his classes at Chapman University: "Special Effects and the College of Pataphysics," in April 2004; "The Increasing Use of Animation and SFX in Contemporary Hollywood," in March 2003; "*Batman*: Myth, Marketing, and Merchandising," in March 2002, and "What a Film Composer Does: Danny Elfman," in December 2004. His feedback as well as his students' greatly contributed to several chapters in the book.

I wrote Chapter 3 while I was a Mellon postdoctoral fellow at Vassar College. Much of the material in Chapters 3 and 5 was presented to the students in my Film 183 course, "Fantasy and Horror," in the fall of 2002: Anine Booth, Sophia Clark, Joshua Ferguson, Thomas Gemelli, Robert Gestone, Michael Gillen, Ashlinn Killeen, Frederick Lash, Ryan Linn, Monica Menendez, Seth Mittelman, Dimitri Otvertchenko, George Peterson, Alice Sackey, and Nicolle Walsh. Our lively discussions greatly helped me clarify my thinking about 3-D animation and special effects and their role in contemporary cinema. I am especially grateful to Ethan Bien for arranging a William Castle retrospective at Vassar. My teaching assistant, Violeta de los Reyes, helped me find numerous articles on Burton.

A project like this is impossible without the help of friends. John Leary provided me with back issues of *Cinéfantastique* and other Burton-related tie-ins. There were the coffee sessions discussing animation in general, and digital animation in particular, with Professor Tom Ellman at Vassar College. I also benefited greatly from the technical expertise of my friend Rain Breaw.

I also spent some interesting hours online with the subscribers to the Elfman Zone website http://www.bluntinstrument.org.uk/elfman/. I am especially grateful to Ian Davis for sending me some interviews with Danny Elfman. I am also grateful to Richard Porton for his help on various issues and to Paul Gulino for advice and encouragement.

I spent many pleasurable hours with my daughter, Ruth, watching and rewatching Burton's films, as well as the films of Mario Bava and Hammer Horror.

There aren't enough words to thank my husband, Warren Buckland, whose support, both critical and personal, was instrumental in the completion of this book. He helped me find stills and did a lot of proofreading, and we had many interesting conversations comparing Burton with Steven Spielberg, as Warren is currently writing a book on Spielberg.

As it happened, the period during which I was contracted to write this book coincided with a period of great upheaval in my life, including two moves, marriage, and several changes in employment. I am extremely fortunate to have David Barker as a publisher at Continuum, and I am very grateful to him for his patience and understanding. Thanks, David, for assigning me this project to begin with and for your infinite patience as I struggled to finish this book with all of that going on.

Author's Note

This book is a study of the work of Tim Burton and how his films fit into contemporary Hollywood filmmaking. To illustrate the points I am making, I have reproduced a few images from especially significant moments in his oeuvre. Each image is a single frame taken from a full-length motion picture and is used here for education purposes pursuant to the fair use doctrine.

My book is not endorsed by or affiliated with any of the performers, directors, producers, or screenwriters who created these movies or by the studios that produced and directed them, and the single-frame images are used here for purposes of criticism and commentary only.

Readers who are interested in seeing these motion pictures are encouraged to buy or rent copies of the movies from authorized sources.

Introduction

Pataphysics will examine the laws governing exceptions, and will explain the universe supplementary to this one: or, less ambitiously, will describe a universe which can be—and perhaps should be—envisaged in place of the traditional one, since the laws that are supposed to have been discovered in the traditional universe are also correlations of exceptions, albeit more frequent ones, but in any case accidental data which, reduced to the status of unexceptional exceptions, possess no longer even the virtue of originality.
—Alfred Jarry Taylor, *Exploits and Opinions of Dr. Faustroll, Pataphysician*[1]

The New Pataphysics

Film critics such as Neil Gabler have complained that the Hollywood cinema of the last twenty years has lost its meaning. Gabler, the author of *Life the Movie: How Entertainment Conquered Reality*,[2] also wrote an op-ed piece in the *New York Times* in the summer of 2002 outlining his position.[3] He coined the term *likeamovie*, claiming that Hollywood no longer works to actually entertain us, to really engage us, but instead delivers facsimiles of real entertainment, films we can follow only because we still remember what real entertainment looks like. According to Gabler, this is not entertainment, but the "illusion of entertainment":

> In most entertainment, the audience responds emotionally, psychologically, intellectually, even physically. There is a level of engagement, and we usually judge entertainment on the basis of how much engagement it elicits. At its simplest, as in so many teenage movies, the illusion of entertainment eschews other forms of engagement for purely physical effects. At its more complex, engagement is replaced by another mechanism entirely. Instead of character development in movies or full-bodied jokes in situation comedies viewers get a set of signals, a kind of code, that advises them how to respond without having to expend the effort, however minimal, that real entertainment demands. You see and hear the signal and you respond as if you were

getting the real thing. Or, put another way, you are given the form and you provide the content.

. . . [I]n effect, these entertainments exist largely as a system of reminders of what we once experienced when we watched real entertainment—movies and television shows that engaged us and made us feel.[4]

What kinds of movies is Gabler referring to? The only example he gives in his article is the Adam Sandler vehicle *Mr. Deeds* (2002), a film with little in the way of special effects but in many ways a poor remake of its original. Gabler argues vehemently that the films he is critiquing are not simply bad formulaic entertainment, which strives to engage using overly predictable means and usually fails. The films Gabler is really attacking involve "a different way of processing what we see." These "illusions of entertainment" get predictable responses, not by actually eliciting an emotional response, but "by cuing the audience in how they are supposed to react." And the audience does react, because "virtually all Americans have internalized the code . . . and are hardwired to respond."

Similar critiques have been leveled against such films as *The Matrix* trilogy (1999–2003) and comic book films like *Hulk* (2003) and *Van Helsing* (2004). For example, on *The Matrix*,

. . . the Wachowskis [brothers Andy and Larry] have synthesized a savvy visual vocabulary (thanks especially to Bill Pope's inspired techno-cinematography), a wild hodgepodge of classical references (from the biblical to Lewis Carroll) and a situation that calls for a lot of explaining.

The most salient things any prospective viewer need know is that Keanu Reeves makes a strikingly chic Prada model of an action hero, that the martial arts dynamics are phenomenal (thanks to Peter Pan–type wires for flying and inventive slow-motion tricks), and that anyone bored with the notably pretentious plotting can keep busy toting up this film's debts to other futuristic science fiction.[5]

On *The Hulk:*

[Screenwriters John Turman, Michael France, and James Schamus] lose sight of the basic requirements of visual clarity, narrative momentum and emotional impact, without which this kind of thing quickly lapses into cultishness or mythomaniacal pretension. Like the raging Hulk himself, a computer-generated Gumby on steroids. . . .[6]

And on *Van Helsing:*

[T]he brawling ghouls, vampires and werewolves wreaking havoc in Dracula's castle under a full moon—to say nothing of the semi-romantic mumbo jumbo passing between Anna and Van Helsing in midfight—are part of a clattering, hectic spectacle that, by the end, has almost completely run out of ideas and inspiration. Which is no great surprise because, despite the rococo obsessiveness of its special effects and its voracious sampling of past horror movies, "Van Helsing" is mostly content to offer warmed-over allusions and secondhand thrills.[7]

Is Gabler correct in arguing that these "warmed-over allusions and secondhand thrills" are indications, not of Hollywood's creative bankruptcy, but of film narration changing, beginning to create meaning in a new way, at least different from the system of classical Hollywood narration that we are accustomed to? The argument of this book is that the answer to this question is yes: yes, filmic narration is changing, though not in a direction without filmic precedent. This does not mean, as Gabler and the reviewers quoted above suppose, that these films mean less—which is not to say that they are better films. I will label this new system of meanings the "pataphysical" way, after the "College for Pataphysicists," originally formed in France in 1948.[8]

My argument in this book is not that current films have "lost" their meaning but that they have come to mean differently, to mean in new ways. In other words, it may be that the movies Neil Gabler is watching appear to be "likeamovies" because a new approach is required to read them, an approach that he is unwilling to take. He is unwilling to let go of the security of classical Hollywood narrative logic and its continuity system of meaning and, furthermore, unwilling to have his old gods satirized.

Pataphysical films have several common characteristics, including some or all of the following. Pataphysical films

1. Make fun of established systems of knowledge, especially academic and scientific
2. Follow an alternative narrative logic
3. Use special effects in a "gee whiz," that is, a blatant, visible way (as compared to "invisible" effects that simulate live action, but without real harm to the actors)
4. Feature thin plots and thinly drawn characters, because the narrative relies more on intertextual, nondiegetic references to be understood

Once we are aware of these characteristics, it becomes clear that pataphysical films are not a recent phenomenon. To the contrary, pataphysical films have been around since the beginning of cinematic history. For example, consider *Le voyage dans la lune* (*A Trip to the Moon*), produced, directed and starred in by Georges Méliès in 1902. *A Trip to the Moon* aims to show the illogicality of logical thinking. Méliès' goal was, as Richard Abel has described, "to invert the hierarchical values of modern French society and hold them up to ridicule in a riot of the carnivalesque."[9] The film makes fun of the scientists by depicting them at first as medieval magicians, as well as generally inept. It shows them discovering that the "face" on the moon belongs to an actual "man," and the moon is also populated with little green men. Méliès himself plays the chief scientist.[10]

The film follows the narrative logic of animation, which focuses on transformation rather than plot development. Even the forces of motion obey laws other than those of physics. For example, a rocket is shot to the moon from a circus cannon, a man flies back to Earth while being towed by a rocket, stars turn into women, a man survives being dunked into a vat of nitrous oxide, umbrellas on the moon turn into mushrooms and grow immensely huge, and a Selenite (a native inhabitant of the moon) disappears in a cloud of dust after being hit.

A Trip to the Moon is a "trick film," a genre of early film predominant around 1896 to 1902, whose narrative was subservient to the special effects, or tricks. It still enchants by its use of special effects, which it uses in both a visible and an invisible way. The flyaway staging would have been "invisible" to contemporary audiences, as it was a convention that was so accepted that it would be read as realistic, but the montage of the rocket returning and the matte shots of the approach to the moon brought audible gasps and made the film enduringly popular in Europe and the United States for years, to the extent it was widely pirated by other companies like the Edison Manufacturing Co., and the Lubin Manufacturing Co.

Compare this film with *The Core* (Jon Amiel, 2003), in which Aaron Eckhart and Hilary Swank lead a team of scientists on a journey to the center of a stilled Earth to nudge the planet's core back into a rotating movement with a couple of nuclear bombs. Each of the team's adventures is highlighted by a series of special effects, and the most memorable moments come from the satire that is Stanley Tucci's rendering of a lead scientist. In terms of its satire of the scientific academy and the use of special effects almost as a plot device, *The Core* and *A Trip to the Moon* have much in common.

Antecedents: The Incoherents and the Surrealists

In the early cinema, trick films and animation films were closely related. We can see this relationship if we compare *A Trip to the Moon* with Emile Cohl's *Fantasmagorie,* an animated film (white lines drawn on a black background) made in 1908 for Gaumont. The thin plot revolves around a stick-figure clown and a bourgeois gentleman who suffer one calamity after another, each calamity a pretext to display a series of special effects, usually illogical metamorphoses. To name just a few, the gentleman's hat and umbrella turn into a movie theater interior; the clown emerges out of the ballooning head of a woman sitting in front of the gentleman and engulfs him; later, an elephant, whose tusks are cradling the clown, changes into a house; the clown then plunges out of a window and loses his head, which Cohl's hand reattaches with a paste brush.[11] *Fantasmagorie* engages us not by a cast of "rounded" characters having a series of experiences that ends with them learning some moral lesson, but by indulging in a series of whimsical transformations that amuse and poke fun at turn-of-the-twentieth-century class pretensions.

Cohl was a member of the Incoherents, a movement he actively participated in from 1882 until its dissolution in 1891. It was founded by Jules Lévy, with the motto "Brothers, we must laugh," which summarized their defiant assault on the decorum of the salons and the Academy.[12] The goal was to exhibit drawings and paintings that caricatured the salon paintings that represented the establishment thinking about art of the day. The Incoherents' exhibits of 1881 and 1884 were so successful that participants were able to donate the large sums earned from entrance fees to charity.[13] As Donald Crafton has noted, Cohl's later filmmaking was heavily influenced by the ideas of the Incoherents:

> [The Incoherents'] common ancestor was [Charles] Baudelaire, but at least three separate movements were discernible: the Symbolism proper of [Stéphane] Mallarmé, [Arthur] Rimbaud's *poésie fantastique,* and [Paul] Verlaine's Decadents. The Incoherents absorbed the general aesthetic program of linguistic renewal proposed in varying formulas by these divergent groups but reacted strongly against their seriousness, introversion, and morbidity.[14]

The Incoherents were nihilists who placed great value on spontaneous artistic expression, who refused to adhere to rules or conventions or to impose any rational structure or order to their art. Cohl's best known work, *Le peintre néoimpressionniste* (Gaumont, 1910), is a film influenced by the Incoherent movement that predicts the pataphysical films of the future in various ways: it shows an artist duping a bourgeois art collector by getting him to buy "blank" canvases, but the film viewer sees that each canvas has an animated scene inserted over it through the use of special effects. Typical scenes include "a cardinal eating lobster in tomato sauce beside the Red Sea" for a red canvas and "Negroes making shoe polish in a tunnel at night," using black leader. In other words, at least two discourses are operating in the film simultaneously, one diegetic (in the story) and one nondiegetic. Both discourses in Cohl's films are humorous and often require repeat viewing in order for a typical audience member to grasp all of the details. Like other Incoherents, Cohl was attracted to the grotesque, distorted images that the Surrealists would later claim had originated in the unconscious, such as hybrids of humans and animals as we saw in *Fantasmagorie*.[15]

Many of the qualities that constitute pataphysical films are characteristic of surrealist films as well. André Breton initiated the Surrealist movement in 1924 with the stated goal of altering the course of the unconscious of society. Qualities of surrealism included an obsession with Sigmund Freud and the unconscious; like the Dadaists before them, the Surrealists cherished the random phrase and the image recorded as if by accident. They took as their notion of beauty the juxtaposition of incongruous elements, in order to attack the familiar and provoke an irruption of otherness. Rosalind Krauss summed up Breton's position:

> In Breton's account, then, the world of real objects has nothing to do with an art of mimesis; the objects are in no sense models for the sculptor's work. The world is instead a great reserve against which to trace the workings of the unconscious, the litmus paper that makes it possible to read the corrosiveness of desire.[16]

Many Surrealists, such as Marcel Duchamp, joined the College for Pataphysics later, so in some ways the surrealist movement can be seen as a predecessor to the pataphysical movement. What the pataphysical approach adds to the satire and the desire to make the subconscious manifest in art of these earlier movements is the use of intertextual references and, often, humor. This is why I have chosen the term *pataphysical* as a name for what I see as a new flowering of a certain approach to filmmaking: because humor, even if it is sly and dry, is always an aspect of these films.

Tim Burton, a Pataphysical Director

The goal of this book is to make a case for a genre of contemporary films I have labeled "pataphysical," using the work of Tim Burton as a case study. Burton is one of the most influential of the pataphysical film directors, as many other directors come to pataphysics by imitating his style. The fact that Burton's most pataphysical films tend to do well at the box office has facilitated the production of pataphysical films generally.

I will begin my analysis of Burton's work in Chapter 1, which presents an analysis of Burton's 2-D animation, from *Family Dog* to the Shockwave animation films based on his book of poems for children, *The Melancholy Death of Oyster Boy & Other Stories*. In the case study of the Shockwave animations, I will analyze how Burton became the poster boy for machinima filmmakers (2-D animators who use game engines and first-person shooter conventions as the basis for their machinima films). Throughout the book, but especially in this chapter, I place these films in the context of the historical antecedents—including the work of Georges Méliès, early animators (Emile Cohl, J. Stuart Blackton, and Windsor McCay), the avant-garde, and 1960s television—Burton has mentioned as inspiration.

Chapter 2 focuses on the antiestablishment message of most of Burton's films. His melancholy heroes, such as Edward Scissorhands, Ichabod Crane, and Batman (usually read as stand-ins for the director himself); his trickster characters, such as Pee-wee, Beetlejuice, Edward Bloom (from *Big Fish*), and Willy Wonka (from *Charlie and the Chocolate Factory*), and his interpretations of everyman characters, such as Leo (from *Planet of the Apes*) and Byron Williams from (*Mars Attacks!*), always emphasize the character's antagonistic relationship with an oppressive establishment. Even his happy characters, such as Ed Wood and Jack Skellington, learn hard lessons. This chapter will focus on his key lead characters and examine their roles as critics of the social order. This built-in critique also has an effect on the film's structure (Burton's films are often accused of having weak plots). Particular attention is paid to his fairy-tale films *Edward Scissorhands*, *Sleepy Hollow*, and *Big Fish*. The chapter also examines the narration of Burton's TV fairy tales, *Frankenweenie, Pee-wee's Big Adventure,* and *Beetlejuice*. As a pataphysical filmmaker, Burton follows an alternative narrative logic, one closely based on the logic of animation.

Chapter 3 looks at Burton's use of special effects, examining his 3-D animation. Burton is renowned for his stop-motion work in films like *Vincent, The Nightmare Before Christmas, Beetlejuice,* and (as producer) *James and the Giant Peach*. He had originally planned to use a great deal of stop-motion animation for his sci-fi satire *Mars Attacks!*, but he was persuaded by Warner Bros. to switch from stop-motion to computer-generated imagery (CGI)—and shave $20 million from the budget. Burton, who had started his career in animation and first made his mark with the stop-motion short *Vincent*, fought the change, until Industrial Light and Magic (ILM) showed him what had been done on *Jurassic Park* and *Jumanji*. Burton's decision-making process basically replicated Steven Spielberg's on *Jurassic Park* just six years before. These two high-profile cases are indicative of a change taking place throughout the industry, where much work traditionally done with stop-motion and animatronics is now carried out with computer-generated graphics. Some critics have even labeled the change "the end of animation history" and pointed out that both practitioners and scholars need to come up with a new definition of what animation is, a positive definition that isn't based on calling animation "not live-action cinema" but puts animation and live action into a new relation to each other. Later in this introduction I will put the relationship of animation and live-action film today into perspective by looking back at the relationship between the two at the very beginnings of film's history.

Chapter 4 focuses on Burton's rendition of *Batman*, which broke all box office records, a runaway success that set a new standard for blockbusters and led to the rebirth of comic book franchise films. The success of the film mystified even its creator. In this chapter, I present a case study of the *Batman* films, demonstrating how high-concept (myth-based) blockbuster films need to be considered in the light of horizontal integration and ancillary markets (especially since 1989) and the role played by total merchandising. Not much room is left in this process for an individual artist, and Burton was removed from the *Superman* production after having worked on it for a year. Yet the pattern set by Burton with *Batman* started a trend that is still noticeable in comic book films like *Spiderman, Daredevil,* and *Hulk.*

Chapter 5 looks at Burton's two recent remakes, *Planet of the Apes* and *Charlie and the Chocolate Factory* (not yet released at the time of this writing), and analyzes how Burton's approach changes when he is dealing with preexisting material.

Chapter 6 takes a careful look at Burton's soundscapes and Danny Elfman's scores for Burton films. Music and memorable soundscapes are an integral part of every Tim Burton film, especially since *Batman*'s dense soundscape and rich score.

Chapter 7 applies the pataphysical analysis briefly to other directors, especially those influenced by Burton. A working list of pataphysical directors includes some people who have collaborated with Burton such as Henry Selick, Nick Park of the Aardman Studios in Britain, and the brothers Quay, as well as other directors who have come to pataphysics on their own, such as Joe Dante, Richard Donner, Barry Sonnenfeld, Luc Bresson, Jean-Pierre Jeunet and Marc Caro, Stephen Sommers, and Roland Emmerich. (The chapter looks at the work of Sonnenfeld, Sommers, and Emmerich.) Taken together, the pataphysical films of these directors earmark the ways in which the horror, fantasy, and sci-fi film genres are changing.

Before I proceed to the analysis outlined above, I need to clarify the historical relationship between animation and special effects.

Relationship between Animation and Trick Films

Film history is characterized by certain grand narratives. For example, it has long been held that it took the earliest filmmakers almost twenty years to establish the basic principles of filmic narration; that silent movies came first, and synchronized sound movies came belatedly after; and that live-action cinema is the umbrella paradigm from which all other mediums, such as animation, are derived. I have reexamined the first of these grand narratives in my book *Alice Guy Blaché, Lost Visionary of the Cinema,*[17] where I argue that early filmmakers grasped the principles of filmic narration well before 1906, and that synchronized sound was the goal of filmmakers from the beginning and was achieved in various formats from 1902 on.

Now let us look at the idea that animation is derived from live-action cinema. Is cinema really a medium separate from animation? Does live-action cinema even deserve to be called a separate medium in the twenty-first century? I no longer think so. Cinema exists only as a manifestation of something else, something bigger and culturally more all-encompassing. We could call this other all-encompassing thing animation. Live-action cinema and animation have an inverse relationship to the one that is usually supposed. Animation is actually the medium that we are all studying. Cinema is just one part of it. Consider the earliest moving picture machines. Most of them projected images, whether it was the Praxinoscope projecting Émile Reynaud's drawings or the cinematograph projecting the images of Louis and Auguste Lumière that gave an illusion of life by being shown rapidly one after the other.

These machines were only one product of the industrial drive to mechanization of the nineteenth and early twentieth centuries. The drive to mechanization was the drive to measure, quantify, and ultimately automate every aspect of life. Moving pictures were born out of a science called motion studies, with the immediate goal of understanding human and animal locomotion in order to devise exercises to perfect the effort of soldiers and to solve the mysteries of flight. The by-products of this investigation were live-action cinema and animation, both born out of the same drive to capture, store, and replay motion at will.

One of the most influential of the motion studies pioneers was Eadweard Muybridge (born in Great Britain but active in the United States), a still photographer who was commissioned by Leland Stanford, the president of the Central Pacific Railroad, to photograph a horse at full trot to demonstrate, once and for all, whether all four hooves left the ground at once at any point. Muybridge worked on this problem for years. Finally, in 1877, Muybridge managed to line up twelve cameras that could take exposures in $1/1,000$ of a second, triggered when the horse broke the cords set across the track. These pictures showed definitively that the horse's hooves did leave the ground in midtrot. Muybridge continued these experiments and photographed many sequences of animals and humans in motion. Muybridge's galloping horse sequences were published in magazines in the form of strips that could be cut out and fit into zoetropes so that home viewers could enjoy the gallop for themselves.

Another motion studies pioneer, Étienne-Jules Marey, began by adapting the photographic rifle that the astronomer Pierre-Jules Janssen had developed to photograph the passage of Venus across the sun, and he was galvanized by the publication of Muybridge's photographs of Leland Stanford's racehorse. In 1883 he was awarded money to erect a building on his Station Physiologique, his center for the study of locomotion. The money also enabled him to hire an associate, Georges Demeny.

At first, Marey used single large fixed plates on which a series of images would be imprinted; however, the overlap of these images made it difficult to decipher the motions he wished to study. By 1888 he had developed the *chronophotographe sur bande mobile,* a motion picture camera that could register up to twenty images a second on paper. Because the roll of paper was not perforated, it wasn't possible to make the images equidistant, thus making it unreliable in the capture and projection of true motion picture images. Until 1892 Marey studied his images of locomotion by cutting them out and then attaching them equidistantly inside a zoetrope, as Muybridge had done. Zoetropes were originally designed to hold hand-drawn or -painted strips, rotate them, and make them appear to move when viewed through a slit: in other words, animation.[18] Live-action cinema and animation were both born out of the same drive to capture, store, and replay motion at will.

Émile Reynaud

As early as 1877, before cinema was invented, before Thomas Edison's kinetoscope of 1895 or the Lumières' film camera in 1896, Émile Reynaud was making and projecting animated bands for his Praxinoscope. From 1892 to 1900 he rear-projected more elaborate bands, which he now called *"pantomimes lumineuses,"* onto a screen by means of a complicated mirror-and-lens system. The images were hand-painted on long strips of transparent celluloid and fitted into a leather band with perforations next to each frame. His apparatus in many ways prefigured that of cinematic projection, though all of the images were hand-drawn and hand-colored by Reynaud himself.

French film historians chose to give the Lumière brothers credit as the fathers of film because they used a single strip of celluloid, which could be mass-produced (the definition of film was based on the Lumière output: it consisted of live action, shot on celluloid, and projected using 35 mm perforated film). This definition was adopted by the Anglo film historians.

But from the perspective of the era of digitization, the era we are in today, it appears that they were wrong, and Reynaud should be given credit as the first animator, first filmmaker, and first film exhibitor, as Reynaud's process and methods were more clearly predictive of today's digital cinema than the Lumière system.

After Reynaud there was not much in the way of animation on film, until Emile Cohl. Cohl was a respected graphic artist and caricaturist who went to work for the film production company Gaumont in Paris in 1908 as a scenarist (the original term for screenwriter). Instead of filming lightning sketches (films of graphic artists drawing humorous images at top speed) or doing trick films with animated objects, as pioneer American animator J. Stuart Blackton had done, Cohl made a film based on 700 individual line drawings using India ink on white paper, which were then photographed, for two frames each, and had the lab print the film in negative, so that he ended up with a white-on-black chalk-line effect. This first effort was *Fantasmagorie* (1908), described above. Crafton has documented Cohl's acknowledged debt of inspiration to Reynaud and to Marey.[19] That *Fantasmagorie*'s hallucinatory images had such an impact, however, was probably due to their seeming spontaneity and to the unusual fluidity of the transformations—perhaps not unlike the gracefully multiplying white lines of Marey's "chronophotographs."

Narration and Animation

It is precisely this fluidity of transformations, typical of animated narration, that carries over to pataphysical films. I will examine this in more detail in Chapter 1, but here is an overview. According to E. G. Lutz, animated narrative is characterized by the following:[20] Animation aims for a laugh for every foot of film. Characters are well defined and in constant movement; the plot is an orderly establishment of parts that lead up to some main point, a succession of distressing mishaps, growing in violence, a cumulative chain of actions, increasing in force and resultant misfortune. The preferred ending has pantomimic action only (no dialogue in titles or voice). Certain concepts, such as humans moving like machines, are always good for a laugh. Certain movements, such as any rotary movement, are used often, because the human mind is fascinated by any rotary movement; so, for example, a victim of a blow must always reel around like a top before he falls, even though this isn't possible in real life. All of this constant motion requires that there be moments of rest, a rhythmic slowing up or pause (such as a character disappearing for a moment behind the house or down the hill). These same characteristics can be found in today's pataphysical films, which add the language of animation to special effects and digital cinema.

Combining Animation and Trick/Special Effects Films

After *Fantasmagorie*, Cohl made a series of films that combined animation and live action, often with trick effects, such as *Songe du garcon du café* (1910) and *Clair de lune espagnol* (1909). Donald Crafton has dubbed these "Incoherent" films because they were so clearly inspired by the Incoherent movement Cohl had belonged to earlier, such as *Le peintre néoimpressionniste* described above. Cohl was not the only one to make "Incoherent" films. Pathé Frères also made *Une excursion incoherente* (1910), in which a couple going to the country on an outing are menaced by demons (shown as shadows), spectral dancers, and a horrifying, sexualized shadow nightmare. What all of these films have in common is that they combine tricks (today we would call them special effects) with animation.

Types of tricks popular in trick films included stop-motion, which created an abrupt series of appearances, disappearances, or substitutions; reverse motion (a flipped dinner table righted itself); multiple exposures (three identical singing heads), coupled with a matte device masking off an area of the camera lens; invisible editing, or cuts that make things disappear on exact framing (also called stop substitution); theatrical devices, such as trapdoors and hydraulics, used to lift objects and people; and enlarging things by bringing them close to the camera in sequential shots.[21] Many in-camera effects today resort to the same techniques.

The earliest animated films used a slight narrative as a pretext to display a series of special effects, just as Méliès' trick films did a few years later. If we look at stop-motion films, such as the films of Ray

Harryhausen (master of stop-motion films in 1950s Hollywood), we see that in stop-motion films special effects and these characteristics of animation are seamlessly combined.

As Crafton notes, when it came to content, early animators were inspired by early stop-motion films; but we must not forget that animation itself is a product of stop-motion substitution, as each drawing is substituted by the next, shot on another bit of film, until the whole gives the impression of movement. We can discuss Blackton's *Haunted Hotel,* for example, both as live-action film and as a trick, or animated, film.[22]

From this quick historical overview it is clear that the paths of cinema and animation were joined at the beginning of their history. It appears that their paths diverged after 1907, when live-action trick films using stop-motion, such as those made by Georges Méliès, fell out of favor, though live-action films to this day rely on the techniques of animation for their special effects sequences. Trick sequences in live-action films, such as films with 3-D animation by Ray Harryhausen,[23] are an area of overlap between cinema and animation, an area where we can see that what we thought were two mediums were really one.

Digitization Brings Special Effects and Animation Back Together

Though the paths of cinema and animation were joined in 1893 in the work of Reynaud, Marey, Demeny, and others, then mostly separated, their paths are joining up again now. The nineteenth-century drive toward mechanization has become in the twenty-first century the drive to digitization.[24] This connection, between animation, early trick films, and the gradual digitization of cinema, has been noted by Michele Pierson in her book *Special Effects: Still in Search of Wonder.*[25] Pierson also notes the change in narration techniques as well as the criticism these films receive for being superficial in their plots (by which critics mean there is little emotional engagement) and by departing from some of the cinematographic traditions of the classical Hollywood cinema such as the use of deep space. However, she does not give the matter the in-depth treatment that I will here. My argument is that this development has led to a new way for films to mean.

Filmmakers such as Tim Burton who are aware of this digitization process and the role that animation plays in it make different kinds of films, films that reflect this awareness. I call these films pataphysical and their filmmakers—those who are already consciously adopting this new way of filmmaking—pataphysicists. We could say that pataphysical films make up a genre, but the term *genre* is applied retrospectively, the way the term *film noir* was.

To say that a film is pataphysical is not a judgment. It does not necessarily mean that it is a better film, nor that it will get better box office. By identifying certain films as pataphysical, or by making a list of characteristics that are typical of pataphysical films, I am taking a more productive approach to the changes in contemporary Hollywood cinema. With this altered set of aesthetic criteria, it should be easier to assess how these films work on their audiences and what is needed to make them more effective. Here is a list of the characteristics of pataphysical films as I see them:

1. The main characteristic of a pataphysical film is its dependence on special effects, whether digital or mechanical. Entire sets may be effects generated, as well as entire characters (that is, for the entire length of their performance). With this reliance on effects usually comes a change in narration and a flattening of the emotional aspects of the characters. It is primarily because of the change in narration and characters that critics deride pataphysical films, with the most common critique being that they are more about style than meaning.

2. Special effects are "visible," or "excessive"; in other words, they call attention to themselves as special effects. The effects do not have to be digital, although they increasingly are. But see the opening of Burton's *Pee-wee's Big Adventure* (analyzed in depth in Chapter 1): all of that parody of mechanical science simply to cook an egg breakfast.

3. The films do not have to be comic ones, although even the most serious films are tongue-in-cheek. See, for example, Johnny Depp's character in *Sleepy Hollow*. In this case, getting away from the scientific explanation is like an emotional revelation, and the character partly solves a problem by sorting out his own memories of childhood traumas.

4. The narrative does not try to be realistic. A true scientific explanation that we would accept in real life would not be acceptable for

the events in the film, though the explanation given may sound scientific. In fact, the events of the film usually satirize or poke fun at scientific discourse. However, once an internal logic for the events of the film are in place, whether the logic be magical, alien, mystical, or pseudoscientific, the film then adheres, most of the time, to the logic of that convention. However, these films also delight in MacGuffins, in stretching the logic of their own conventions to the breaking point.

5. The narrative excesses and MacGuffins[26] make sense when the spectator is aware of additional texts or discourses outside of the film, and their meaning harks back to that. In other words, these films cannot be viewed in isolation, but must be understood in relation to other texts. Few contemporary films are meant to be standalone texts, but rather intermediate texts, drawing meaning from and feeding meaning into other media forms such as commercials, print ads, television shows, previous and later films, comic books, games (both board and computer), novels and other books, magazines, newspapers, the Web, paintings, music videos—in other words, whatever is out there.[27] This is especially true of pataphysical films.

Pataphysical Films Are Typically Lambasted by Critics, Whether or Not They Do Well at the Box Office

One reason why critics always find that the narration of pataphysical films falls short is because they are judging the narration of these films by the standard of the classical Hollywood aesthetic, a standard that rarely applies. Even when it does apply (compare *Taking Lives* [D. J. Caruso, 2004] to Alfred Hitchcock's thrillers), the film seems dated. The aesthetics of the classical Hollywood cinema are no longer the correct measuring stick to use in judging these films; rather, other aesthetic systems, such as those of animation, are.

Pataphysical films often tend to follow the same narrative logic and rules of narration and character transformation as animation—specifically, the narration of cartoons. If we judge these films as a form of animation, then their reliance on special effects is really a manifestation of the fact that these films are really animated, the flat characters more about physical metamorphosis than dramatic revelation. One reason why other critics have not noted this connection (although some have—see especially references to the work of Lev Manovich and Sean Cubitt in Chapter 1) is that animation itself is not taken seriously, this in spite of the fact that, both historically and conceptually, it is probably safer to say that live-action cinema is a subset of animation than that animation is some poor cousin to live-action cinema. The dependency of live-action cinema on animated films was very clear at the beginning of film history, and now it is becoming clear again in pataphysical films.

What does that mean for contemporary film scholars and filmmakers? It means that in order to understand these films, we need to understand animation better, and we need to look at the subjective use of these techniques in the films; that is, we need to look at how filmmakers, whether directors, writers, or special effects artists (as we have entered a new era where special effects artists should be given their due credit as auteurs), intended their films to mean. This meaning has to be assessed in the text's action (the story being told), the comments within the film on the action, and its relation to other, discrete texts that are related to it. My hope is that this book will help with that process.

Notes

1. Alfred Jarry Taylor, *Exploits and Opinions of Dr. Faustroll, Paraphysician* (1907), trans. Simon Watson (Boston: Exact Change, 1996).

2. Neal Gabler, *Life the Movie: How Entertainment Conquered Reality* (New York: Vintage Books, 1998).

3. Neal Gabler, "Just Like a Movie, But It's Not," *New York Times*, Week in Review, Aug. 4, 2002, pp. 1 & 3.

4. Neal Gabler, "Just Like a Movie, But It's Not," *New York Times*, Week in Review, Aug. 4, 2002, pp. 1 & 3.

5. Janet Maslin, "The Reality Is All Virtual, and Densely Complicated," *New York Times*, March 31, 1999.

6. A.O. Scott, "Tall and Green, but No 'Ho, Ho, Ho,'" *New York Times*, June 20, 2003.

7. A.O. Scott, "Full Moon, Romance and a Demon Rustler," *New York Times*, May 7, 2004.

8. Alastair Brotchie, ed., *A True History of the College of Pataphysics*, translated by Paul Edwards, Atlas Arkhive: The College of Pataphysics, number IX, part I, London: Atlas Press, 1995. Limited edition.

9. Richard Abel, *The Ciné Goes to Town: French Cinema 1896–1914*, updated and expanded ed. (Berkeley: University of California Press, 1998), p. 65.

10. As Abel notes, the nonmagicians in the film don't fare very well either—the only women are in support roles, played by a ballet corps, their aid in launching the rocket obviously sexualized, and the Selenites on the moon are half crustacean, half primate, a biological and colonial composite "other." Abel, ibid., p. 72.

11. A comprehensive series of frames from the film, as well as an analysis, can be found in Donald Crafton's *Emile Cohl, Caricature, and Film* (Princeton, NJ: Princeton University Press, 1990), pp. 258–266.

12. The Paris Salon was originally an officially-sanctioned semi-public exhibition of works by members of the Académie royale de peinture et de sculpture. See http://en.wiki pedia.org/wiki/Paris_Salon.

13. Crafton, *Emile Cohl*, pp. 31, 33.

14. Ibid., p. 257.

15. Ibid., pp. 29–34, 257–258.

16. Rosalind Krauss, "No More Play," available at http://www.artchive.com/giacometti/krauss.html.

17. Alison McMahan, *Alice Guy Blaché, Lost Visionary of the Cinema* (New York: Continuum, 2002). See especially chapters 1 and 2.

18. Alison McMahan, "Film Technology before 1914," in *Encyclopedia of European Cinema*, ed. Elizabeth Ezra (Oxford and New York: Oxford University Press, November 2003), pp. 22–25.

19. Crafton, *Emile Cohl*, p. 122.

20. E. G. Lutz, *Animated Cartoons: How They Are Made, Their Origin and Development* (1920) (Bedford, MA: Applewood Books, 1998), pp. 223–241.

21. McMahan (2003), p. 38.

22. I am grateful to my student Julie Turnock for this insight. See her master's thesis, "*Un Truc Extraordinaire*: Early Cinema, Diegesis, and *Trucage*" (University of Amsterdam, August 2001).

23. For a comprehensive overview of the work of Ray Harryhausen, see *Ray Harryhausen: An Animated Life*, by Ray Harryhausen and Tony Dalton, foreword by Ray Bradbury (New York: Billboard Books, 2004).

24. For a more in-depth treatment of this issue, see Alison McMahan, "The Drive to Mechanisation and Digitisation," Ch. 3, *The French Cinema Book*, edited by Michael Temple & Michael Witt, London: BFI Publishing, 2004, p. 42–49.

25. Michele Pierson, *Special Effects: Still in Search of Wonder*, ed. John Belton (New York: Columbia University Press, 2002). The key portion of her argument can also be found in her article "CGI Effects in Hollywood Science-Fiction Cinema 1989–95: The Wonder Years," *Screen*, 40.2 (Summer 1999): 158–176.

26. MacGuffin is the name given by Hitchcock to a plot device that holds no meaning or purpose of its own except to motivate the characters and advance the story. Used mostly in thrillers.

27. This intertextuality and intermediality can develop naturally but are more often part of the overall marketing plan; see Chapter 4 for a detailed account of how this works. More recently, it was announced that the Universal movie *Van Helsing* will be made into a television series by NBC, part of NBC's overall policy of "cross-pollination," in which various pieces of its media empire promote other parts of the same empire. See Elizabeth Jensen, "NBC Welcomes Promotion Synergy," *Los Angeles Times*, Business section, May 14, 2004. See also the use of "interstitial commercials," which come out just before and in conjunction with a film's theatrical or DVD release, that incorporates popular characters from a film (for example, the influence of *Men in Black II* in the Sprint commercials featuring the black-suited company salesman).

1

BURTON DOES 2-D:
FROM ANIMATION TO MACHINIMA

I think best when I'm drawing.

—Tim Burton[1]

Given Burton's visual flair, it is perhaps no surprise that he began his professional life in animation, a medium in which anything is possible, where constraints of imagination, time and place have little meaning. In many ways Burton's movies can be seen as animated exercises shot as live-action, since they deal with characters and situations that exist outside the realms of reality. [Says Burton,] "People ask me when I'm going to make a film with real people. What's real?"[2]

Mark Salisbury's comments on Tim Burton articulate the basic concept on which this book is organized. However, the fact that Burton began his professional life as an animator can be misleading, as he was producing, directing, and starring in live-action films, shot in Super 8, which he made with a group of friends, from his teens into his early twenties. Unfortunately, these films are now lost, though I did find a cryptic reference on the Internet to *The Island of Dr. Agor* (1971), made when Tim Burton was thirteen.[3]

Burton loved to draw as a teenager. At fourteen, he even won a poster contest for a litter campaign. (The logo was "Crush litter," and the posters were pasted on the sides of town garbage trucks for a year.) Burton also made pocket money by painting his neighbors' windows for Christmas and Halloween decorating. He credits the encouragement of one of his teachers in high school for the fact that he got a scholarship to the California Institute of the Arts when he was eighteen.[4]

20

The institute is located in Valencia, California, twenty-two miles northeast of Burbank, Burton's childhood home. Walt and Roy Disney established the school in 1961. In 1975 the Disney estate gave Cal Arts a $14 million endowment to train animators for their TV studio. In 1976 Burton started as a scholarship student in the film department. Burton notes that "[a]t Cal Arts we would make Super 8 movies: we made a Mexican monster movie and a surf movie, just for fun. But animation—I thought that might be a way to make a living."[5]

Disney had a practice of hiring (Burton described it as a "draft"[6]) student animators right out of the Cal Arts program. Usually the studio executives looked at seniors, but they often hired lowerclassmen as well. This made the atmosphere among the animation students very competitive, as everyone wanted Disney to pick them; at the time, animators did not have many other places to go for employment. Burton loved to draw, but he was feeling financial pressure because in his third year his scholarship was taken away, the result of some bureaucratic mix-up. Burton was in the financial aid office arguing for its reinstatement every day, even as he prepared his final project for the year, a pencil test animation entitled *Stalk of the Celery Monster*, in which a Frankenstein type of doctor, aided by a huge, veiled mountain of an assistant, seems to be conducting evil experiments on a female patient. Finally, the mad scientist is revealed to be an ordinary dentist, as he cackles, "Next, please . . ." to the other patients in the waiting room.

A clip from *Stalk of the Celery Monster* can be seen in the A&E *Biography* episode "Tim Burton: Trick or Treat." Even this brief segment reveals some stylistic details that would become Burton trademarks: a lead char-

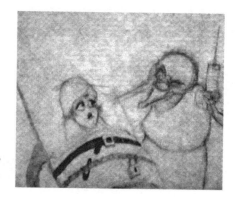

The monstrous scientist from *Stalk of the Celery Monster* about to torture a bound female.

acter whose actions and intent are misunderstood; an unwilling (and often, as in this case, almost deformed) assistant; the mad-scientist theme; and lovely women either being restrained by a madman or looking directly out at us, their already overly large eyes made larger by their expression of terror. According to Rick Heinrichs,[7] *Stalk of the Celery Monster* got the attention of the Disney headhunters because, unlike most of the other students who used their films to perfect various animation techniques, Burton used his to tell a story and to create a complex set of relationships between a group of characters.[8] Nobody was more surprised than Burton when he was selected in 1979:

> As the years went on, the competition, the films, would get more elaborate, there was sound, music, even though they were basically pencil tests. The last one I did was called *Stalk of the Celery Monster*. It was stupid, but I got picked. It was a lean year, and I was lucky, actually, because they really wanted people.[9]

By hiring him, Disney gave Burton a source of income and an identity—the identity of an animator, which he retains to this day. But the price was very high. His first assignment was working on *The Fox and the Hound* (Art Stevens, 1981), under the supervision of Glen Keane. Burton had a lot of respect for Keane: "He was nice, he was good to me, he's a really strong animator and he helped."[10] But he hated the job of drawing "all those four-legged Disney foxes, I just couldn't do it. I couldn't even fake the Disney style. Mine looked like road kills. So luckily I got a lot of far-away shots to do."[11] As a result, Burton's first year at Disney was miserable, and he gradually sunk into a depression, sleeping fourteen hours a day (he learned how to sleep at his desk with

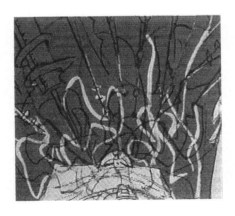

The electrical zapping lines of torture from *Stalk of the Celery Monster* will be seen again as life-giving in *Frankenweenie.*

The scientist in *Stalk of the Celery Monster* is revealed to be a mere dentist, and the whole horror story a projection of our dental fears.

his pencil in his hand), or hiding in his closet or under his desk, or walking down the hallways after his wisdom teeth had been removed, letting the blood stream out of his mouth. However, when he did work, he worked fast, and apparently enough to make sure that he didn't get fired.

Part of the problem is that the Disney Company as a whole was in the middle of an identity crisis. The animation department had shrunk from a high of 650 artists to 200. In 1979, the year Burton started at Disney, Disney's Chief Animator Don Bluth left, taking with him seven other animators and four assistants, to produce feature-length animated films for Steven Spielberg. The success of Don Bluth's *An American Tail* gave Disney its first taste of real competition in the animation field.[12] Burton was quite sensitive to the sense of disorientation and confusion in the atmosphere, with movies like *Herbie Goes to Monte Carlo* contrasted with films like *Tron* (for which Burton did some in-between work). Disney's internal divide was characterized by the contrast between the remnants of the old-style animators, "just a couple of zany gag men in a room,"[13] as Burton put it, and the new people struggling to take Disney into the digital era.

Burton's situation improved when he was given the job of conceptual artist on the film *The Black Cauldron*, a movie a decade in the making. *Cauldron* was unique for various reasons: it was the only Disney film to get a PG rating, it had no songs, and it had a rather dark story line. More important, for Michael Eisner,[14] at least, it had some of Disney's first use of computer-generated images in several scenes. The use of computer animation was quite effective, especially in the darker scenes of combat toward the end of the film; one reviewer noted that the digital artwork "gives some of the scenes a surprisingly effective three-dimensional appearance (one tracking shot up the side of a dark castle with lightning flashing is particularly impressive)."[15] Eisner credited the digital innovation at Disney to Glen Keane and John Lasseter (the latter would go on to produce *Toy Story,* the first fully computer-animated movie),[16] though, like Burton's, none of Keane's animation made it into the film.

Cauldron was a failure at the box office, and Disney took it off the shelf for thirteen years. The reasons have more to do with the story than with the animation (although the figure of Taran seems to be a bland copy of Arthur in *The Sword in the Stone*). Though based on the first two books of Lloyd Alexander's *The Chronicles of Prydain* series, the film seems to be aiming for the *Star Wars* audience; Taran's sword even looks like a light saber. Many critics, including Roger Ebert,[17] also noted the resemblance of the climax to that of *Raiders of the Lost Ark*, though the same critics said the visual treatment rose above this copying.

The film's real problems are with the story. Taran starts out as an assistant pig keeper, and in the end he returns the magic sword he has used in several battles in order to resume being an assistant pig keeper (instead of returning the magic sword because he has grown into his warrior role sufficiently to no longer need it). Darker fantasy films are designed to help children face the rigors of adult life, but this one gives a conflicting message, about Taran's aspiring to be a warrior, actually saving his world, along with the princess, a couple of friends, and the prophetic pig from a fate worse than death, but then walking away from his leadership role. In addition to this major flaw, the film is marred by smaller plot holes: the wizard that Taran works for sends him out unprepared and does nothing to help him (all of his help comes from strangers), and the pig's prophetic powers are vastly underused, considering the situation in which the characters find themselves. Most of the logic of Lloyd Alexander's world (a world very similar to that of J. R. R. Tolkien's *Lord of the Rings*, since both are based on the same set of British myths) is completely lost in the *Cauldron* screenplay.

Burton resented the fact that none of his conceptual drawings were used in the final film: "I basically exhausted all of my creative ideas for about ten years during that period. And when none of it was used . . . I felt like a trapped princess."[18] However, the experience was probably not a complete waste. It seems that Burton was aware of the film's story flaws and learned something from *Cauldron*'s failure, as his *Sleepy Hollow* has a very similar plot, in a very similar world, and ignores key elements of its source material in a very similar way, but without the problems we see in *Cauldron*. (For a more in-depth comparison between the two films, see Chapter 2.)

Burton was not the only one who was chafing at Disney's schizophrenic atmosphere of dictatorialness and confusion. Others working at the company felt the same way, and they banded together with Burton on weekends and whenever they had spare time to make two live-action films, *Doctor of Doom* (1980) and *Luau* (1982). Neither film is available for public viewing, although clips from each can be seen on the A&E *Biography* video *Tim Burton: Trick or Treat*. *Doom* was filmed in black and white on video, with a deliberately bad overdubbing in order to make something that looked like a foreign import from the sixties, with Burton playing Dr. Doom. *Luau* is an energetic homage to beach-blanket movies and other B movies, complete with song-and-dance numbers, with Burton starring as the disembodied head of "The Most Powerful Being in the Universe."[19] Among the Disney colleagues who worked on these films with Burton was John Musker, who, along with Glen Keane, Burton's original mentor at Disney, would go on to help usher Disney into a new era, an era characterized by the extensive use of digital technology, with films like *The Little Mermaid* and *Beauty and the Beast*.

Though none of Burton's conceptual artwork for *Cauldron* was used in the final film, it did get the attention of Disney executive Julie Hickson, who enabled Burton to produce the stop-motion short *Vincent*, in 1982 (I discuss this film in depth in Chapter 3). After *Vincent*, Burton made another short at Disney, *Frankenweenie* (see Chapter 2), which led directly to his being tapped as director for his first commercial live-action feature film, *Pee-wee's Great Adventure* (see Chapter 2 for a discussion of *Pee-wee*'s narration and Chapter 3 for a discussion of its special effects).

For all intents and purposes, Burton left 2-D animation behind when he departed from Disney in 1984. Once his success as a live-action director gave him enough clout, he used it to make a stop-motion film, *The Nightmare Before Christmas*, and at the time of this writing (fall of 2004), he has another stop-motion film, *The Corpse Bride*, in production (release set for early fall 2005). Although he designs and produces these films, he usually does not direct them himself, nor does he do any animation work, leaving that to others, such as Henry Selick.

Burton continues to carry a sketchbook with him wherever he goes and renders key life events, such as the birth of his son in 2003, in drawings. 2-D animation is something he returns to when he has time, when he needs emotional solace, or when he is invited to do so. For example, in 1985 Brad Bird, who had worked on *The Fox and the Hound* along with Burton at Disney, asked Burton to do some design work on *Family Dog*, an animated episode of Steven Spielberg's *Amazing Stories*. Bird wrote and directed the episode, which was part of a showreel he and Burton had produced while they were at Disney.[20] Bird would write and direct a sequel episode in 1992, this time with music by Burton's regular composer, Danny Elfman (and a musical theme by John Williams). Eventually the two episodes were turned into a series produced by Amblin Entertainment in 1993, with Burton as executive producer.

Family Dog shows the typical suburban family life from a dog's point of view. The family consists of Mom and Dad (looking like flabby versions of the Jetsons); Billy, a gap-toothed kid with a maniacal expression and an unruly mop of red hair; and Buffy, the little sister who greatly resembles the sister in *Vincent*. Each member of the family is completely self-absorbed and uses the dog as a sort of screen for the projection of his or her own neuroses, whether it is Mom indulging in a long tirade about how she has to wait on everyone, Dad blaming and beating the dog for his own smelly fart in front of company, Billy torturing him with a vacuum cleaner, or Buffy dressing him up as a doll and throwing a tantrum if the dog so much as bares his teeth at her. However, the dog gets his own after Dad takes him to obedience school (the female dog trainer has a helper who is reminiscent of the hulking assistant to the mad dentist in *Stalk of the Celery Monster*). He uses his new assertiveness to first chase burglars out of the house, then joins the burglars in a series of robberies and lives a glamorous underworld life with them. When the burglars chafe at being called "the dog gang" in the press, the dog turns them in and returns to his suburban family. The sequel episode ends with the dog attacking Dad when he returns home late and has forgotten his key. About *Family Dog*, Burton said: "I just love the idea of trying to do something from a dog's point of view. I don't know why, but I always relate to dogs. Edward Scissorhands is like a dog to me."[21]

There would be a long gap between Burton's design work for *Family Dog* and his next animation outing, but for the fans of his animation, it would be worth the wait. In 1997 Burton published a collection of twenty-three poems entitled *The Melancholy Death of Oyster Boy & Other Stories*, all about misfit eccentric children, that focused on the horror of childhood with a sweetening dose of humor.[22] The key character in the collection is Stain Boy, who is introduced in a poem of the same name. The poem compares Stain Boy to Superman and Batman, and notes:

> He can't fly around tall buildings,
> Or outrun a speeding train,
> The only talent he seems to have
> Is to leave a nasty stain.[23]

The reference to Batman and Superman are pointed, as Burton had spent a year (in 1997–1998) developing a feature film for Superman and had been removed from the project against his will. His solace was to create his own superhero, a boy who could do no more than to leave a nasty stain. Only two of the stories are about Stain Boy (*Stain Boy's Special Christmas* is about Stain Boy getting a dry cleaned suit for Christmas and covering it with stains in less than ten minutes). Of the other stories, three are about mismatched couples (*Stick Boy and Match Girl in Love*, *Junk Girl*, and *The Pin Cushion Queen*), four are about parents who are horrified by their misfit children (*Robot Boy*, *The Melancholy Death of Oyster Boy*, *Mummy Boy*, and *Anchor Baby*), fourteen are about freaks without references to parents (*Staring Girl*, *The Boy with Nails in His Eyes*, *The Girl with Many Eyes*, *Stain Boy*, *Voodoo Girl*, *The Girl Who Turned into a Bed*, *Roy the Toxic Boy*, *James*, *Brie Boy*, *The Pin Cushion Queen*, *Melonhead*, *Sue*, *Jimmy, the Hideous Penguin Boy*, and *Char Boy*), and three stories feature the continuing adventures of heroes we have already met (*Stain Boy's Special Christmas*, *Stick Boy's Festive Season*, and *Oyster Boy Steps Out*). Looked at in terms of Burton's favorite themes, five of the stories are about Christmas, and one is about Halloween.

The *Los Angeles Times* described Stain Boy as a "splotch, a blob with legs, an ink stain that one might see on a Rorschach test,"[24] but the *New York Times* said: "Inspired by such childhood heroes as Dr. Seuss and Roald Dahl, Mr. Burton's slim volume exquisitely conveys the pain of an adolescent outsider. Like his movies, the work manages to be both childlike and sophisticated, blending the innocent with the macabre."[25]

The same review quotes Burton on his inspiration for the book: "I was quiet but early on, I got deemed as weird," he said. "When someone says that and the whole world starts believing it . . . by the time I was a teenager, I *felt* weird."[26]

In late January 2000 the papers were announcing Stainboy's (his name was changed from two words to one when he went digital) transition to the Web. The San Francisco–based netcaster Shockwave.com invited several well-known filmmakers, including *South Park* creators Trey Parker and Matt Stone, comic book icon Stan Lee, and Tim Burton, to produce animated Flash programming for the Web. Burton was dubious at first but agreed after he had a glimpse of Shockwave's Macromedia Flash Player technology (Macromedia owns Shockwave.com). Burton agreed to produce twenty-six original animated episodes of two to five minutes each. Shockwave paid for all production of the shorts and retains the Internet rights to the character; Burton gets all the ancillary rights. If *Stainboy* wasn't enough of a hit online to carry over to film or TV, "Burton dryly pointed out, perhaps the characters could be featured 'in an ice show in Las Vegas.' "[27] In addition, Shockwave had plans to develop digital trading cards and interactive games designed by Burton himself.[28] In a deal similar to that brokered for the *South Park* creators, Burton also got a small percentage of Shockwave.com.[29] The deal was announced at the Sundance Festival, and Burton was quoted as being excited about "the kind of textures" he could get with Flash technology.[30]

The *Stainboy* Series

Burton feels that "medium and idea share a chemistry. For some stories you have to wait for the right medium. I think [the Internet's] the perfect forum to tell a sad little story like this one. Stainboy is a character that doesn't do much. He's just perfect for four-minute animations."[31] Burton also chose Stainboy as the animated frontispiece for his Web site, www.Timburton.com, an otherwise inactive site.

The plan was for Burton to create, write, and direct the new series. Burton did a series of original watercolors, pencil sketches, and gray-on-gray washes that were accented with pastel colors and took them to Flinch Studios, a twenty-two-person animation and Web-media production studio based in Los Angeles (the company has since relocated to Florida). Flinch was formed in 1997 by President Chris Takami and CEO and Creative Director Tony Grillo, whose backgrounds were in the video game and CD-ROM animation world of the early '90s. It was the first studio Burton visited, and he found their style to his liking; it also helped that both Burton and Flinch were represented by the William Morris Agency. Burton charged them with creating a series of animations that would be as different from the garish look of Saturday morning cartoons as possible, with an emphasis on the bizarre characters in realistic settings and using minimal effects (not even animation's characteristic stretching or squashing). Flinch's first challenge, then, was to duplicate the watercolor look of Burton's storyboards in Flash. (With subsequent episodes Burton used other mediums, moving from watercolor to gouache to oil paint; by episode 4 Flinch was using 3-D volumetric rendering.) Shockwave was considerate enough to assign them a special technical team for the task, in order to guarantee that the *Stainboy* episodes could be viewed without the need to download any special plug-in.

The second challenge was the animation itself: although Stainboy and his partner, Stare Girl, are superheroes of a sort, they are very inactive. They are drawn with fragile lines, and the pacing of their activity is quite different from that of traditional cartoons. According to art designer Will Amato, "Our goal was to create an animation that was not driven by incident or event. We wanted to create a story that—if they wanted to—the characters could just curl up and fall asleep."[32]

To support a smooth production effort, the Flinch team front-loads Tim Burton with as much assistance as possible. They take rough ideas and turn them into storyboards, then develop vectorized versions of characters early in the production process, making it easier to animate them once script and storyboard are approved.

Shockwave initially wanted Flinch to use bitmaps for the characters. They experimented with this technique on Stainboy, creating a body out of one or two bitmaps, then drawing twenty different heads and masking the heads onto the same body. They quickly found that the resulting files were huge, too large for Web transmission. In the end, Flinch went with vector-based solutions that required the use of transparencies and transparent gradients to handle Burton's muted color palette of grays and off-grays:

Will Amato created what he calls a "baroque arrangement of multiple layers." Other experiments involved scans that were mimicked in Flash. In most cases, Amato says, "I could get the Flash file to be a smaller file than the scan." Finally he developed a combination of semi-transparent gradients and a wash look to create a multi-layered world. Controlling the gradient and using four to five layers of transparency enabled Flinch to achieve the look they were after for any given character. . . .

To convey every little tick and gesture of Burton's original watercolors, Flinch handcrafted them in Flash at a high resolution. "We wanted to create an effect that looked like a brush had painted them onto the screen," Amato says. "I found a way to paint the gradient, as if it were popped right into wet watercolor. I did it section by section of the drawing. It was a deliberate effort to mimic Tim's pure gesture. I was an art forger."[33]

Flinch succeeded in making the image file small, but there was not much that could be done to reduce the size of the audio files. Each episode has a heavy use of sound effects, a rich score composed by Danny Elfman, and Burton regulars to voice the characters. For example, Lisa Marie voiced Match Girl, and Glenn Shadix voiced Sergeant Dale and other minor characters. Dialogue was recorded into a handheld Sony digital audiotape (DAT) recorder (someone from Flinch would simply go over to Shadix's house and get the needed audio), then sent right into the computer.

To date, Burton and Flinch have produced only six of the planned twenty-six episodes of *Stainboy*. Burton became extremely busy directing his "reimagining" of *Planet of the Apes* (2001) and wasn't able to plan any more episodes. However, the six episodes, now available for viewing on www.atomfilms.com, give us a fairly rounded view of Stainboy's world and some of his past history.

The first episode establishes the pattern for the rest by introducing us to Stainboy as some kind of detective that Sergeant Dale sends on special missions. In this case, his assignment is to deal with Stare Girl, though once Stainboy arrives at Stare Girl's house and we see her staring at herself in a mirror, it is hard to understand what threat she poses. The two enter into a staring contest. Stainboy struggles to stay awake, then finally uses his staining ability to loosen a ceiling lamp that crushes Stare Girl to death. The episode has what will become a standard coda of Stainboy going back to the police station and getting a gruff, insult-laden statement of thanks from Sergeant Dale. Elfman's score for the episode consists of theremin wails very similar to what he did in *Mars Attacks!*

The second episode is entitled *Toxic Boy*, who was called Roy the Toxic Boy in the book. Toxic Boy eats noxious garbage, and his home is filled with foul substances. The smell is disturbing the neighbors, which is why Sergeant Dale sends Stainboy to investigate. Toxic Boy almost kills Stainboy with his acidlike vomit, but Stainboy evades him and kills Toxic Boy in turn with an air freshener in the shape of a Christmas tree. After Toxic Boy falls dead into the dog dish, his Chihuahua comes in and takes a bite out of his head, turns blue, and dies.

The third episode, entitled *Bowling Ball Head*, gives Stainboy a villainous opponent for the first time (also voiced by Glenn Shadix), in a form of a huge bowling ball head that kills bowlers (because they have cheapened the sport). This episode is scary and effective, worth repeated viewing.

Episode 4, *Robot Boy*, gives us additional insight into Sergeant Dale: he has been married at least three times, and his favorite TV show is *Cops without Tops*. Sergeant Dale sends Stainboy to deal with Robot Boy because he is causing brownouts. As Stainboy enters Robot Boy's home, he sees a copy of the magazine *Mechanics Confidential* (the issue blares the headline "Man Turns Son into Hedge Trimmer"). Behind him various pieces of junk metal form themselves into Robot Boy, who immediately tries to kill Stainboy. Robot Boy chases Stainboy until he reaches the end of his power cord, which comes out of the wall, deactivating him. Stainboy returns to the police station, Robot Boy parts in tow, to find that Sergeant Dale is throwing a "topless cop" party. In spite of his success, Stainboy is not very welcome. As in the poem, in a later episode we see Robot Boy serving as a garbage can.

Episode 5 pits Stainboy against Match Girl, whom Sergeant Dale describes as "an old flame of yours." Before Stainboy can do anything, Match Girl lights herself and blows up a gas station.

The last episode is entitled *Birth of Stainboy*. Although Stainboy dutifully reports to Sergeant Dale, there is no mission for him, so Dale sends him home. Stainboy falls asleep and in his dream relives his birth (which is shown to us from his point of view), his parents' horror, his uncontrollable ability to leave hideous stains everywhere, and his parents' decision to put him in the Burbank Charity Home for Unusual Cases, where he meets other *Oyster Boy* characters: Brie Boy, The Girl with Many Eyes, Jimmy the Hideous Penguin Boy, and The Boy with Nails in His Eyes. This episode contains a lot of in-jokes, such as a monster hand rising out of the muck on TV, and numerous references to other *Stainboy* installments.

The first episode in the series went online in October 2000, and within the first six days it had generated over a million hits. Every time a new episode was released, the high volume of traffic for *Stainboy* slowed down the servers at Shockwave.

Critical response was positive. For example, *Variety* praised "the simplicity of the ink and watercolor drawings, the odd details in each frame. . . . and the skillful way Burton uses colors against the black-and-white backgrounds." The same article also had high praise for Elfman's score.[34]

Shockwave had pursued animations by Hollywood talent as a response to financial pressure; while the *Stainboy* series was in production (produced with a grant from Compaq), some staff members were laid off, even as the company pursued advertising, sponsorship, and merchandising opportunities and considered a subscription model for their series. *Stainboy* was an experiment in developing revenue streams for the Web, but it did not succeed, at least not financially.

However, as a result of the *Stainboy* series, Burton became a hero and role model for the machinima crowd.

Machine (The Computer) + Cinema = Machinima

Lev Manovich has argued that cinema and its conventions are the dominant cultural interface of our time, and that the language of cinema is being remediated[35] in newer cultural forms appearing in various other media. Although I find the concept of a cultural interface to be attractive and useful, I don't agree that cinema is the dominant cultural interface. Rather, I think animation deserves that honor. It is important to reevaluate the relationship between animation and live-action cinema in order to understand motion picture art in the twenty-first century. It must be clear to anyone who has read this far that the films of Tim Burton often refuse to be labeled cinema or animation, forcing us to reevaluate our understanding of both. A careful study of machinima will prove my point, that animation is our dominant cultural interface, and not (classical Hollywood) live-action cinema.

The term *machinima* means films made by machines, and the history of the machinima movement is closely linked with the development of first-person shooter games, their approach to graphic design, and their methods of distribution. As a matter of convenience, let's say it all started with the first truly "immersive" 3-D game, *Wolfenstein 3D* (id Software, 1992), the first recognizable first-person shooter. (Steven Poole has pointed out historical antecedents in his book *Trigger Happy*.)[36] *Wolfenstein* first put the player into rooms, separated by doors, with walls receding realistically into the distance and populated with bots (non-player characters) that took the form of Nazi soldiers for the player to destroy. There was no texture on the walls or ceilings, so only the walls moved with forward movement, and the bots looked two-dimensional, as they were drawn with bitmapped sprites whose pixels enlarged as they got closer. *Wolfenstein* made another innovation, which was adopted by the genre, to include a representation of hands (the player's hands) clutching a gun at the bottom of the screen. The gun is not used for aiming, but it does make the player feel incorporated into the space.

The creators of *Wolfenstein 3D* were John Romero and John Carmack, cofounders of id Software. *Wolfenstein 3D* was innovative in another way as well: the first of its three levels was distributed for free over the Internet, as shareware. The complete game and two other variations of the game, that is, new games using the same engine, were sold via retail. Id Software built on its success by producing *Doom*, with a graphics engine designed by John Carmack and Tom Hall leading the game and map designs, a job completed by John Romero when Hall left. Romero also designed the game's map editor. Jay Wilbur, id's PR man, would leak bits of information about *Doom* before it came out, so that by the time the shareware was available from the University of Wisconsin's server in December 1993, the server was overrun with people trying to download *Doom*.

Up to four people could play one game at a time, and games like *Deathmatch,* in which players went after each other instead of after bots, became popular, earning first-person shooters the ire of many educators, politicians, and parents. No one seemed to recognize that all first-person shooters have done is put the player in the role of the tomcat of the cartoon series *Tom and Jerry* or the sheriff in *Road Runner*, substituting fantasy weapons for the cartoon's elaborate booby traps. Also rarely noticed is that first-person shooters encourage the formation of clans and a cooperative play mode for games such as *Capture the Flag*. Regardless of the critical outcry, *Doom* set the standard for subsequent first-person shooter games, such as *Quake, Quake II* (also developed by id Software), and *Unreal* (by GT Interactive).

But what was really special about *Doom*, or, more accurately, about id Software's marketing strategy, is that, along with the game, the company released the source code of the game itself. Once gamers had familiarized themselves with the game, they could improve game levels, add sound effects, or build new levels altogether. Some of these fan-created levels became so popular that they then became incorporated into the game, as *Quake*'s *Capture the Flag* has been. It was a brilliant marketing strategy, as it created a large community of people who were committed to the game. And each new version of the game brought with it a new and improved game editor.

Customizers of *Quake* could use *Quake*'s editor to make a racing game or a flying game, and someone even made *Quess* (*Battle Chess* meets *Quake*) and *Quake Rally*, a patch that brings arcade-style racing into the world of *Quake*.

What exactly does a game editor allow a player to do? First of all, there is the level, or map, or environment design. Then there are the character avatars, models that can be outfitted with "skins," or specific characterizations—a digital version of paper dolls. There is the design of weapons and tools and ways of customizing the environment through lighting and sound. Players with some programming skill can modify the game code itself; the resulting modifications are called "mods," and the people who modify them, the "mod community." Game levels have two main parts: interactive sequences, such as battles, and noninteractive sequences, also known as cut scenes. Cut scenes are very similar to traditional film sequences. The first machinima films were not actually films but players saving their own record-breaking game play in order to post it to the Web and show off their prowess or that of their *Quake* clan. This practice was eventually extended to cut scenes (sequential, noninteractive sequences within an interactive game, usually used for exposition or emotional identification with a character).

The first machinima filmmakers came out of this mod community; in other words, they were gamers first and filmmakers second. One player known only as "CRT" (later identified as David Wright) created a mod called Key Grip, which made movie editing available to *Quake* gamers. According to the press reports that I have read, the machinima era began in 1996, when a *Quake* clan called The Rangers produced a demo called

Diary of a Camper, which was really a movie. *Quake* players used the game as a virtual movie set to produce the movie based on a prerehearsed script.[37] Hundreds of machinima films have been made since, and gamers quickly realized that learning something about filmmaking would help them in their efforts. Those who knew shared what they knew with those who didn't, primarily in the form of tutorials posted on Web sites like Machinima.com and Gamasutra.com.[38]

The term *machinima* itself was actually coined by the members of The Strange Company, based in Scotland, who also developed the portal Machinima.com and wrote most of the filmmaking tutorials to be found there. Strange Company produced the now classic example of machinima filmmaking, *Eschaton*, based on the writings of H. P. Lovecraft.

Another well-known producer of machinima films is the New York–based ILL Clan, who produced *Apartment Huntin'* and *Hardly Workin'* using the *Quake* engine. *Apartment Huntin'* made history when it became the first machinima film to stream on *Wired*'s animationexpress.com Web site. The ILL Clan had to ask permission from id Software to do so, as the code is still id's. This is one reason why machinima remains a hobbyist's form of filmmaking. To remedy this, Strange Company is working on a set of film-editing tools using the *Lithtech II* (Monolith) game engine that they hope can be used to produce works for sale. Other ways of making machinima pay include using machinima films as portfolio samples to get a job in the gaming industry. Companies use their machinima portfolio to get advertising contracts.

Most machinima films run less than ten minutes in length and are downloadable for free on the Web. There are also machinima film festivals, and more established short-film sites such as Atomfilms are now showing machinima films. A typical machinima film is produced by first writing a script, then rehearsing and recording the actors' vocal performances, then creating a visual world using the game editor (*Unreal* and *Half-Life 2* are currently the most popular) to first create a map of the world and then to populate it with objects and models (characters). Once the models are built, the game editor is used to animate them. The game modelers are fairly limited in what they can do, so figures often look very boxy, but those with the skill and the means can use commercial 3-D modeling packages such as Discreet's 3D Studio MAX and then export their finely modeled object into their new level (the mod) or to their film. As such, machinima production has much in common with films that depend heavily on CGI, such as *Final Fantasy* (2001), and traditional animation films.

It is not surprising, then, that machinima filmmakers looked to Burton as one of their own after the release of *Stainboy*.[39] Although *Stainboy* is a 2-D animation and most machinima is 3-D (though Flinch did move into 3-D volumetrics with the fourth episode), the format, type of story, methods of production, and, most importantly, distribution (and the fact that Burton was paid for his work) made him a role model for machinamists everywhere.

Machinima versus Cinema

If we start out with the assumption that machinima is a new form of cinema, then it's clear that the opportunities and limitations of machinima are leading to certain changes in film language. For example, a 360-degree pan, or circling camera, difficult to achieve on a film set, is very easy to do in machinima and as a result tends to be overused. Slow motion (slo-mo) is necessary to make action sequences read clearly, and not, as in films, as emotional emphasis (slo-mo is generally avoided in customized game levels altogether). Fade-to-black is used between scene changes, not to indicate the passage of time, as it does in traditional films, but to cover up the fact that a new digital map is being loaded. Instead of talking about point of view (POV) or depth of field, machinima filmmakers talk about field of view (FOV). A wide FOV (90 degrees) comparable to that of a fish-eye lens, is typical for mod applications, but 52 degrees is closer to a standard cinematic depth of field (25 mm).

Mod designers and machinima filmmakers have numerous forums for active discussion between themselves on the Web, and by reading these discussions, it is possible to see how this new genre is evolving. In my research I focused on the tutorials for the mod community that aimed to help developers make better machinima. Most of these tutorials were written by people who were not actually filmmakers themselves, though some of them had done special effects work for film. In every case, when a mod-customizer-cum-machinima filmmaker had a query about how to do something, the tutorials recommend the classic cinematic solution— even when this solution was very difficult to achieve in machinima. For example, machinamists are advised to cut on the action, even though this is incredibly difficult to do in a game editor. A more limited, and therefore cinematic, FOV is recommended. Circling camera, typical in games, is discouraged except for a rare emotional effect, as are overdone uses of slow motion, such as the bullet effect familiar to us from films like *The Matrix*. Machinamists yelped with delight when new shareware enabling lip sync became available, though sync was typically not very important in game levels.

The message of these machinima tutorials is loud and clear: when forced to choose between the visual conventions of first-person shooters and cinema, the machinamists are encouraged to choose the conventions of cinema. The texts most recommended are Steven Katz's *Film Directing: Shot by Shot* and *Film Directing: Cinematic Motion,*[40] and Daniel Arijon's *Grammar of the Film Language.*[41] The machinima tutorials refer to these books as "film theory," although film theorists see them as guides to the options available to the film director in the staging of a sequence, practical handbooks for filmmakers, and not theory at all, especially since they limit themselves to classical Hollywood cinematic language.

Cinematic Interface or Animation Interface?

This overlap between cinema and animation is analogous to an overlap that existed at the beginning of cinema's history. The first filmmakers were really the animators, people like Émile Reynaud, who drew images on acetate by hand and linked them on perforated leather strips. Early trick films, which relied heavily on stop-motion animation, were an outgrowth of the same approach to movement, the motion studies approach,[42] best known to us through the work of Muybridge and Marey.[43]

The production of animation itself gradually became more mechanized. At first, artists like Emile Cohl,[44] who began making animated films for Gaumont and The Lux Film Company (a French film company that had a branch in Fort Lee, NJ) in 1908–1909, and his U.S. counterpart, Windsor McCay,[45] had to produce every drawing for an animated film by hand. The laboriousness of this process was often highlighted in films, and live action and animation were combined in order to reach the one-reel standard length while still staying within budget. The only difference, at this early stage, between live-action cinema and animation was the source of the image.

This is even truer today than it was in the early 1900s, as live-action images, artificially produced photographs, and animation work, whether produced using rotoscoping, motion capture, key framing, or computer simulation techniques, are all combined in films ranging from *Star Wars: Episode II—Attack of the Clones* (2002) to *Dinotopia* (2002) to *A Beautiful Mind* (2001). Lev Manovich, in his book *The Language of New Media* (2002), has argued that when the history of media is considered as a whole, live-action cinema will be a small chapter. In the same book, written before the advent of machinima, he explains his theory of cinema as a cultural interface, or cinema as the conceptual prism through which we understand our culture in general. Based on what I know about early cinema and what I see in digital cinema, netcinema, and machinima, I would argue that it is more likely that animation is the dominant cultural interface of our time, with the language of cinema being a subset of it, and not the other way around. If we understood cinema as a subset of animation, instead of treating animation as the bastard relative of cinema, as is usually done, then we could, for example, better appreciate the relationship between trick film techniques, such as the stop-motion techniques used in early cinema, in the special effects of artists like Ray Harryhausen, and in the digital versions of stop-motion that have been standard in Hollywood films since *Jurassic Park*. The film and television industries are still in the process of making the conversion from analog to digital production, but already even the most straightforward dramatic films, like *A Beautiful Mind,* are filled with digital effects quite similar to those used by machinima artists (I am thinking now, in *A Beautiful Mind*, of the change of seasons outside Nash's window at Princeton and the moment when he tosses his desk out the window—all effects achieved with a combination of studio set and digital technique). If I am correct, and animation really is our dominant cultural interface, then the way of the future has already been paved by artists working in the computer game industry and its offshoots such as machinima.

Animation Narrative

Although most of Tim Burton's work has been live-action fiction film, he has often been accused of having no sense of plot, or of not caring about narrative. However, anyone who is familiar with the conventions of animation narration can see that often these are the conventions that Burton is following, and not those of classical Hollywood cinema. In other words, most of Burton's films are pataphysical, each in a different way. One characteristic that singles out many of Burton's films, especially his early work, is that they are actually closer to animation in their narrative conventions.[46]

In the rest of this chapter I will outline the key aspects of narration in animated films, especially the type of films that influenced Burton (he has expressed a special fondness for Chuck Jones's cartoons, for example). One of the most readable accounts of animation aesthetics is by Maureen Furniss, *Art in Motion: Animation Aesthetics*. Furniss divides animation structures into linear and nonlinear. A linear structure has a plot moved forward by dialogue, with an emphasis on humor and a sense of closure. Disney's animated imitations of Hollywood live-action cinema are typical examples.

Silent-era animation was characterized by more of a gag structure, with one funny incident after another and little or no plot development. These were extensions of music hall routines. Often these films were initially structured around a chase scenario (just as many early live-action films were) and man's hapless relationship with machines. Sight gags often imitated the live-action cinematic humor of Buster Keaton, Charlie Chaplin, Harold Lloyd, and Stan Laurel and Oliver Hardy. Another borrowing from vaudeville was the "direct address" to the camera by an animated character, also characteristic of live-action early cinema, especially comedies.

Because the pace and emotions were more important than the plot, early studios such as the Max Fleischer Studio (1919–1942) created a story mood chart to illustrate the "degree of emotional pace" in its cartoons.

Nonlinear animation narrative can be cyclical or thematic. In a cyclical narrative, there is no goal to achieve, less emphasis on expectation and fulfillment, and no closure to mark the end of the experience. Its strength is showing unity and renewal, as opposed to consumption. Furniss uses the work of Faith Hubley, (the renowned independent animator who worked in NY [1988–2001]) as examples of this type of animation.

Nonlinear animation can also be structured around patterns or music. Compilation films with work by various artists often are based on a structure of patterns and variation.

Animation films with a thematic structure tend toward stasis rather than move forward, or even in a repeated pattern. In that respect, they can be described as meditative or poetic in nature, exploring an experience, emotion, or other abstract concept in depth. They also tend to be highly subjective and often rely on abstract imagery, which might provide the only means of expressing an ineffable notion. However, even in relatively thematic works, there can be a sense of building toward a final moment in the film, for example, in a meditational, relatively abstract film.

Abstract animation often lacks characters with which to identify, no diegesis to transport the viewer to a different time and place, and no closure to provide an artificial sense of understanding of the film's meaning.

Abstract motion pictures are often about the need to expand our ability to see, experience, and comprehend things in day-to-day life. They challenge the viewer to participate in the process of creating meaning and require repeated viewing. Abstract animation defies the naturalized logic of forward-moving cause-and-effect narrative. Rather, it tends to be developed around an aesthetic of thematic stasis or cycles.[47]

Most animated films do not fall squarely into one type but rather mix types in one film, so even a very abstract film will have some kind of theme and plot.[48] For example, an animated film built on a thematic structure can use a pattern of a series of metamorphoses to provide a sense of ambience rather than a record of physical actions.[49]

Anarchic Animation

The intended venue for an animated film and its available budget will often determine its aesthetic. Television animation tends to be more linear, independent animation more abstract. Animation films with a limited budget will resort to cost-saving methods, such as those used by the United Productions of America (UPA) in the 1940s: held poses, simplified character design, and abstract backgrounds. Before the imposition of the Hays Code,[50] animation was routinely subversive, with wide use of racist humor, slapstick violence, and sexual angst and innuendo.

Burton has specifically cited the animation work of Chuck Jones (most of it produced for Warner Bros., Burton's "home" studio), the creator of Road Runner, Roger Rabbit, and many others. Burton mentions Jones's adaptation of Dr. Seuss's *How the Grinch Stole Christmas* as an inspiration for *The Nightmare Before Christmas*.[51] In a tutorial on the DVD *Chuck Jones: A Life in Animation*, (2000)[52] Jones lists the key ingredients in his typically anarchic animations:

1. Zip-outs (characters leave the frame in a flash instead of walking or running out)
2. Anticipation (character uses a countermove to inform us of an upcoming move, like a windup motion)
3. Primary and secondary action (a primary physical action, such as hitting a wall, will be followed by the secondary movement of the character's clothes)
4. Overlapping action, when moving in one direction and moving in the other direction are shown simultaneously
5. Cartoon exaggeration, such as adding muscles to a body that a human doesn't have
6. Natural animal movement
7. Anthropomorphism: making an animal seem like a human (Jones says it was easier to make animals seem human than to make humans seem human, so he stuck to animals)
8. Animation of minutiae, such as the slightest change in expression in a character looking at the camera

Many avant-garde animators, such as Jan Svankmajer,[53] see themselves more as magicians than animators. To a certain extent this is true of Burton as well, especially in his emphasis on setting the scene and creating an atmosphere, rather than on action. Although Burton has directed more live-action films than animated films, we will see in the following chapters that his films often share many of the characteristics typical of a Chuck Jones cartoon.

Notes

1. Lynn Hirschberg, "Drawn to Narrative," *New York Times Sunday Magazine*, November 9, 2003.
2. Mark Salisbury, ed., *Burton on Burton*, rev. ed. (London: Faber & Faber, 2000), p. xv.

3. On IMDB.com list for Tim Burton, *The Island of Doctor Agor* (1971) is listed as written and directed by Tim Burton. The user comments include an entry by "Richard Gonzalez," who claims to have seen the film and summarizes it as follows: "Very well done super 8 film filmed around Burbank and surrounding areas, such as the old L.A. zoo in Griffith Park and the beaches of Malibu, where Dr. Agor (Burton) met his drowning death at the hands of his half man–half animal creations. Tim made great use of the bear and lion cages at the old L.A. zoo to house his 'experiments.' The cast consisted of friends and classmates." The fact that this entry was posted on April 1 (April Fool's Day) makes it more likely to be a joke than anything else.

4. Burton in Salisbury, *Burton on Burton*, pp. 6–8.

5. Ibid., p. 7.

6. Ibid.

7. Rick Heinrichs met Burton when they were both students at Cal Arts. Heinrichs has worked on almost every Burton film since *Vincent* as production designer, art designer, or special effects consultant.

8. Jim Smith and J. Clive Matthews, *Tim Burton* (London: Virgin Books, 2002), p. 9.

9. Burton in Salisbury, *Burton on Burton*, p. 8.

10. Ibid., p. 9

11. Ibid.

12. Michael Eisner with Tony Schwartz, *Work in Progress* (London: Penguin Books, 1998), pp. 171–172.

13. Burton in Salisbury, *Burton on Burton*, p. 13.

14. Michael Eisner: CEO and Chairman of the Board of Walt Disney Co. from 1984–2004.

15. James Kendrick, "The Black Cauldron" http://www.qnetwork.com/?page = review&id = 113.

16. Eisner, *Work in Progress*, pp. 172–173.

17. See his review of *The Black Cauldron* at www.rogerebert.com

18. Burton in Salisbury, *Burton on Burton*, p. 12.

19. For a complete plot summary and description, see Smith and Matthews, *Tim Burton*, pp. 10–19.

20. Taylor White, "Other Weirdness," *Cinefantastique* vol. 20 no. 1/vol. 20 no 2. (November 1989): 85.

21. Burton in Salisbury, *Burton on Burton*, pp. 52–53.

22. Tim Burton, *The Melancholy Death of Oyster Boy & Other Stories* (New York: Rob Weisbach Books, 1997).

23. Ibid., pp. 26–27.

24. Booth Moore, "Social Confidential," *Los Angeles Times*, February 10, 2000.

25. James Rayn, "Oyster Boy and Other Misfits," *New York Times*, November 2, 1997.

26. Ibid. Emphasis in original.

27. Greg Miller, "Tim Burton to Animate Cartoons for Shockwave," *Los Angeles Times*, January 28, 2000. Home Edition, Business Section, page C-3.

28. Ellie Kieskowski, "Tim Burton's Animated Series 'Stainboy' Premieres: Shockwave .com Announces New Fall Line-Up and Online Store," http://www.streamingmedia.com/ r/printerfriendly.asp?id = 6231.

29. Laura Randall, "Burton's Shorting Shockwave: Director brings 'Stain Boy'" to the Net, Takes Stake in Company," *Hollywood Reporter*, January 28, 2000; Greg Miller, "Tim Burton to Animate Cartoons for Shockwave," *Los Angeles Times*, January 28, 2000.

30. Juan Morales, "A Stain on Humanity: Director Tim Burton Brings His Brilliantly Bizarre Artistic Vision to the Web," *Detour*, April 2000.

31. Burton, quoted in Dean Delandreville, "Hollywood Is Streaming," http://www.zdnet.com/devhead/stories/articles/0,4413,2600198,00.html, as quoted in Smith and Matthews, p. 220.

32. Sam McMillan, "Flinch Studios Makes Its Mark with Tim Burton's Stain Boy," http://www.designinteract.com/features/stainboy/.

33. A user-friendly demo of Flinch's animation process can be seen on Flinch's Web site, www.Flinch.com.

34. Ramin Zahed, "Stainboy," *Variety*, November 13, 2000.

35. That is, the new medium is using the aesthetic system of the older system, such as computer games using cinematic conventions.

36. Steven Poole, *Trigger Happy: Videogames and the Entertainment Revolution* (New York: Arcade Publishing, 2001). Another good history of computer games is Steven L. Kent, *The Ultimate History of Video Games, From Pong to Pokémon and Beyond—The Story Behind the Craze That Touched Our Lives and Changed the World* (Prima Publishing, Roseville, CA 2001).

37. Katie Salen and Tommy Pullotta, "Shoot First, Play Later: Filmmaking with Gaming Engines," *RES* 3.2 (2000): 48–53. See also Colin Williamson, "This Is Quake II: What Are You Going to Do About It?", *PC Gamer* 4.10 (October 1997): 98–122.

38. On www.machinima.com, see especially the online essays by Gordon Madonald, Hugh Hancock, and Ian Mulliner, among others.

39. Scott Smith "Tim Burton: Dark Prince of the Web," *Res* 3.2 (Spring 2000), pp. 44–48.

40. Steven D. Katz, *Film Directing: Shot by Shot* (Culver City, CA: Michael Wiese Productions, 1991), and *Film Directing: Cinematic Motion* (Culver City, CA: Michael Wiese Productions, 1992).

41. Daniel Arijon, *Grammar of the Film Language.* (London: Focal Press, 1982).

42. For more on this, see Alison McMahan, "The Quest for Motion: Moving Pictures and Flight," in *Visual Delights: Essays on the Popular and Projected Image in the Nineteenth Century,* ed. Simon Popple and Vanessa Toulmin (Trowbridge, UK: Flicks Books, 2000), pp. 93–104.

43. Marta Braun, *Picturing Time: The Work of Étienne-Jules Marey (1830–1904)* (Chicago and London: University of Chicago Press, 1994). See also Marey's own book, *Du mouvement dans les functions de la vie* (Paris, 1868).

44. For the definitive study of Cohl, see Donald Crafton, *Emil Cohl, Caricature, and Film* (Princeton, NJ: Princeton University Press, 1990).

45. An excellent study of early animation is Donald Crafton, *Before Mickey: The Animated Film 1898–1928*, (Chicago and London: University of Chicago Press, 1993). Also of interest is E. G. Lutz, *Animated Cartoons: How They Are Made, Their Origin, and Development* (Bedford, MA: Applewood Books, 1998 (facsimile of original published in 1920)). The best history and analysis of prefilmic animation toys (or optical toys, as they are sometimes called) is in Laurent Mannoni, *Le grand art de la Lumière et de l'ombre—archéologie du cinema,* trans. Richard Crangle, in *The Great Art of Light and Shadow: Archeology of the Cinema,* with an introduction by Tom Gunning and a preface by David Robinson, Exeter Studies in Film History (Exeter: University of Exeter Press, 2000).

46. As an interesting comparison, Maureen Furniss notes that Frank Tashlin's animated works for Columbia, Warner Bros., and Disney during the 1930s and '40s are strongly influenced by live-action conventions, while the live-action features he directed are very cartoony. See Maureen Furniss, *Art in Motion: Animation Aesthetics* (London: John Libbery, 1998), p. 6.

47. Ibid., p. 252.

48. Ibid., pp. 102–103.

49. Ibid., p. 242.

50. The Hays Code was a self-regulatory code of ethics in Hollywood in force from 1934 to 1968. It especially prohibited showing sympathy for criminal activity.

51. James Clarke, *Animated Films* (London: Virgin Film, 2004), p. 265.

52. *Chuck Jones: A Life in Animation* DVD, Warner Home Video, 2000.

53. Svankmajer is a Czech surrealist filmmaker/animator whose work has influenced Tim Burton, Terry Gilliam, and others.

2

BURTON AND NARRATIVE:
FROM HIS TELEVISION WORK TO *BIG FISH*

*There's always problems in my movies. I'm not one of American's greatest storytellers.
I think if the things I've done have worked, they've worked on another level.*

—Tim Burton[1]

*Having begun his career as an animator at Disney, Burton has, some say, continued
to turn out animated movies ever since—only his films feature animated human beings
rather than cute cutouts.*

—David Mills[2]

Early Television Work

Perhaps fortunately for Burton, he was given the opportunity to really
learn his craft as a director on two television fairy tales. The first, made
in 1982 on a $116,000 budget, was *Hansel and Gretel*, with an all-Asian
cast and with Disney executive Julie Hickson serving as executive producer. She also wrote the screenplay for Burton to direct. (Hickson later
wrote a feature-length screenplay for Burton to direct called *True Love*,
about two boys who battle for the love of a girl. One of them is a
"Japanese Dr. Wu–type whose bedroom houses a full laboratory where
he busily concocts formulas, allowing him to metamorphose into a series
of weird, Transformer-type monsters."[3] However, they were never able
to get the project off the ground.)

Burton made certain changes to the well-known tale, such as making
the father a toymaker rather than a wood cutter. Additionally, all the

characters are played by men, as is typical of the Japanese Kabuki theater, with the witch wearing traditional Kabuki garb. There is also a "crazed" karate battle between Hansel and Gretel and the witch at the end; as one reviewer put it, "the Brothers Grimm meet Bruce Lee."[4] The cast, all nonactors, was led by Michael Yama (playing the witch and the mother) and Jim Ishida (the father). Some of the cast members did not speak English very well. This, along with the fact that the project was off-lot and that Burton had trouble stretching the material to fill the forty-five-minute slot (the program was intended for the newly established Disney Channel), tested Burton's mettle, and he was not always successful in dealing with the problems. For Burton, communicating to a large group of people, something not demanded from him as an animator, was particularly trying:

> It's funny, if you've never made a movie with actual people, you think you can do it, you don't see any reason why you can't. It looks very easy. But there is something about it that's abstract. So it was a good learning experience for me.[5]

Nevertheless, Burton used his opportunity well, both to learn and to show what he could do in terms of special effects on a low budget, working again with his team from *Vincent* Richard Heinrichs (who did the models) and Stephen Chiodo (who made the sets). According to Taylor L. White, the special effects included "front projection, forced perspective and a handful of impressive stop-motion shots. . . . [A]lso impressive is a number of on-set gags, most notably the witch's house built from sweets and edibles, where the walls ooze like jelly donuts."[6] Burton fondly remembered "a little duck toy that turns into a robot and a gingerbread man. He was a weird little puppet who forces Hansel to eat him."[7] The experience with the special effects undoubtedly served Burton well when he later made *Beetlejuice*.

Unfortunately, at least for Burton's fans, *Hansel and Gretel* was aired only once, late on Halloween in 1984, and is not currently in distribution.

In 1985, after Burton had made *Frankenweenie* (discussed below), which featured Shelley Duvall, Duvall invited him to direct *Aladdin and His Wonderful Lamp*, an episode of Showtime's *Faerie Tale Theatre* series for which she was the host and executive producer. Burton was honored to be asked, especially because name directors like Francis Ford Coppola usually directed. Also, it would be his first production away from Disney.

As with *Hansel and Gretel*, Burton was faced with a format over which he had little control, and a tight budget. Again, Burton brought on Rick Heinrichs and Stephen Chiodo for model and effects work. Burton had a week to produce the show, which was shot on videotape with three cameras, a new format for him.

The episode, which is still available on video, features Leonard Nimoy, as the evil magician who first leads Aladdin to the magic lamp, and James Earl Jones, as the narrator, the Genie of the Ring, and the Genie of the Lamp. Burton was less starstruck working with them than he had been with Vincent Price on *Vincent* (see Chapter 3): "Again, I got a chance to see great actors at work; every actor has a different way of working and so I was observant and learned from that."[8]

The story begins with Aladdin, played rather blandly by Robert Carradine, as a happy-go-lucky fatherless lad about town who survives by pickpocketing and petty thievery. He encounters a magician who claims to be his long-lost uncle. Though Aladdin and his mother are doubtful, they are pleased to be fed and at the prospect that the uncle will set Aladdin up in business (Aladdin wants to start a marble shop). But the uncle's real goal is to have Aladdin go to a cavern in the desert and steal a magic lamp from its magical guardians. The cave features a humorous use of forced perspective (and a sight gag based on forced perspective, as Aladdin is seen in profile crawling through arches that become progressively smaller and smaller), the kind of external-to-the-narrative joke that Burton would use increasingly in his later films. There are two magic trees in the cave that have fruit that turns into jewels when picked. The lamp itself is held in place by a hand protruding from the mouth of

Aladdin from *Aladdin* in the magic cave menaced by monsters that are reminiscent of some of Burton's animated creatures.

a large fish. When Aladdin steals the lamp, monstrous figures on the wall come to life and appear ready to chase him (although we never see them actually come off the wall). When Aladdin refuses to give his uncle the lamp, the uncle locks him in the cave. However, Aladdin manages to escape with the help of the Genie of the Ring. When he returns to town, he catches a forbidden glimpse of the sultan's daughter as she goes to her bath and promptly falls in love. He sends his mother to plead his case to the sultan, with the jewels he took from the fruit tree as gifts. However, the grand vizier convinces the sultan that he himself is a better match. Meanwhile, Aladdin discovers the lamp's hidden powers accidentally and gets the genie to help him win the princess (played as a desirable sugar plum, but without much personality, by Valerie Bertinelli). The sultan is fond of bizarre toys, and Aladdin gets his attention by having the genie provide him with a sort of television (which seems to show only cartoon-like fairy tales) and by building a new palace overnight. However, once Aladdin is happily married, his uncle manages to steal the lamp from the princess, and Aladdin has to struggle all over again to get it back, which he and the princess manage to do in collaboration.

The story's moral (the script was by Mark Curtiss and Rod Ash) seems to be that good fortune can come to the undeserving, but they have to earn it in order to keep it. For Aladdin, this means showing kindness to the class of poor folk he came from and being polite, as well as firm, with the genie (which does not extend to freeing him as it does in some versions of the tale), who has a deliciously reactionary sense of humor, played to the hilt by James Earl Jones. This blatant message about paternalism as the ennobling characteristic of the upper class is overlaid by a more subtle one: although the transfer of power (the narrator makes it clear that it is Aladdin who takes over when the sultan dies, and not the princess) goes through the Princess, she is not allowed to rule or even to be looked at by others, ensuring that she lives her life in virtual isolation. As if to emphasize this, her boudoir greatly resembles that of Jeannie's (from the television series *I Dream of Jeannie*) in her bottle, as does the shape of the castle that Aladdin has the genie build for her. The fact that Aladdin can discard her whenever he pleases is also alluded to by the genie, who protests that he doesn't want to build anything too fancy if Aladdin isn't fully committed to the relationship. The themes of personal and civic responsibility and the allusions to class conflict would return in later Burton films, especially *Big Fish,* discussed later in this chapter, and Burton's reimagining of *Planet of the Apes* (discussed in Chapter 5). The image of the imprisoned love interest returns in *The Nightmare Before Christmas,* but without the depth seen here.

Aladdin is worth revisiting not only because it serves as a time capsule of American social mores of the early 1980s, but for the performances of James Earl Jones and Leonard Nimoy, marked contrasts to their work in *Star Wars* and *Star Trek.*

Frankenweenie

Between the two TV productions, Burton directed *Frankenweenie,* a fairy tale that was originally meant to be distributed theatrically, along with the 1984 re-release of *The Jungle Book* (Wolfgang Reitherman, 1967). The film was rescheduled to be released at Christmas with the re-release of *Pinocchio* (Hamilton Luske and Ben Sharpsteen, 1940). However, after a couple of test screenings for mothers with six- to nine-year-old children, it was determined that the film was too dark and macabre. There was some discussion of pairing it with *My Science Project* (1985), but this did not come to pass. In the end, *Frankenweenie*'s only theatrical release was in a few art houses.[9] It was the third time Burton had worked on a film for Disney that had not found its audience. Burton left the studio soon afterward.

Unlike the two fairy tales he directed for television, Burton had complete control over *Frankenweenie.* He wrote the story, which was adapted for the screen by Lenny Rip and executive produced by Julie Hickson. The project was shot in black and white on color film stock, with a shooting schedule of fifteen days and a budget just under $1 million. It

Young Victor Frankestein re-animates his dog in *Frankenweenie.*

starred Shelley Duvall and Daniel Stern as the Frankensteins and Barrett Oliver as their son, Victor Frankenstein. Victor is a ten-year-old boy living in a peaceful suburb with his parents and his dearly beloved bull terrier, Sparky, who stars as a dinosaur in the opening movie-within-a-movie that Victor has made. While Victor is playing ball with Sparky, the dog runs into the street (the ball and street are shown from the dog's point of view) and is hit by a car. (The ball bounces away forlornly, a move borrowed from Fritz Lang's *M* as a way of indicating a death that is not shown onscreen.) After the dog is buried in a pet cemetery, Victor tries to get back to his life, but nothing really wakes him from his depression until a science teacher shows Victor and his classmates how frog legs can be made to move with a jolt of electricity. This inspires Victor, who runs home, borrows his mother's toaster and sundry mechanical items from the garage, and builds a lab in his room. (Burton even managed to get the original *Frankenstein* lab equipment designed by Kenneth Strickfaden.) Part of the lab consists of a bicycle, used upside down, a motif that would reappear in *Pee-wee*. He then digs up Sparky's body from the cemetery. He is helped along by an electrical storm and succeeds in reanimating Sparky, now covered with scars and patches of mismatched skin that Victor seems to have borrowed from other dogs.

Victor tries to keep the dog's existence a secret from his parents and neighbors, but although Sparky leaks water through his stitches when he drinks, he is still an active dog and runs around the neighborhood, frightening the neighbors. The neighbors inflate the danger he presents to such a degree that they turn into a hysterical mob, even though Victor's parents try to explain and introduce them to the dog at a formal party at their house. The mob chases Victor and Sparky onto a miniature golf course, where they take refuge in a windmill. Someone sets the mill on fire, and it collapses; Sparky drags an unconscious Victor out in time

The electrical charge is augmented by spinning bicycle wheels in *Frankenweenie.*

but is crushed himself. This selflessness calms the mob and changes their opinion, so they use jumper cables to collectively reanimate Sparky again.

Although only twenty-five minutes long, *Frankenweenie* manages to match and, in a skewed way, replicate all of the key moments of James Whale's *Frankenstein* (1931), starring Boris Karloff. In turn, Burton's later effort, *Edward Scissorhands*, can be seen as a remake of *Frankenweenie*, except the neighbors in *Scissorhands* fail to reach the level of understanding and new tolerance, even helpfulness, that happens in the shorter film. The climactic scene in the windmill is also replicated and extended in *Sleepy Hollow*. To a certain extent, the moment of understanding is in *Sleepy Hollow* as well, when Ichabod Crane realizes that he has misjudged Katrina Van Tassel and returns to save her.

Frankenweenie is a clear homage to Whale's *Frankenstein* and other horror films of the 1930s, but it also has numerous connections to cartoons: for example, the way the accident is shown from the dog's point of view (although we don't see the dog's reaction, as we would in a cartoon), and Sparky is clearly a progenitor of the bull terrier Burton designed for the cartoon series *Family Dog*. Victor Frankenstein is also in many ways a cartoon character: completely given over to his obsession, in this case his love for his dog; cut off from those around him (although his parents are cheerful and supportive, they don't seem to know their son very well and never touch him, even when they tuck him in at night); able to bring about fantastical metamorphoses, whether creating a lab out of household items or bringing a dead and buried dog back to life. Like most cartoon characters, Victor himself remains unchanged by the end of the film, although his neighbors, at least, seem to have altered in relation to him. However, the affinity between *Frankenweenie* and certain kinds of cartoons lies in that fact that many cartoons are loosely based on fairy tales and that many cartoons parody classic live-action films. In the case of *Frankenweenie*, the resemblance to cartoons is minor and incidental, more the result of mining similar sources than anything else. However, there is a certain affinity between the rapid transformations that occur, Victor's isolation from those around him, his unrealistic scientific genius, his unrelenting focus on the object of his obsession, and the temporary nature of death that is similar to what we associate with animation as a genre. *Frankenweenie* doesn't fully qualify as a pataphysical film, as the effects are invisible within the conventions of its genre, but Victor Frankenstein would qualify as a pataphysical character.

Though *Frankenweenie* was the first time Burton had worked with professional actors, Shelley Duvall, as I noted earlier, was impressed enough to invite him to direct an episode of her *Faerie Tale Theatre* series for Showtime. *Frankenweenie* also got him his first job directing a feature film, as a friend at Warner Bros., Bonnie Lee, made sure to show it to the various executives. Eventually it was seen by Paul Reubens, the creator of the television character Pee-wee Herman, who had a green light from the studio to make a feature film based on his character. Reubens had just rejected the director suggested to him by Warner and had a week to find a suitable replacement or lose his go-ahead. After watching just the opening of *Frankenweenie*, Reubens knew he'd found his director. (Interestingly, both Reubens and Burton had attended Cal Arts at the same time but had never met there.)

Pee-wee's Big Adventure

Pee-wee's Big Adventure (1985) is the most blatantly cartoon-like of Burton's live-action films (it even includes two short cartoon sections as well as several scenes of stop-motion animation). Like many cartoons, it parodies other genres. What's special about *Pee-wee* is that almost all the genres being parodied are taken right from 1970s television, from the sporting event opening, the product-placement shots of the bike (Burton specifically mentions late-night TV commercials for kitchen products as a source of inspiration), the police series (Burton specifically refers to *CHiPs.*), soap opera series like *Dynasty*, and underwater action sequences from *Tarzan*. The chase sequence at the end shows a series of B movies being shot on various Warner Bros. soundstages, including a Godzilla movie, a Christmas movie, and a beach-blanket bingo movie. But most of all *Pee-wee* is an homage to the road movie.[10] On the DVD commentary for the film, Burton notes repeatedly that what he enjoyed the most about making the film was the opportunity to try his hand at different genres, which gives us the impression again of a young director making a conscious effort to learn his craft.

Like young Victor in *Frankenweenie*, Pee-wee is obsessed with, and apparently only has warm feelings for, his gleaming red bike. The film opens with him dreaming of winning the Tour de France with it. When he awakens, we see that though he is a grown man, his approach to life is basically that of a prepubescent boy, with a roomful of toys, long minutes spent putting tape on his face just for fun, a fear of women who want anything from him other than to ride bikes, fix bikes, or help him look for his bike. At the same time he is something of a mechanical genius, with an elaborate machine set up to make breakfast (which would be echoed later in Vincent Price's cookie factory in *Edward Scissorhands*) and a fondness for magic tricks. Pee-wee's bike is the envy of all the real boys on the block, and after he refuses to sell it to Francis (Mark Holton), the local bully, Francis manages to steal it from him, even though Pee-wee has attached it to a mechanical clown (apparently played by Burton, according to the DVD commentary) with endless miles of chain. After Pee-wee calls in the police and organizes a neighborhood search, Francis fences the bike and refuses to admit to his guilt, even after Pee-wee bests him in a Tarzan-versus-alligator-style wrestling match in his bathtub. Pee-wee consults a psychic, who tells him his bicycle is in Texas, in the basement of the Alamo, and Pee-wee starts off on his road trip in search of his bike. He gets a ride from Mickey (Judd Omen), an escaped convict, and helps him evade capture at a roadblock by dressing as a girl and pretending to be Mickey's girlfriend. However, when it is his turn to drive, he has an accident (there is a beautiful cartoon moment when the convertible top acts as a parachute and lowers the car gently to the ground), and Mickey unceremoniously leaves him at the side of the road. Then he is picked up by a trucker, the ghost of Large Marge (Alice Nunn), whose facial transformation is another cartoon moment (see Chapter 3). Marge leaves him at a rest stop, and it is only when Pee-wee goes inside that he learns his driver's identity. The rest stop has two large dinosaur statues, and Pee-wee ends up having a

Pee-wee and Mickey on the road together in *Pee-wee's Big Adventure.*

night-long heartfelt conversation with Simone, the waitress (Diane Salinger, who would play the Penguin's mother along with Reubens as the Penguin's father in *Batman Returns*), who dreams of going to France. This gets her boyfriend, Andy (Jon Harns), jealous, and the two get into a clearly cartoon-inspired fight around the dinosaurs, with Andy menacing Pee-wee with a large dinosaur bone. Pee-wee ends up hopping a freight train and singing songs with a hobo, and finally gets to the Alamo, which turns out not to have a basement at all (though the mostly improvised tour led by Jan Hooks is hysterical). Heading home, Pee-wee impresses a group of Hell's Angels by dancing to "Tequila" in platform shoes. They give him one of their motorcycles, but he immediately has an accident and ends up in the hospital, where he dreams a stop-motion dream of a dinosaur eating his bicycle (see Chapter 3). However, he sees his bicycle on TV and heads to the Warner Bros. studio lot to reclaim it. He steals the bike back and is chased by the security guards all over the lot, including a memorable run through the soundstages.

Critics who have repeatedly noted that Burton's films are poorly plotted are making their comments from the perspective of classical Hollywood narrative, in which the lead character should have some kind of moral revelation that changes his life. Pee-wee has no such revelation; yet, in spite of his self-absorption, he seems to have a large number of friends and makes friends wherever he goes. Many of his friends seem to be as eccentric as he is, and we are led to question those who are depicted as relatively normal, such as Francis's father, by the mise-en-scène: for example, the family room at Francis's house is filled with big game trophy heads and large stuffed animals that enhance Francis's bully persona.

The plot of *Pee-wee's Big Adventure* is circular and episodic, with each episode structured around a gag or a series of gags. This is clearly a more cartoon-like structure. Animation scholar Harvey Deneroff has noted the differences between traditional animation scripts and screenplays. He points out that, before the advent of television animation, animation writers often started out as animators, and, because animation studios did not have story departments until the sound era, they tended to switch back and forth between those two roles throughout their careers. (As a result, animation writers are represented by the animator's union, The International Alliance of Theatrical Stage Employees (IATSE) Local 839, to this day, and not the Writer's Guild of America, as screenwriters are.) The different backgrounds for the different types of writers led to stories that were subservient to gags, rather than the other way around. Deneroff quotes Walter Kerr's discussion of Harold Lloyd's Hal Roach films:

> The gags and the situations . . . were provided by a stable of idea-men, [who were] not so much writers as split second improvisers who could match wits with one another in an office or on the set before the comedians came to work for the day. . . . All studios producing comedies had staffs of this sort. . . .[11]

As Deneroff points out, the usual procedure in the silent era was for the studio head to call in some of the animators for a conference, out of which a "story" would come. This is similar to the animation script meetings at Disney that Burton remembers:

> There were still the remnants from the old days at Disney, there were still people who would say, "Let's do another *Fantasia*," guys from the old school where they didn't have scripts, just a couple zany gag men in a room who'd say, "Let's get [Louis] Prima in here and work up a little number." Those guys were still around. It was cool.[12]

Even when Disney set up a story department, it did not produce scripts in the traditional sense, but rather storyboards, and these storyboards were only at one remove from the model charts of the silent era. (A model chart is a series of drawings of a cartoon character from different angles, in different poses, for the various animators to use as a guide in order to maintain visual consistency in the character.)[13]

The story of *Pee-wee's Big Adventure* was developed in much the same fashion: Reubens had created the character in the late 1970s, when he was a member of the Los Angeles improvisation group The Groundlings, which trained many later members of *Saturday Night Live*. It was a Groundlings practice that members write material for other members, and Phil Hartman, another member who ended up coauthoring the script for *Pee-wee*, wrote sketches for the Pee-wee character there. So *Pee-wee's Big Adventure* was created in much the same way as a classic cartoon: it began with Reubens's character and was developed through a series of loosely connected gags. Reubens had originally conceived of the movie as a retelling of the Pollyanna story, with Pee-wee coming to a small town and ending up making everybody happy. One day Reubens was walking with his managers on the studio lot and noticed that other people used bicycles to get around the lot, and he voiced a desire to have a bicycle himself. A few days later his managers presented him with an elaborate vintage bicycle similar to the one designed for the film, and Reubens knew immediately he had to drop the Pollyanna idea and write a completely new story about Pee-wee's obsession for his bike.[14] Burton described the writing sessions for *Pee-wee* in much the same way he had described the writing sessions at Disney:

> It started with Paul [Reubens] and one of the writers, Phil Hartman. . . . Those guys were really good and funny, and working on that movie was a lot like being in animation and having a story meeting; even though the script was really good, we'd sit around and come up with ideas. It was very exciting to me to be around them because they were funny. In improv, they base everything on knowing what their character is and letting go from there.[15]

The character of Pee-wee is an androgynous man-boy character (one reviewer called him an "aging elf"[16]) with amazing mechanical aptitude, a prepubescent attitude toward sex, and an obsessive love for his bicycle. By the time Burton signed on to direct the film, the character was fully formed and even established in the public mind. After auditioning for *Saturday Night Live* and not being chosen, Reubens had borrowed money from his family and staged *The Pee-wee Herman Show*, a series of set pieces that parodied American television from the 1950s and 1960s, at the Roxy Theatre on Sunset Strip. The show was aimed at adults and was laden with sexual innuendo. It was eventually made into an HBO special, which led to Reubens appearing several times as Pee-wee on *Late Night with David Letterman*.[17] Burton had seen the show and was a fan,[18] but he was concerned with working with such an established character. However, he finally agreed because his sensibility and Reubens's own were so in tune with each other, and because the film would give him the opportunity to try his hand at various genres.[19] Most of what, with hind-

As in *Frankenweenie,* the spinning bicycle wheels in *Pee-wee's Big Adventure* represent both a sense of loss and a sense of menace.

sight, seem to be truly Burtonesque touches are in the set design. These include Pee-wee's bathroom window, which turns out to be a fish tank; the spinning bicycle wheels behind Pee-wee's head, when he realizes his bicycle has been stolen; and the breakfast-making machine. All of them are animation-style moments, moments that involve metamorphosis or externalizations of a character's emotion. On the DVD commentary, Burton refers to the moment when the convertible's top opens and acts as a parachute to save Pee-wee and Mickey from a fatal car crash as "Felliniesque," but it can also be considered an animation moment, when an object's visible properties are exaggerated to humorous effect.

Critics compared the film to David Lynch's *Blue Velvet* (1986),[20] and to Vittorio De Sica's *The Bicycle Thief* (1948), "without the realism." Smith and Matthews focus on the fact that *Pee-wee* is a road movie, and compare it to *Wild at Heart* (David Lynch, 1990), *Easy Rider* (Dennis Hopper, 1969), *The Grapes of Wrath* (John Ford, 1940), and *It Happened One Night* (Frank Capra, 1934). They note that the road movie has built-in obstacles to creating a coherent narrative, and most filmmakers get around this by having two or more people on the trip and having the development occur between them. By having Pee-wee alone on his trip, a sense of coherence is lost, which is exacerbated by the fact that Pee-wee seems to have learned nothing from his experience.[21]

Though many of these comments are valid, to compare *Pee-wee* to a classical or postclassical Hollywood film, or any film with a classical narration, is to miss the point. A more appropriate comparison, if we insist on comparing Pee-wee to a classically narrated film, would be to *E.T.* (Steven Spielberg, 1982). Burton has several moments of subtle homage to *E.T.*, such as Pee-wee's moment of flight on his bicycle as he crosses the river, and most notably the shot of Pee-wee and Dottie (Elizabeth Daily) riding away on their bicycles at the end of the film and being silhouetted against a view of a sunset that is on a drive-in screen. (The latter scene also closes the loop with the moment at the opening of the film, when an animated band of cyclists roll along the bottom of a billboard advertising the Tour de France that appears in Pee-wee's dream.) Also comparable are the ways the two films are told from a child's perspective, with the hero's nightmares and fears being expressed by their environment. Both films are aimed at primarily younger audiences; the key difference is one of tone.

A more critically appropriate approach to *Pee-wee* is to see it as one of the first clear exemplars of a new genre, the pataphysical film. Once we admit that we are dealing with a different set of genre conventions, then we are no longer comparing apples and oranges. Pataphysical films need to be classed with animation, with films whose special effects sequences serve the same function as animation, and with films that follow the storytelling conventions that we associate with stories for very young children—stories that are filled with redundancies, that are episodic, that are unrealistic, and that often do not show a character undergoing a classic Aristotelian catharsis, or learning a lesson; after all, catharsis is a quality of tragedy, of myth, but not necessarily of comedies and fairy tales. These focus more on preparing the young and uninitiated for the world by familiarizing them with some aspect of it in exaggerated form. Burton described his own relationship to the Pee-wee character as follows:

> I've always felt close to all the characters in my films. I've always felt I *had* to be, because when you're doing something you're putting your life into it, and there has to be aspects to all the characters that are either a part of you, or something you can relate to, or something that is symbolic of something inside you. I *have* to connect. The Pee-wee character was just into what he was doing, and when you grow up in a culture where people remain very hidden, it was nice that he didn't really care about how he was perceived. He operated in his own world, and there's something I find very admirable about that. He's a character who is on his own, who is able to operate in society, and yet he's also sort of an outcast. Again, it's that whole theme of being perceived as this weird thing. In some ways, there's a freedom to that, because you're free to live in your own world. But it's a prison in a way. It's how I felt when I was an animator at Disney.[22]

Beetlejuice

On the surface, Burton's approach to *Beetlejuice* (1988) seems similarly episodic and disjointed in its comedy. Certainly there are similarities to the look of *Pee-wee*—it's very stagy, there is an emphasis on bright colors, with settings that refer to American iconic environments such as the storybook New England village and the Maitlands' rambling, rustic home, which resembles a large doll house more than anything else, contrasted to the New York urban artist loft look that Delia Deetz brings with her when she moves into the Maitlands' house and starts to redo it. However, *Beetlejuice* is an ensemble film, with the members of the ensemble arranged in perfect symmetry: the ghost couple (the Maitlands, played by Alec Baldwin and Geena Davis), with their servant/clown, Beetlejuice (Michael Keaton); the human couple, the Deitzes (Jeffrey Jones and Catherine O'Hara), with their servant/clown, Otho (Glenn Shadix); and the Deitzes' teenage Goth daughter, Lydia (Winona Ryder), who serves as a bridge between the two worlds.[23] Both groups are feeling pressure from outside forces: the Maitlands from their "caseworker for the dead," Juno (Sylvia Sidney), the Deitzes from the businesspeople from the city (led by Dick Cavett and Robert Goulet) that they are trying to impress. We don't see much of the city world the Deitzes are from (they bring it with them in the form of Delia's menacing sculptures), but we do see the underworld that the Maitlands must prepare themselves for by haunting their own home for another 125 years: the sand world that surrounds the house, filled with menacing caricatures of the sandworms from David Lynch's *Dune*; (1984) the "fish tank full of bizarre creatures," as Vincent Canby[24] referred to it, which the film describes as a "death for the dead"; and, most imaginative of all, the idea of death as a large, unwieldy bureaucracy, run by other dead, all still marked by the signs of how they died, from the explorer whose head was shrunk by cannibals to the human cinder, a man who burned to death after smoking in bed.

The plot is as follows: The Maitlands are very much in love, and in love with fixing up their house. They are beginning to think about starting a family. They take a trip to the hardware store for supplies, and on their way back they are in an accident, their car goes into the river, and they drown. However, they themselves do not realize this until they reenter their house. They find a guidebook for the deceased and discover the entrance to the bureaucratic offices of the dead, only to be told by their caseworker that they need to haunt their own home for 125 years. If they try to leave the house, they find themselves in the desert with the sandworms. Meanwhile, their house has been sold, and the Deitzes move in. Delia, with the help of her interior designer, Otho, immediately starts redecorating. The drastic changes she makes alarm the Maitlands, but their own attempts at haunting are rather ridiculous, so they call on Beetlejuice, the "bio-exorcist" who is trapped in the model of their town that Ian Maitland built, to get rid of the Deitzes. Bringing Beetlejuice in is rather a mistake. Though he succeeds in convincing the

Deitzes and their guests that the house is haunted, this just encourages them to start a business exploiting the ghosts, while Beetlejuice, whose libido is still very active, tries to force Lydia to marry him, or her friends, the Maitlands, will be forced to join the ranks of the truly dead. Through joint effort they succeed in getting rid of Beetlejuice, and then the Deitzes and the Maitlands agree to share the house on terms acceptable to all, with the Maitlands essentially taking over the job of parenting Lydia, who gives up her Goth ways.

The screenplay was an original, written by Michael McDowall (an author of horror novels), with a story by McDowall, Burton, producer Larry Wilson, and Warren Skaaren (who rewrote McDowall's script). The basic concept clearly owes a debt of inspiration to the *Topper* trilogy: *Topper* (Norman Z. McLeod, 1937, starring Cary Grant), *Topper Takes a Trip* (Norman Z. McLeod, 1939), and *Topper Returns* (Roy Del Ruth, 1941), as well as a *Topper* television series in 1953 and a *Topper* TV movie in 1979. (Another *Topper* movie appeared in 1992.) In the original *Topper* story, a ghostly couple haunt a friend who is still alive. What the *Topper* films share with *Beetlejuice*, primarily, is the comic treatment of death. According to reviewer Anne Thompson, the original script was "darker and less humorous" and went through a long, arduous rewrite and development phase before Burton was given the go-ahead by the studio. The problem, apparently, was the difficulty in developing a cohesive tone.[25]

The film was made on a very tight budget of $13 million. There were over three hundred effects done during production, costing $1 million, a tiny budget for that number of effects (Alan Munro and Rick Heinrichs led the effects department), and the movie grossed over $73 million in the United States alone.

Although the film did excellent box office, reviews were rather mixed, if not downright negative, such as Vincent Canby's:

> There are funny ideas in the screenplay, but either they are undeveloped by the writers or they are thrown away through what appears to be Tim Burton's shapeless direction. This may not be an oversight, but, rather, the influence of a kind of television comedy show in which gags don't grow one out of another but succeed one another, randomly.[26]

Similarly, Kim Newman writes:

> The director doesn't yet have the discipline to structure a movie as more than a series of individual skits. The down-to-earth Maitlands should be the backbone of the film, but too often they just play stooges to Betelgeuse or

the Deetzes [sic], and Burton's anything-for-an-effect approach is exemplified by the yanking in of "guest stars" Robert Goulet, Dick Cavett and Sylvia Sidney to no real purpose. And yet the film keeps pulling itself together. . . .[27]

Although Newman, who reviews Burton's films regularly,[28] is more favorable of the film than Canby, both reviewers were unable to understand what they were seeing: that *Beetlejuice* represents the birth of a new genre, the genre that I have labeled "pataphysical," of which the *Scream* series of films (starting with *Scream* in 1996) are probably the most extreme example. Pataphysical films make fun of established systems of knowledge, especially academic and scientific ones, which often take the form of turning conventions (including genre conventions, as genre conventions are based on what we accept to be true at any given moment) on their head. In *Beetlejuice*, this convention reversal starts at the very beginning, with the film's leads, the Maitlands, being killed off in the first ten minutes; the rest of the film consists of the ghosts' efforts to rid the house of humans, instead of the other way around, as is usually the case.

Pataphysical films usually follow an alternative narrative logic, a logic based on conventions other than those of classical Hollywood cinema; this is the characteristic the reviewers have the most trouble with, as they are attached to classical narrative and consider any work that doesn't follow the formula to be weak. This blind spot means that they don't see the alternative narrative structure that is in place; in the case of *Beetlejuice*, as with *Pee-wee*, the narrative structure is closer to animation narrative than to traditional Hollywood narrative. Burton himself emphasized that the narration of the script was part of what drew him to the project:

> [A]fter Hollywood hammering me with the concept of story structure, . . . the script for *Beetlejuice* was completely anti all that: it had no real story, it didn't make any sense, it was more like stream of consciousness. That script was probably the most amorphous ever. It changed a lot, but the writer Michael McDowall (sic) had a good, perverse sense of humor and darkness, and that was the good thing about it. It had the kind of abstract imagery that I like, with these strange characters and images floating in and out.[29]

To be clear, the fact that a film follows an alternative logic in its narration does not free it from the requirement to be faithful to its own conventions. *Beetlejuice* has some glaring inconsistencies—if everyone in the afterlife is kept in the state they were in at the moment of their death, why don't the Maitlands look like drowned corpses? And when Beetlejuice is "killed" for the second time, why doesn't he join the "Death for the Dead" world, instead of ending up in the waiting room where the Maitlands went? An alternative form of narration also doesn't free the film from the need to make the characters sympathetic. As Jim Smith and J. Clive Matthews note, "whilst no one is evil (not even Betelgeuse) there aren't any genuinely sympathetic characters either. The Maitlands are twee, the Deitz's are ghastly, and Lydia is just a pompous adolescent. . . ."[30] Burton defended the characterization of the Maitlands: "I never saw the Maitlands as one hundred per cent good; they had their problems. The whole gist to me with them was that these are people who like being boring. It's like that thing in old movies where the bland characters need to get goosed a little . . ."[31] The problem of character sympathy is not as extreme in *Beetlejuice* as it is, for example, in *Cabin Boy*, a film discussed in Chapter 3, which Burton produced. Of course the issue is one that needs to be addressed first by the screenwriter(s), and it is often a glaring weakness in pataphysical films. For Burton, the problem of likeability in the hero did not go away, as similar criticisms were leveled at his vision of *Batman*. Burton finally seemed to get a handle on it with *Edward Scissorhands* and *The Nightmare Before Christmas*, both scripted by Caroline Thompson, a pataphysical writer par excellence with a gift for combining the strange and the sympathetic (she also wrote *The Addams Family* (1991), for example).

The aspect of pataphysical films that is most difficult for viewers steeped in classical (and even postclassical) Hollywood cinema is the fact that these films emphasize highly stylized set design and visible (to the point of being-in-your-face) special effects, and have thin plots and thinly drawn characters, because the narrative relies more on intertextual, nondiegetic references to be understood. They are most easily grasped by younger viewers who, like Burton, absorbed their pop culture from television instead of out of books, and are well versed in the multiple references and comments built into the films. Alain Garsault, who reviewed *Beetlejuice* for *Positif*, understood this aspect of the film:

> *Beetlejuice* counts on the knowledge base that fans of fantasy films will bring to this one. [Burton] is a true master of comedy. He combines the comic, the fantastic, and the horrific into one vital, inventive whole, and does so with a joy in creating illusions that harks back to one of the still-vibrant sources of our art: [Georges] Méliès.[32]

In spite of being doubly dead, *Beetlejuice* had an afterlife as a children's cartoon TV series (1989–1991, Warner Bros. Television), which Burton produced.

Edward Scissorhands

Scissorhands (1990) is, to this day, the film that defines Burton in most people's minds. He commissioned novelist Caroline Thompson to write the screenplay while he was working on *Beetlejuice*, then sold the script with himself attached as director as a package to Fox after Warner's seemed reluctant to take it on. The idea of a man with hands for scissors had been with him since childhood, and a simple drawing of a man with scissors for hands, in a punk-style costume, was all he gave to Thompson to begin with. To Burton, the character reflected something about how he had felt as a child, about the conflict between the inner and outer selves, about the teenage dilemma of wanting to touch but not being able to.[33]

Caroline Thompson, who is also credited as an associate producer on the film, defined the story as a fable, a story not to be taken literally but nevertheless with a meaning that is easily understood.[34] The plot closely follows that of James Whale's *Frankenstein*, as did *Frankenweenie*, which makes *Scissorhands* look like an extended rewrite of the shorter film. But, as Burton pointed out:

> I always loved monsters and monster films. I was never scared, I simply loved them, for as long as I can remember . . . King Kong, Frankenstein, Godzilla, Creature from the Black Lagoon—they're all quite similar, and only differ in terms of costume design and makeup. . . . I found that most monsters were completely misunderstood. They usually had more sensitive souls than the human characters around them.[35]

Johnny Depp as Edward in
Edward Scissorhands.

The story of *Scissorhands* is as follows: The local Avon Lady, Peg Boggs (Dianne Wiest), desperate to find new customers, drives up the hill to a mysterious, Gothic-style mansion, where she discovers a nearly mute young man (Johnny Depp) with scissors for hands living alone in the ruins. She takes him home out of pity, and he is welcomed with varying degrees of enthusiasm by her husband, Bill (Alan Arkin), and her son, Kevin (Robert Oliveri). Her teenage daughter, Kim (Winona Ryder), is away on a camping trip, but Edward is immediately attracted to her picture on the mantel. Peg dresses him in her husband's clothes and puts makeup on him to cover the scars on his face, then has a barbecue to introduce him to the neighbors. Edward's innocent curiosity is very endearing, though most of the neighbors find him frightening. Still, he manages to find ways to make himself useful, from trimming the hedges into fantastical animal shapes, to grooming dogs' fur into equally fantastical shapes, to finally, as the ladies of the neighborhood get used to him, cutting their hair in fanciful styles. The film satirizes the suburban lifestyle by showing how empty these women's lives are; they are not shown overwhelmed by housework and child care but rather as lazy, with not enough to occupy them, filling their time with gossip and, in the case of at least one woman, Joyce (Kathy Baker), casual affairs. The husbands all mow their lawns and drive to work, or return home from work, in synchronized time. One neighbor, a religious fanatic (O-Lan Jones), immediately accuses Edward of being a representative of the devil, but since she was ostracized to begin with, the others ignore her.

The only other person who has a negative reaction to Edward at first is Kim, who comes home late one night to find Edward on her waterbed; she screams in terror, and this frightens him, so he ends up puncturing the waterbed beyond repair. Kim is dating Jim (Anthony Michael Hall), a local jock/tough guy who also has a negative reaction to Edward. Kim

Edward's ruined mansion is surrounded by lovely topiary in *Edward Scissorhands*.

gradually warms up to Edward, however, and begins to find his inno-
cence, shyness, and sensitivity a welcome contrast to Jim's heavyhanded,
macho behavior. This only angers Jim more; Edward also alienates Joyce,
who has attempted to seduce him and been rejected, and now wants
revenge. Jim stages a robbery of his own home, using Edward's special
hands to jimmy the locks, leaves Edward behind when the security system kicks in and the house locks down again. Joyce adds her accusing
voice to that of Esmeralda, the religious fanatic, who is now accepted by
the group of neighborhood women even as Edward is rejected by them.
As Kim's preference for Edward becomes clear, Jim goes into a drunken
rage and almost runs over her brother Kevin with his van. Edward saves
the boy in time, but he accidentally cuts the boy's face in the process,
just moments after he had accidentally cut Kim's hand. The uneasy
neighbors now make up their minds and turn into a vengeful mob,
driving him out of the neighborhood and back up to his ruined mansion.
Jim's rage is murderous, and he attacks Edward, who kills him in self-
defense. Kim witnesses it all and tells the mob that the boys have killed
each other. Edward is left alone in the empty mansion again, and the
mob calms down and returns home, the women still wearing the hair-
styles that Edward had arranged for them.

The movie itself is framed as a fairy tale told by a grandmother to her
grandchild, as the child watches it snow outside and wants to know
where snow comes from. We realize that the grandmother is Kim, and
that the snow comes from Edward carving ice sculptures at top speed,
one of which is always of Kim as she looked when she was young, a
figure Edward has endowed with angel's wings.

The main difference between *Scissorhands* and most of Burton's previous films is that *Scissorhands* is not a comedy. It is a fairy tale that ends
sadly instead of happily, as *Frankenweenie* and *Beetlejuice* did. Although

Winona Ryder as Edward's angelic muse
in *Edward Scissorhands*.

65

there are funny moments (mostly resulting from Burton's gentle satire of life in Southern California suburbia), the overwhelming feeling is one of pathos. Another significant difference is the relatively minor use of special effects, most of them in-camera. There was a lot of work with makeup, at least for Johnny Depp in the title role, and the Stan Winston Studio created the scissors-for-hands.

Although, of all Burton's films to date, *Scissorhands* has the most coherent narrative, reviewers still found it fit to critique Burton's narrative structures:

> Clearly, this time Burton, a director noted for his visual style but often faulted for his story structures, is trying to engage not only our eyes but our hearts and minds as well.[36]

> All of the central characters in a Burton film . . . exist in personality vacuums; they're self-contained oddities with no connection to the real world. It's saying something about a director's work when the most well-rounded and socialized hero in any of his films is Pee-wee Herman.[37]

Once again, there is a problem here of perception: with *Scissorhands* especially, the fact that the film has a melancholy tone, instead of a comic one, again leads viewers to expect a classical Hollywood narrative format. But in spite of the genre change, Burton is still making a pataphysical film: yes, it is dramatic and not comic, yes the effects are fewer than in *Beetlejuice,* but *Scissorhands* is still a pataphysical film. There is still a dialogic blend of genres, but the dominant one is not drama, but fairy tale. Fairy tales do not have realistic plots: they are peopled with characters who can do the impossible, like the inventor, played here by Vincent Price, who (as we see in flashbacks later in the film) creates Edward out of a factory robot and a cookie heart, or Edward himself, who is unable to touch but can produce dazzling works of art in the form of topiaries, hairdos, groomed dogs, and ice sculptures. When judged as a realistic

Vincent Price as Edward's inventor in *Edward Scissorhands.*

drama or a social commentary on suburban life, *Scissorhands* leaves much to be desired. But when judged as a fairy tale, its initial and continuing popularity is clearly understandable:

> If people didn't line up to see this stuff by the tens of millions, Burton would be earning comparisons with such cult directors as John Waters and David Lynch instead of Lucas and Spielberg. Yet against all expectations, he's struck a nerve in the mass audience—an apparent longing for wacky unpredictability, for moody surrealism and explosive humor, for a taste of the light fantastic. The reason, says [screenwriter Caroline] Thompson, is simple: "David's [Lynch's] obsessions are the obsessions of a nineteen-year-old, and Tim's are the obsessions of a twelve-year-old. And this is much more a twelve-year-old's culture."[38]

Scissorhands marks Burton's return to fairy tale as the narrative structure for his films, but this time applied and manipulated in a sophisticated way, blended with humor and pathos, the lessons of his early TV work clearly well learned. Looking over his film output from the beginning to *Big Fish*, it is clear that the fairy-tale narrative structure suits him even better than that of animation; he would not use animation narrative structure again in live-action films except for *Mars Attacks!*

Obviously, animation narrative and fairy-tale narrative have much in common, which perhaps excuses David Mills, one of the reviewers who picked up on the animated narrative structure in Burton's early films, for saying it applied to all of his films up to *Sleepy Hollow*.[39] In his films that used stop-motion animation (as *Mars Attacks!* was going to, initially), Burton returned to a combination genre-narrative with animation as the dominant narrative structure; in *The Nightmare Before Christmas*, the animation structure was combined with a fairy-tale structure, and in *Mars Attacks!* with a certain brand of '50s alien-invader-sci-fi structure. But with *Scissorhands*, *Sleepy Hollow*, and *Big Fish*, he would use a hybrid genre-narrative in which the fairy-tale structure was dominant. (With the *Batman* films he experimented with a heroic myth structure, which he perfected, in his own inimitable way, in *Ed Wood* and would use again in his *Planet of the Apes*, as we will see later.)

To further add to the genre melting-pot, Burton's fairy tale films (*Edward Scissorhands*, *The Nightmare Before Christmas*, and *Sleepy Hollow*) as well as his myth-films (*Batman*, *Batman Returns*, *Ed Wood*, and *Planet of the Apes*) are also examples of modern Gothic, with their gloomy and mysterious settings, menacing or nostalgic soundtracks, the oppressive weight of the past upon the present, supernatural and human evil, and a set décor that is usually an excessive combination of medieval and rococo design styles. It is also worth noting that in classical Gothic tales human evil was often incarnated in the maleficent aristocrat, an oppressive father figure; but this is one element that Burton routinely dispenses with, instead showing father figures, from Vincent Price's inventor in *Scissorhands* to Martin Landau's portrayal of Bela Lugosi in *Ed Wood* to Charlton Heston's cameo as the dying father ape in *Planet of the Apes* as positive role models and sources of love. In fact, a keystone of Burton is that every hero's task is to become his father.

Sleepy Hollow

The story of *Sleepy Hollow* (1999) is set in 1799. Ichabod Crane (Johnny Depp) is a forensic police detective, a Victorian-style scientist caught in what is still very much a Gothic Revival America. The legal system he works with cannot comprehend his desire to do autopsies. In order to be rid of him for a while, the authorities send him to the remote village of Sleepy Hollow, to investigate a series of mysterious decapitations.

Ichabod enters the village of Sleepy Hollow in the 1949 Disney cartoon, *The Adventures of Ichabod and Mr. Toad.*

Johnny Depp as Ichabod enters the village of Sleepy Hollow in Tim Burton's *Sleepy Hollow.*

Sleepy Hollow is a bucolic farm village, its vaguely Dutch architecture fitting in perfectly with the early fall colors, but as Ichabod walks down the main street, the villagers close their windows against him. Finally, he enters a house where a party is taking place. There he sees a young woman, Katrina Van Tassel (Christina Ricci), playing a game that seems a cross between Blindman's Buff and Spin the Bottle within a circle of admiring young men, including Bram von Brunt (Casper Van Dien). Ichabod gets caught up in the game unwittingly, and the blindfolded Katrina gives him a kiss, which leads to instant romantic sparks between the two. This is immediately noticed by the possessive Bram, but Ichabod walks away from the confrontation and is invited by Baltus Van Tassel (Michael Gambon), Katrina's father and the town's wealthiest landowner, to stay with them while he conducts his investigation. Ichabod meets with the town's elders—Van Tassel, the Reverend Steenwyck (Jeffrey Jones), Magistrate Philipse (Richard Griffiths), Doctor Lancaster (Ian McDiarmid), and Notary Hardenbrook (Michael Gough). The elders tell him that the decapitations are surely the work of the Headless Horseman, a Hessian mercenary who died in the Western Woods some twenty years earlier. Once the mystery is unraveled, what has occurred is this: Lady Van Tassel (Miranda Richardson), Baltus' second wife, had come into his household as nurse to his first wife, looking for revenge for a grievance to her own family years ago and to get rich. She ensures that Katrina's mother dies and quickly seduces Baltus into marrying her. Because she is the daughter and sister of a witch, she uses her witchcraft to bring the Hessian back from the dead to do her bidding; he will decapitate whoever she says as long as she has his head. At her bidding the Hessian kills almost everyone Ichabod meets on the first night, as well as Baltus' servant Maspeth and Bram von Brunt. It appears that he has also killed Lady Van Tassel, but she has staged her death (substituting her servant girl's body for her own) in order to put Ichabod and Baltus off track. Lady Van Tassel is also responsible for killing her sister and her servant girl Sara, as well as Katrina's mother.

Ichabod at first rejects the story of the Hessian, but after he witnesses the death of Magistrate Philipse, he realizes that the stories are true. At first, he has what appears to be a nervous breakdown, but he quickly comes out of that, declaring that the Horseman might be supernatural, but he is controlled by a living human. Ichabod then applies a rational, scientific method to finding the killer. His method leads him to suspect

The Headless Horseman from *The Adventures of Ichabod and Mr. Toad.*

Christopher Walken as the Headless Horseman in *Sleepy Hollow.*

Baltus, but Baltus is killed by the Horseman, then Katrina herself, in spite of his growing attraction to her. However, his method leads him back to Lady Van Tassel, and he returns to the village just in time to save Katrina from a fiery death in the windmill. In the end the Horseman takes Lady Van Tassel to hell with him on his black horse.

As Smith and Matthews have noted, the plot has a few logical inconsistencies, the most salient of which is why Lady Van Tassel would fake her own death.[40] How could she then return from the grave and claim Van Tassel's land without suspicion? The size of this loophole is reflected in the clunkiness of Lady Van Tassel's long monologue at the end of the film, when she explains her method and motivations.

The original screen story was written by Kevin Yagher and Andrew Walker (*Se7en*); the screenplay was by Andrew Walker and later doctored by playwright Tom Stoppard. Yagher and Walker had originally sold the idea to Scott Rudin as a low-budget horror film, with an emphasis on a murder occurring every five minutes. Originally Yagher, a makeup and special effects artist, was slated to do the effects and direct, but the project languished at Paramount. When Burton was released from his *Superman* contract, in 1998, Rudin sent him the script. It was also Rudin who suggested bringing Stoppard on board for the rewrites.[41]

The story has fairly little to do with Washington Irving's novella, *The Legend of Sleepy Hollow*, originally published in *The Sketch Book of Geoffrey Crayon, Gent,* in 1819. In Irving's story, Ichabod is a schoolmaster, tall, gaunt, and gangly, but vain and arrogant enough to think he can win the luscious Katrina's heart, someone he loves because she is the heiress to a wealthy landowner. According to the story, he is a good schoolteacher and very good at bringing extracurricular cultural activities to his little village, as well as a good dancer, but he is superstitious, and Bram von Brunt plays on his superstition by dressing as a headless horseman, chasing Ichabod home late on Halloween night, and throwing a lighted jack-o'-lantern at him for good measure. Ichabod runs out of town in terror, never to return, leaving Bram free to marry Katrina, who was just leading Ichabod on anyway, in order to make Bram jealous. The story does make much of the fact that Ichabod, from Connecticut, is an outsider to this little farming community, which is still very Dutch in its outlook and customs.

Burton was actually more familiar with the 1949 Technicolor Disney animation version from *The Adventures of Ichabod and Mr. Toad,* narrated by Bing Crosby (one of his teachers at Cal Arts had worked on the Disney film).[42] The Disney cartoon follows the story fairly faithfully, but it emphasizes the Grand Guignol elements, which Burton would later expand upon in his own version of the film: Ichabod's first walk down the village street, the way Katrina is surrounded by a circle of male admirers, the charmed way Ichabod succeeds at getting Katrina's attention in spite of his natural clumsiness and overall lack of social grace, the prominence of a covered bridge, the way the Horseman chases Ichabod (even the bit when Ichabod rides his horse backwards comes from the cartoon), the threatening look of the Western Woods, and the twisted appearance of the trees in the mist and the dark.

Perhaps because the visual elements of the film are very Gothic, authors such as Paul Woods claimed that *Sleepy Hollow* "was the first Gothic horror movie in Tim Burton's career."[43] But yet again, Burton is making a hybrid genre film that combines two structures—fairy tale and horror—and the fairy-tale structure is the dominant: Ichabod, the hero, is sent on a quest, the quest consists of various smaller difficult tasks (seeking the advice of the Witch of the Woods, conducting various unpleasant autopsies, digging up the Hessian's grave, among others), with the help of unexpected and odd helpers (the murdered Maspeth's son and Katrina herself). He eventually solves the problem by proving himself as a man, which in his case means incorporating the reality of magic and the spirit world into his forensic, deductive methods (however, his method is always shown as being right throughout the film—it just works better once he accepts witchcraft as real). By confronting his personal deficiency, the hero is able to reconcile the masculine (the rational method) and the feminine (here represented by witchcraft), and therefore not only is able to solve the mystery and bring peace to the village, but can marry Katrina and look forward to a new, enriched life.

The horror elements in the film are all visual. As many reviewers pointed out, and the designers themselves acknowledged, the overall atmosphere of the film (with sets designed by Rick Heinrichs) was influenced by Hammer movies,[44] especially the Christopher Lee vehicle *Dracula Has Risen from the Grave* (Freddie Francis, 1968) and *The Curse of Frankenstein* (Terence Fisher, 1957). The influence of Roger Corman horror films, especially those starring Vincent Price, is also obvious, and a subtle debt to German expressionism can also be noted. In some instances, especially the windmill scene, Burton is also quoting his own work in *Frankenweenie*. As noted in Chapter 1, he seems to have benefited from his experiences with *The Black Cauldron*, as the plots of the two films are similar, but *Sleepy Hollow* improved on specific issues that were problematic for *Cauldron:* the lead character has a clear character growth arc, which also helps him heal from a childhood trauma (featuring what is for Burton a rare portrayal of an evil father); the magic in the film is central to the main conflict; and, most important of all, both his allies and his opponents are as imbricated in the central conflict as he is, if not more so.

But the most obvious homages are to Mario Bava's films, especially *Black Sunday* (*La maschera del demonio*, 1960), most notably in the flashback sequence when Ichabod's father (Peter Guinness) murders his mother (played by Burton's then-partner, Lisa Marie). In Andrew Walker's original script, Ichabod's mother was a "child of nature" who would burn cannabis leaves in the fireplace to get high or eat wild mushrooms in order to hallucinate that she could fly. Ichabod's father condemns her to death not only for using drugs herself but for encouraging her son to join in her experiences. In the final film, the direct allusions to drugs are mostly removed, though still basically there, and more emphasis is put on the father reading the mother's activity as witchcraft.

The goriness of the murders and the autopsies in *Sleepy Hollow* are typical horror fare, as is the way the Horseman chases down his victims, especially the red-headed child, whose death is another illogical moment in the film (it has been carefully set up that the Horseman kills only those he is ordered to kill or to defend himself; the child falls into neither category). However, it is such a stunning set piece that no one really seems to mind.

The most horror-influenced aspect of the film is the serial-killer psychopath that is Lady Van Tassel, a standard character in low-budget horror. Nevertheless, the film hardly emphasizes her; all the emphasis is on Ichabod, who is a typical young-prince-on-a-quest figure. Unlike the original Ichabod Crane, this Ichabod takes full advantage of Depp's beauty, with no makeup used to extend his nose or enlarge his ears, even though Depp himself wanted to do that. Rather, Ichabod's outsider status is all created through performance, with Depp offering a stark contrast between Ichabod's persistent investigative, rational nature and his deep-seated, reflexive antipathy to anything dirty, messy, insect-like, or at all scary. In his director commentary[45] on the *Sleepy Hollow* DVD, Burton described Ichabod as a "male action adventure hero who's portrayed like a thirteen-year-old girl." This is somewhat reminiscent of the approach taken in *Pee-wee's Great Adventure*, in which a grown man plays a prepubescent boy. Most of the moments of humor in the film come from the contrasts in Depp's performance.

Sleepy Hollow is yet another permutation of the pataphysical film: the narration is again unrealistic, following the logic of fairy tales combined with certain horror elements. As a result, the characters, except for Ichabod himself, are rather thinly sketched, as they are all there in service of the fable. There is a heavy use of visible special effects, mostly in front of the camera, some of which comment on themselves. For example, Bram von Brunt pretends to be the Headless Horseman (in a sequence taken directly from the Disney cartoon), and later the "real" Headless Horseman appears. There is elaborate makeup for Christopher Walken, who plays the Horseman with filed teeth, and Miranda Richardson as the Witch of the Woods. The moment when she is possessed is highlighted by her eyes popping out on stalks, much as Large Marge's did in *Pee-wee*.

The film is heavy with invisible special effects as well. Many of these effects are the old-fashioned type, with most of the exteriors (especially the Western Woods) built on soundstages and finished with classical Hollywood–style backdrops. There are also many digital effects: sky replacement scenes that extend the painted backdrops, enhanced digital matte paintings, and entire live-action skies replaced with digital versions and much digital painting added to live plates. Even the waving grass along the riverbank is digitally animated. The outdoor representation of Sleepy Hollow was actually built outside so that the filmmakers could get wide vista shots, and smoke was used to link the village location to the Western Woods location on the stages. The two locations were also linked by a similar use of forced perspective. "Tim and I treated *Sleepy Hollow* like a big stop-motion animated movie," Heinrichs commented, "emulating the graphic style of smaller-scale stop-motion and foreshortened miniature setups. We wanted to be in that same 2D/3D zone."[46] Matching the lighting of the indoor and outdoor sets was a challenge, eventually solved by using large cranes to light the exterior sets, cranes which then had to be digitally removed. Some locations were never even built but existed only as digital matte paintings, such as the Van Tassel manor exterior. Blue screen was used to remove the Headless Horseman's head, and a digital collar was added to his cape afterwards. Of the other numerous decapitations, half were achieved digitally, and half through Kevin Yagher's practical effects. The blood that gushes from Ichabod's mother when she falls out of the iron maiden is also digitally rendered, so that the filmmakers could choreograph the flow of the blood. This effect was used again on the Tree of the Dead when it spurts blood. And because Miranda Richardson plays herself and her sister, whom Lady Van Tassel decapitates at one point, the decapitation was done using a split screen that merged two separate background plates. "There was a lot of CGI and digital post, it's all invisible. All the camera moves were wild [that is, there was no motion control], and that shows in the material—it's very free," said Paddy Eason, supervising visual effects designer.[47]

Although the digital effects were numerous, they were mostly invisible. We do not realize the blood pouring from the iron maiden is digital, or that the Van Tassel manor is a matte painting. The visible effects went with the killings and beheadings for the most part, and the fact that these were theatrical effects instead of digital ones added to the film's sense of realism. It is the beginning of Burton's move away from a preponderance of effects in service of an animation-style narrative. Although, as quoted above, he was inspired by the style of the Disney cartoon, the heavy mix of horror with fantasy and suspense makes this a different kind of pataphysical film, less reliant on jokes that only make sense outside of the narrative and interstitial references to communicate its theme. The greatest pleasure the film provides is watching Ichabod Crane, forensic detective, make the transformation from young bachelor to a man willing to commit to a family, from forensic scientist with no faith to an investigator who has a mind open to anything, even the irrational.

Big Fish

After producing a series of increasingly myth-based films (*Ed Wood, Batman, Batman Returns, Planet of the Apes*), Burton returned to the fairy-tale structure with *Big Fish* (2003), based on the novel of the same title by Daniel Wallace, originally published in 1998. Although the novel is subtitled "a novel of mythic proportions," it is, in fact, a fairy tale: William Bloom (Billy Crudup) is on a quest to really understand his father, Edward Bloom (Albert Finney) as Ed senior, Ewan McGregor as the young Ed), who is dying. All of his life, his father has hidden behind a series of tall tales and jokes. After reviewing all of the key tales his father has told him all his life and in his conversations with his father as he lays dying, William gradually realizes that he will probably never really see his father as his really is; instead, he inherits (and in the course of the novel, successfully internalizes) his father's way of reinterpreting experience, and glossing over the more unpleasant aspects of that experience through tall tales. This is a fairy tale and not a myth, because it focuses on a narrow family dynamic—Billy is not a king, or in fact, a leader of any kind, and neither is his father (unlike, for example, Batman, who is always depicted as one third of a trio that controls and protects Gotham, the other two being the police commissioner and the mayor). And the tales he tells, his quests, are entirely quotidian, but exaggerated to a delightful degree: selling bizarre, useless products, like the Handimatic, door-to-door, catching the world's biggest catfish, and rescuing a female bather (who turns out to be a mermaid) from a water snake (which turns out to be a stick).

It is fairly easy to read between the lines in the novel and see what William Bloom claims he cannot find: Edward Bloom is a salesman, but not a very successful one; he spins great tales about his courtship and love for his wife, but in fact spends years driving back and forth between wife and mistress; he tells tall tales of rescuing a town, but in fact this is a metaphor for taking up with a young, outcast girl who lives in that town. When his interest in the girl wanes, her house reverts to its swamplike state, with her along with it.

We actually learn less about William Bloom in the book than we do about Edward. Burton's film compensates for this by making William (here called Billy, the same name Burton chose for his son, who was born at the same time) a journalist in France, married to a French photographer (Marion Cotillard), who is about to become a father himself for the first time. It is his own impending fatherhood and the self-doubt that comes with it, more than his father's final illness, that move Billy to try to find out the truth about his father. So Billy takes his wife back to his childhood home in Alabama and has to put up with hearing his father tell her all of the stories yet again.

As he helps his mother clean out the attic, he discovers objects and documents among his father's possessions that point to at least some of what his father says as truth: his father did serve in the military and was missing in action for a short time; he was a traveling salesman, selling a mechanical device that looked like a robotic hand; and so on.

One of the weaknesses of *Big Fish*'s screenplay (by John August) is that it wants to adhere to the "one true love" philosophy of most fairy tales, and so it glosses over Edward Bloom's attraction to the girl in the swamp (in the film, she is from the town of Specter, a town that the film first depicts as magical but later brings back as real). This dissipates the whole message of the book—that Edward Bloom uses tales to conceal his own human weaknesses, both in his own eyes and in the eyes of his family. Apart from that, the decision to combine Specter with the town that Bloom buys and reinvigorates in the book is an inspired one, as it pulls together various of the novel's disparate threads, just as the circus location does. However, the subplot in which Edward works for three years for free, included to provide just a few bits of information about the woman he will marry, rings false (and is not in the book), though it does lead to some incredible visual sequences that are Burton at his best, including Danny DeVito as a circus ringmaster who is also a werewolf.

The reason that *Big Fish* fails is not that it is a fairy tale, but that it is *only* a fairy tale. Burton made all of his other films as genre hybrids, starting with *Pee-wee*, which combined cartoon with '70s road picture. *Big Fish* is sometimes reminiscent of the way Burton jumped from genre to genre in *Pee-wee*, but here these jumps seem excessive, rather than successful. The story needed a second, underpinning genre, subordinate to the fairy-tale genre, that dominates in order to work. Horror might have worked, as it did for *Sleepy Hollow,* if Edward Bloom were shown to tell his tall tales as a way of gently leading his son into a world that would otherwise be sordid, often trivial, and ultimately depressing—the world of Arthur Miller's *Death of a Salesman,* for instance, to which the *Big Fish* screenplay seems to owe some (but not enough) debt of inspiration.[48]

To sum up our discussion of Burton's fairy-tale films, it is clear by now that just because we can label a film pataphysical does not mean that it is necessarily good. There are better pataphysical films; Burton has made a few of them. *Big Fish* is not one of them, though it does contain some of the most beautiful, and most artfully rendered, cinematic sequences of Burton's career.

Notes

1. Daniel Cerone, "Reigning Bats and Dogs: Tim Burton Rides High with 'Batman' Sequel, 'Frankenweenie,'" *Los Angeles Times*, March 12, 1992.

2. David Mills, "One on One—Tim Burton," *Empire*, February 2000.

3. Taylor L. White, "Other Weirdness," *Cinefantastique* vol 20 no 1/vol 20 no 2, (November 1989), p. 85.

4. Ibid.

5. Mark Salisbury, ed., *Burton on Burton,* rev. ed. (London: Faber & Faber, 2000), p. 27.

6. Taylor L. White, p. 85.

7. Salisbury, p. 31.

8. Ibid., p. 40.

9. Jim Smith and J. Clive Matthews, *Tim Burton* (London: Virgin Books, 2002), p. 33.

10. *Pee-wee's Big Adventure* DVD (2004) distributed by Warner Studios.

11. Harvey Deneroff, "In the Matter of Writers and Animation Story Persons," in *Storytelling in Animation: The Art of the Animated Image, Vol. 2,* ed. John Canemaker, published in conjunction with the Second Annual Walter Lantz Conference on Animation (Los Angeles: American Film Institute, 1988), pp. 33–34. Deneroff quotes Walter Kerr, *The Silent Clowns* (New York: Knopf, 1975), p. 108.

12. Burton in Salisbury, *Burton on Burton*, p. 13.

13. Deneroff, "In the Matter . . . ," p. 34.

14. *Pee-wee's Big Adventure*, DVD commentary.

15. Burton in Salisbury, *Burton on Burton*, p. 47.

16. Vincent Canby, " 'Beetlejuice' Is Pap for the Eyes," *New York Times*, May 8, 1988.

17. Smith and Matthews, *Tim Burton*, pp. 37–38.

18. Ibid., p. 39.

19. From the DVD commentary by Burton and Reubens.

20. Ann Lloyd, "Pee-wee's Big Adventure," *Films and Filming* 394 (July 1987).

21. Smith and Matthews, *Tim Burton*, p. 43.

22. Burton in Salisbury, *Burton on Burton*, p. 44.

23. Alain Garsault, "Méliès retrouvé," *Positif* 336 (February 1989): 61–63.

24. Vincent Canby, " 'Beetlejuice' is Pap for the Eyes." This is a time when "the creation of movies that don't offend has become an art."

25. Anne Thompson, "Tim Burton's Tasty *Beetlejuice*," *Movieline*, April 8, 1988, p. 22.

26. Vincent Canby, " 'Beetlejuice' Is Pap for the Eyes," *New York Times*, May 8, 1988.

27. Kim Newman, "Beetlejuice," *Monthly Film Bulletin* (August 1988).

28. Paul Woods, ed., *Tim Burton: A Child's Garden of Nightmares* (London: Plexus, 2002), collects reviews by top critics for Burton's films, from *Vincent* to *Planet of the Apes*.

29. Burton in Salisbury, *Burton on Burton*, p. 55.

30. Smith and Matthews, *Tim Burton*, p. 66.

31. Burton in Salisbury, *Burton on Burton*, p. 68.

32. Garsault, "Méliès retrouvé," (my translation).

33. See DVD commentary. *Edward Scissorhands*, DVD, 10th Anniversary Edition, 20th century Fox Home Video, 2003.

34. "Making of" featurette on the DVD.

35. Originally quoted in (filmdiesnt 24/1993) (46), as quoted in Helmut Merschmann, *Tim Burton: The Life and Films of a Visionary Director* (London: Titan Books, 2000), pp. 45–46.

36. Steve Brodrowski, "Edward Scissorhands," *Cinefantastique* (February 1991).

37. Roger Ebert, "Edward Scissorhands," *Chicago Sun-Times,* December 14, 1990.

38. Frank Rose, "Tim Cuts Up," *Premiere* (January 1991). Reprinted in Paul A. Woods, *Tim Burton: A Child's Garden of Nightmares*, Ultrascreen Series (London: Plexus, 2002), p. 63.

39. David Mills, "One on One—Tim Burton," *Empire* (February 2000).

40. Smith and Matthews, *Tim Burton*, pp. 212–214.

41. Mark Salisbury, "Graveyard Shift," in *Total Film* (February 2000) and *Fangoria* (November 1999), also reprinted in Paul A. Woods, ed., *Tim Burton: A Child's Garden of Nightmares*, p. 151.

42. Mark Salisbury, "A Head of the Game," *Fangoria* 189 (January 2000), pp. 32–36.

43. Photo caption by Paul A. Woods, ed., *Tim Burton: A Child's Garden of Nightmares*, p. 147.

44. Hammer Film Productions, based in the U.K., is best known for low budget horror films it produced from the late 1930s to the early 1960s, many starring Christopher Lee.

45. Directors Commentary, *Sleepy Hollow* DVD, Paramount Studio, 2003.

46. Mark Cotta Vaz, "A Region of Shadows," *Cinefex* 80 (January 2000): 91.

47. Ibid., p. 108.

48. However, some level of melancholy does come through, and is rumored to have affected Spalding Gray, the clinically depressed storyteller, who jumped off a bridge just hours after having seen *Big Fish* (Alex Williams, "Vanishing Act," *NYMetro.com*, http://www.newyorkmetro.com/nymetro/news/features/n_9787/index.html). This is not the first time that a suicide has been connected to Burton's darker film work; *Vanity Fair* (David Edelstein, "Tim Burton's Hollywood Nightmare," *Vanity Fair*, November 1994, pp. 124, 129–134) implied that *Batman* set designer Anton Furst commited suicide partly because Burton abandoned him as a friend. (This charge was rehashed by Ken Hanke in *Tim Burton: An Unauthorized Biography of the Filmmaker*, Los Angeles: Renaissance Books, 1999, pp. 121–122.) These easy pop-psychology associations are, of course, ridiculous, but it does point to the fact that the darker aspects of Burton's films clearly speak to our melancholy sides.

3

BURTON DOES 3-D: HOLLYWOOD'S
TRANSITION TO CGI

I t all started with *Vincent*.

Actually, Tim Burton's lifelong love affair with stop-motion animation began when he was a child. His love of Godzilla movies led him to fantasize as a youngster that he would one day be the actor inside the Godzilla suit; by the time he was a teenager, he and a handful of friends were making Super 8 movies in Burbank. One of these was a stop-motion animation film, which Burton recalled quite clearly:

> We made a wolfman movie, and a mad doctor movie, and a little stop-motion film using model cavemen. It was really bad and it shows you how little you know about animation at the beginning. These cavemen had removable legs—one was in the standing position, and the other was in a walking one—and we just changed the legs. It's the jerkiest animation you'll ever see. I used to love all those Ray Harryhausen movies—*Jason and the Argonauts, The Seventh Voyage of Sinbad*—they were incredible, I loved stop-motion animation as a kid. And as you get older, you realize that there's an artistry there too, and that's what you're responding to.[1]

Vincent

Burton began his commercial 3-D animation career with *Vincent*, a five-minute combination of stop-motion and 2-D animation that he made with Rick Heinrichs when both were still Disney employees. Burton had been working as a conceptual artist on *The Black Cauldron* (1985),[2] but none of his ideas were used in the final film. However, his conceptual work got the attention of Disney producer Julie Hickson and studio vice president Tom Wilhite, who gave him $60,000 to produce an animated film based on a children's story that Burton had already written.

The Walt Disney Company was willing to fund such experiments because studio executives were desperate for a new sense of direction. Walt Disney had died in 1967, making *The Jungle Book* (1967) his last film. The studio had been in the doldrums since then, and the animation department heads were looking for a change. They were even considering making a children's movie using 3-D animation, but they hesitated because of their unfamiliarity with the process. One of the ideas they were toying with was a shift from traditional cel animation, with which Disney had for so long been associated, to a completely different style. Burton and Heinrichs felt that they "could convince the hierarchy that a feature-length, model-animated film with the Disney logo on it could be commercially viable, and *Vincent* was [their] way of showing them."[3] *Vincent* featured 3-D characters made from ball-and-socket models, as well as 2-D cel animation in a high-contrast, black-and-white style. This new approach was partly inspired by Disney's own practice of making 3-D models for its 2-D animators to work from, as Rick Heinrichs described:

> Disney likes to make sculptures of the characters for its animated movies so that animators can hold three-dimensional things in their hands. Tim and I learned that you can combine the graphic look that makes most of the design elements of a two-dimensional picture with something three dimensional. It finally came to fruition in *Vincent* . . . showing us we could have the best of both. We loved that expressionistic approach then, and Tim still strives for it in all his work.[4]

Though the studio had provided the $60,000 budget, the project had "off the lot" status—meaning Burton and Heinrichs had to supply their own materials and find their own space. As a result, they were able to make the film with little interference at the Dave Allen studio across town.

The film is a very creative combination of 2-D cel animation and 3-D stop-motion animation. It begins with a black screen, with Burton and Heinrichs receiving equal credit for the film. Then the longest 2-D animation sequence begins: a black cat (vaguely reminiscent of the poster image for the film *The Tomb of Ligeia,* starring Vincent Price) emerges from behind a skeletal tree and hops onto the top of a brick wall, and

The opening of the title sequence for
Vincent is 2-D.

the title appears on the wall in quasi-Gothic lettering. The cat walks to the end of the wall and jumps into the window of a 3-D house—the first of many such seamless transitions from 2-D to 3-D. Inside the house, the cat, now a 3-D model, sidles up to Vincent, who is playing the tune on a recorder that we have heard since the opening credits. The music is a score by Tom Hilton, with melodic variations on "In an Egyptian Marketplace" and J. S. Bach's Toccata and Fugue in D Minor.[5] When Vincent picks up the cat, the voice-over narration, performed by Vincent Price, begins:

> Vincent Malloy is seven years old
> He's always polite and does what he's told
>
> For a boy his age he's considerate and nice
> But he wants to be just like Vincent Price

On this last line a stop-substitution, masked by a quick dissolve, transforms Vincent the boy into Vincent the boy-as-Vincent-Price, complete with long cigarette holder and gown vaguely reminiscent of Vincent Price's costume in *Pit and the Pendulum* (Roger Corman, 1961). He blows cigarette smoke in the air—a 2-D detail in an otherwise 3-D scene. He is still holding and petting the cat, who has been purring contentedly with its eyes closed, but when it smells the smoke, the cat looks at Vincent and, startled by the transformation, screeches and leaps out of Vincent's arms.

Similar transformations occur on the beat of every second verse for the rest of the film. Vincent, still in his Vincent Price berobed persona, walks into the next room, where we see his little sister and two dogs:

> He doesn't mind living with his sister, dog and cats,
> Though he'd rather share a home with spiders and bats

On the word *bats,* Vincent pulls a cord, which turns off a light but leaves a pyramid-shaped lighted area that fills with fluttering bats. Again, the transformation is smooth and seemingly instantaneous, all in 3-D, though the areas of light and shadow are indicated by 2-D drawing. The references, and the transformations that occur along with changes in lighting, continue. Vincent's aunt comes to visit and switches on the light; Vincent the boy allows himself to be patted on the head, but then he transforms into the Vincent Price–mad scientist persona, specifically inspired by the film *The House of Wax* (Andre de Toth, 1953), which was originally a 3-D film, meant to be watched with 3-D glasses. Like his hero, Vincent the boy lifts his aunt up on a chain and drops her into a vat of boiling wax. Still in his mad scientist guise, he transforms his dog, Abercrombie,[6] into a "horrible zombie," and the two skulk through the dark and misty London streets looking for victims.

Several critics have compared *Vincent* to the German Expressionist film *The Cabinet of Dr. Caligari* (Robert Wiene, 1920), as well as *Nosferatu—A Symphony in Terror* (F. W. Murnau, 1922) and *M* (Fritz Lang, 1931). Burton himself described it as "Dr. Caligari meets Ray Harryhausen,"[7] though the only obvious connection to Harryhausen is that the film is stop-motion. According to Burton, the primary source of inspiration was not *Caligari*, but the work of Dr. Seuss (Theodor Geisel):

> I certainly saw pictures of [*Caligari*], in any monster book there were pictures of it. But I didn't see [the film] until fairly recently. I think it probably has more to do with being inspired by Dr. Seuss. It just happens to be shot in black and white, and there's a Vincent Price/Gothic kind of thing that makes it feel that way. I grew up loving Dr. Seuss. The rhythm of his stuff spoke to me very clearly. Dr. Seuss's books were perfect: right number of words, the right rhythm, great subversive stories. He was incredible, he was the greatest, definitely. He probably saved a bunch of kids who nobody will ever know about.[8]

The 3D Vincent Malloy imitates his hero, Vincent Price, while blowing 2-D smoke in *Vincent.*

The "London" set is the closest thing the film has to anything from *Caligari*. There are other details that could be seen as Gothic, but once we are alerted to the debt of inspiration owed to Dr. Seuss, the homage to Seuss seems visible in many details: the areas of action illuminated with pyramid-shaped spotlights that highlight the crooked checkerboard wallpaper; the sinuous wainscoting; the twisted skylights; the long, silhouetted staircase that looks more like the teeth of a handsaw than steps, with a tiny, crooked door perched at the top; the feathered quill pen and the penultimate image of a door and floor that are curved out of shape in a hallucination that seems to be filmed through a fish-eye lens.

Jim Smith and J. Clive Matthews have pointed out that the plot of *Vincent* refers to stories by Edgar Allan Poe (the story Vincent reads is a conflation of "The Fall of the House of Usher"[9] and "The Premature Burial,"[10] as well as filmic adaptations of these stories directed by Roger Corman, many of which starred Vincent Price: *House of Usher* (Corman, 1960); "The Black Cat,"[11] which Corman made into a segment of his *Tales of Terror* with Vincent Price in 1962; and *The Premature Burial* (Corman, 1962) which did not star Price. Vincent's high-collared coat in the mad scientist scenes and the electrical equipment in the lab seem to be obvious homages to *Frankenstein* (James Whale, 1931).[12] These stylistic references are fleeting, whereas the rhymed couplets and the alternations between light and dark, the child's version of a Gothic fantasy and parental insistence on daylight and the suburban status quo, that happen on the poetic beat are much more reminiscent of Dr. Seuss. Vincent's obsession with Poe stories and Vincent Price movies is similar to the obsession of Dr. Seuss's characters in stories like *Green Eggs and Ham* (1960) and *And to Think That I Saw It on Mulberry Street* (1937). The plot of *Vincent* is vaguely similar to that of *The Cat in the Hat* (1957) and *The Cat in the Hat Comes Back* (1958), both horror stories about two children

The stairs leading to Vincent's room are right out of a Dr. Seuss illustration in *Vincent*.

locked in a house with a mad feline visitor who systematically wrecks all the household symbols of middle-class suburban life.

In *Vincent*, by contrast, it is his mother's order to go outside—"If you want to you can go outside and play/it's sunny outside and a beautiful day"—that drives Vincent to his final attack of Gothic fantasy—"I am possessed by this house/and I can never leave it again." Vincent's final visions are a conflation of his imaginings, from killer zombie dog, aunt-in-wax, and beautiful, undead wife represented in a mix of 2-D and 3-D animation, until Vincent collapses on the floor, dead or fantasizing that he is dead, as the camera withdraws and allows him to be submerged in a pool of darkness as he quotes the final lines from Poe's "The Raven"[13] "And my soul from out that shadow that lies floating on the floor/ Shall be lifted Nevermore."[14]Apparently Burton meant for Vincent to be fantasizing his own death, as he has commented that by the end of the film, "the kid basically has the impression of not living . . . even though it's in his own mind."[15]

Smith and Matthews have described this film as having death as a theme but no actual killing.[16] This seems disingenuous, when we clearly see Vincent preparing to dip his aunt in wax, and though we don't see her actually sink into the wax, we later see the effects; we also see Vincent going out with his dog in search of victims, Jack the Ripper style, and we can only assume that, like the character in the Edgar Allan Poe story, Vincent-as-mad-scientist is responsible for burying his "wife" alive. Of course, all of these killings or intents to kill are fantasies, but they are clearly depicted, leaving little to the imagination.

It was probably these representations of killing, the fact that Vincent might be dead at the end, or the idea that a child could harbor so much rage that led one of the Disney executives to ask for a "happy ending," which Burton successfully opposed:

> They wanted it to have more of an upbeat ending, but I never saw it as being downbeat in any way. It's funny, I think it's more uplifting if things are left to your imagination. I always saw those tacked-on happy endings as psychotic in a way. They wanted me to have the light click on and have his dad come in and go, "Let's go to a football game or a baseball game." That was my first encounter with the happy ending syndrome.[17]

Getting Vincent Price to narrate the story was a real coup, both emotionally and commercially, for Burton. This is how Price remembers it:

> [Around the end of 1981] [t]hey asked me to come down and meet Tim and Rick Heinrichs. . . . So I went down to Disney and they showed me the

drawings and mock-ups they had planned for this short film, as a sort of tribute to me. Tim recited the poem for me and asked me to narrate it. I was really struck by his charm and enthusiasm, so I said yes. Tim is really in love with film and is a wonderful kind of mad fellow. I thought it was marvelous of Disney to give these two kids a chance to make the film. They were only about 20 when they did it. . . .[18]

Price's narration was recorded in one day in December 1981, before the animation had been developed,[19] but his relationship with Burton did not end there: he acted again in *Edward Scissorhands,* and Burton has produced a documentary homage to Price called *Conversations with Vincent* (working title), which has not been released because of conflicts over the rights.

Burton said of Price:

He was very supportive. I always had the feeling he understood exactly what the film was about, even more than I did; he understood that it wasn't just a simple homage, like "Gee, Mr. Price, I'm your biggest fan." He understood the psychology of it, and that amazed me and made me feel very good, made me feel that someone saw me for what I was, and accepted me on that level. . . . It's a scary proposition meeting somebody who helped you through childhood, who had that affect on you, especially when you're sending them something that's showing that impact in a kind of cheesy, children's book kind of way.[20]

Burton later asked Price to give voice to Santa Claus in *The Nightmare Before Christmas,* but the actor by then was in failing health and had to bow out.[21]

Although *Vincent* received the Critics' Prize at the Annecy Animation Festival in France, as well as favorable comments at festivals in Los Angeles, Chicago, and Seattle, Disney released it theatrically in only one Los Angeles theater for two weeks, as an opener for *Tex* (1982), starring Matt Dillon.[22] It was then shelved and did not become available to the public until the release of the *Nightmare Before Christmas* Special Edition DVD.[23] The concept of producing 3-D animation at Disney suffered a similar fate, and nothing along those lines would happen at the studio for another decade, when Burton returned with *The Nightmare Before Christmas.*

Disney financed two more short films of Burton's: *Frankenweenie* (discussed in Chapter 2) and *Hansel and Gretel* (1982). For *Hansel and Gretel* Burton took the opportunity to pay homage to the design style and color schemes of his beloved Godzilla movies. He loaded the program with special effects, including front projection, forced perspective, and a little stop-motion by Rick Heinrichs and Stephen Chiodo, who had done the honors on *Vincent*.[24]

Burton did not use any stop-motion in *Frankenweenie*, his last film for Disney as a contract employee, nor did he use any in the version of *Aladdin and His Wonderful Lamp* (1984), which he directed for *Faerie Tale Theatre*, even though Heinrichs and Chiodo again provided the special effects, including a tunnel embedded with cartoon skulls that would be echoed later in *Pee-wee's Big Adventure*.[25]

Pee-Wee's Big Adventure

In Chapter 2, I analyzed how the narrative in Burton's first feature film, *Pee-wee's Big Adventure* (1985), was structured and its relationship to cartoon narration. *Pee-wee* is in essence a road picture, a series of disparate episodes linked by Paul Reubens's performance as a man-child who is searching desperately for his stolen bike. Each episode is shot in the style of a different kind of film genre, from sports to coming-of-age to slapstick comedy. There is a long, complex, and very funny sequence at the end when Pee-wee makes his way across various Warner Bros. soundstages where different movies are being filmed, from a *Miracle on 34th Street* and *Angels with Dirty Faces* style drama to a beach-blanket bingo film to a Toho Godzilla movie, complete with Japanese director. The scene includes an actor in a Godzilla suit who ends up in a sleigh with a Santa Claus careening across the Warner Bros. lot, almost a flash-forward to the stop-motion animated feature *The Nightmare Before Christmas*, a film Burton wouldn't make for several more years but which he had already designed and storyboarded. Another reference to *Nightmare* is the skeletal reindeer that delivers Pee-wee's toast, taken directly from the reindeer design for *Nightmare*.

Although Burton was focusing on the live-action directing in *Pee-wee*, he included two brief stop-motion sequences. A wonderful moment is a one-and-a-half second replacement animation by Stephen Chiodo, who transformed the ghost of Large Marge into a pop-eyed ghoul. Large Marge already had a hairdo and wide-eyed stare reminiscent of the bride of Frankenstein in James Whale's 1935 film of the same name. The moment that Pee-wee realizes Marge is a ghost, eternally doomed to drive her bus along the same strip of highway, is when her staring eyes expand, her mouth becomes impossibly large and opens wide, revealing irregular, rotting teeth, and her long, stop-motion tongue uncurls toward Pee-wee, like the tail of a noisemaker, followed by her protruding eyeballs that pop out on springs. There are similar moments in *Beetlejuice* (using rod puppetry manipulated by three puppeteers[26]) and *Sleepy Hollow.*

There is also an homage to the stop-motion dinosaur movies that Burton loved, though only in the briefest of scenes: Pee-wee dreams that a red tyrannosaur (a rubber doll with glowing white eyes) walks onto a miniature set and picks up his bicycle in its mouth, then begins to chomp on it with its huge teeth. All of this is intercut with alternating shots of a stationary puppet of Pee-wee from behind and shots of the live Pee-wee from in front and above, that is, from the point of view of the dinosaur. Although there was not much of a budget for this animation, the intercutting of the live Pee-wee with a model Pee-wee is reminiscent of Ray Harryhausen's sequence in *Clash of the Titans* (1981), when close shots of Calibos' expressive face are intercut with rear long shots of a puppet representing Calibos. Burton also has a brief reference to his film *Vincent*, when Pee-wee walks down an alley, preceded by his own huge shadow—the reverse of the shadow of Abercrombie, the zombie dog, that follows Vincent through the London fog.

Beetlejuice

In his next film, *Beetlejuice* (1988), Burton had a bigger budget, though at $14 million, it was not huge, with only $1 million earmarked for special effects. This meant that the plethora of special effects required

Pee-wee's toast-delivering reindeer would appear again in *The Nightmare Before Christmas* and is an homage to Méliès.

had to be done mostly on-set and in-camera. These effects included creature creation and makeup, opticals and miniatures, blue screen, forced perspective, motion-control cinematography, and, not surprisingly, replacement and stop-motion animation. In most cases the stop-motion was tightly interwoven with live-action and puppetry.

The most important stop-motion is in the sand planet, the infernal environment populated with carnivorous sandworms that the Maitlands find surrounding their house after they have died. The sand planet was a mixture of three elements: a real set, puppetry, and stop-motion. Alan Munro, a former storyboard artist on his first outing as effects supervisor, realized that a twelve-foot-deep set with forced perspective (the distortion of the shape and scale of different set pieces and props that stand between the actor and the back of the set or background image, giving the impression of great depth on a shallow set[27]) would be cheaper and easier than using blue screen for the actors, as had been originally planned. A six-foot-long rod puppet worm was built out of latex and foam to dive through the sand dunes, maneuvering through channels in the sand. Forced perspective was used with the worm as well, with "sand flings" and clouds added optically later. A larger puppet of the worm's head, with a mouth that could open to reveal another, inner worm, was

The miniature of the Maitland's house in *Beetlejuice* looks like the real thing in the fast-moving opening camera move . . . until the spider appears.

The forced perspective hallway in *Beetlejuice* resembles the one Burton used in *Aladdin*.

Delia Deitz is imprisoned by her own sculpture, brought to life with stop-motion, in *Beetlejuice*.

This shot of Barbara Maitland on the worm's back in *Beetlejuice* combines live action with stop-motion.

also built. Burton made the decision to augment the puppetry sequences with stop-motion, and hired Doug Beswick to build a three-foot version of the worm's head and upper body and the inner worm head. To make the worm move quickly, Munro skip-framed Beswick's animation.[28] The worm originally had three stop-motion sequences, although one of these was dropped. The two remaining scenes include the worm's first appearance, when it rears out of the sand and reveals the inner worm. The worm's last appearance in the film also includes some stop-motion of the worm with Barbara Maitland on its back, breaking through the ceiling, eating Beetlejuice, and disappearing through the floor.

The banister that turns into a snake was also originally planned as all-puppetry, but Burton was not happy with the results; he insisted that the snake be redesigned as stop-motion and hired Ted Rae to do the job. Rae chose to make a realistic-looking three-foot snake body with a cartoon version of actor Michael Keaton's face. A larger rod-servo version of the puppet was used for shots in which the snake crawls between Delia Dietz's foot and under her dress and for the dialogue shots, and the snakelike eyes were achieved with rotoscoped animation (in which additional animated detail is hand-drawn over the already existing image).

The last bit of stop-motion animation in *Beetlejuice* takes place when Delia Dietz's sculptures come to life and trap the Dietzes so that they cannot stop Beetlejuice from marrying their daughter. The movement of the treelike sculpture was modeled after the labored walking of a dinosaur, while the other sculpture inched along the ground like a worm.[29] In total, the film has 300 effects shots, of which 15 are stop-motion.

Cabin Boy

Burton did not use stop-motion for *Batman, Edward Scissorhands,* and *Batman Returns*. After *The Nightmare Before Christmas,* discussed below, he produced *Cabin Boy* (1994) with Denise Di Novi, apparently intended as an "affectionate spoof of Harryhausen's *Sinbad* films."[30] It was a story by Chris Elliott and Adam Resnick, written and directed by Adam Resnick, with stop-motion by Doug Beswick and Yancy Calzada, both veterans from *Beetlejuice* (the latter uncredited).

Cabin Boy is an interesting but ultimately failed film, a fairy tale about an effeminate and arrogant aristocrat, played by Chris Elliott, who graduates from his posh and protected boarding school and sets out to get on a ship that will return him to his father and his predetermined post helping run his father's business empire. Unlike the very macho and muscle-bound actors who played Sinbad in the Harryhausen films, who were fatherly toward their crewmen, seemingly without fear, and coldly gallant to women, Elliott's character is very much a boy, whiny, cruel, and inconsiderate, and an extremely arrogant abuser of his father's power and influence. His bad attitude gets him dumped out of his limousine before he arrives at his ship (modern limos and nineteenth-century sailing ships, along with eighteenth-century fashions, are all combined). He ends up getting lost and boards a run-down fishing ship called *The Filthy Whore* by mistake, where he is forced to earn his passage by working as a cabin boy. This leads to a taming-of-the-shrew-like conversion, and he is rewarded at the end by finding true love with a woman who is determined to swim around the globe. He chooses to stay at sea with *The Filthy Whore* and her crew so that he can retain his new personality and be near his mermaid-like love.

The film has two stop-motion animation sequences, which stand out for their quality and because they include rare moments of warm feeling in the film. One is a brief animation of a "shark man," a character with a human upper body and a shark's lower body, as he slices through the water with his tail. A longer (eighteen-shot) sequence is of an "iceberg monster," reminiscent of the monster (a rod puppet) at the North Pole in the 1912 film by Georges Méliès called *A la conquête du Pôle* (*Conquest of the North Pole*). In true Harryhausen style, the iceberg monster sequence creates a solid illusion that the stop-motion character interacts with the actors, poking one actor with its finger, and is attacked by the sailors with harpoon and oar, with Elliott's character stepping on its toe, a moment when it shows emotion convincingly, especially when its hand is melted away, much to the monster's surprise. The final coup de grâce is when one of the sailors sprays the monster with coffee and the monster's beautiful wickedness begins to melt, ending with its shattering into icy pieces on the deck.[31] Burton had another homage to Méliès in *Nightmare* in the form of the skeleton reindeer that pull Santa's sleigh (which was also in *Pee-wee's Big Adventure*, as the toy reindeer that drops Pee-wee's bread into the toaster).

The Nightmare Before Christmas

As we've seen, Burton had originally made *Vincent* with the hope that it would persuade Disney to produce a longer 3-D animation film. Once

Sally, the patchwork girl from *Nightmare Before Christmas*.

Jack Skellington tries to cook up Christmas in *Nightmare Before Christmas*.

done with *Vincent*, he prepared numerous drawings and wrote a story-poem that followed the rhythms of *The Night Before Christmas*, and Rick Heinrichs produced a model of Jack Skellington, the lead character. Burton's original intention was to have Vincent Price narrate what he thought would be a short film or a TV Christmas special similar to Dr. Seuss's *How the Grinch Stole Christmas* (Chuck Jones, 1966, narrated by Boris Karloff) or the "animagic" musical with Burl Ives, *Rudolph the Red-Nosed Reindeer* (Rankin-Bass Productions, 1964). Burton then took his materials and showed them to anyone at Disney who would look at them. Burton compared the process of shopping the project to being in "that show *The Prisoner*; everybody's really nice, but you know you're never going to get out, it's not going to happen . . . as you proceed, it becomes less and less of a reality."[32]

Once Burton was chosen to direct *Pee-wee*, he had to set *Nightmare* aside, but apparently he never stopped thinking about it. After his success with *Pee-wee*, *Beetlejuice*, and *Batman*, the time seemed right to try it again, and he had his agent, William Morris, "ask around" at Disney to see who owned the property. Apparently, Disney did, though when Burton developed it, he wasn't even sure if he was a Disney employee or not:[33] "There's this thing you sign when you work there, which states that any thoughts you have during your employment are owned by the thought police."[34]

That Disney owned the property turned out to be a good thing. David Hoberman, then president of Disney's Touchstone Pictures, was overjoyed to have an opportunity to bring Burton back into the Disney fold, and he agreed to produce not only *Nightmare* but *Cabin Boy* and *Ed Wood*—the latter a project that Columbia had put into turnaround. Hoberman even allowed Burton his wish to make *Wood* in black and white. *GQ* described Hoberman as "bent on making the flat-footed Touchstone into a haven for the hip and the bankably outré."[35] And why not? Burton had yet to make a flop.

The first surprise with *Nightmare* came with Burton's decision not to direct it himself: "If I had [directed it], I'd be dead before I ever saw the final version . . . the reason I originally got out of animation is because I didn't have the patience for it."[36] Instead, the task of directing went to Henry Selick.[37] Selick chose to base Skellington productions in San Francisco, where he lives and where there is a large pool of stop-motion professionals. Burton traveled there a few times while making

Batman Returns and *Ed Wood*, but he basically entrusted Selick with realizing his vision. In the "making of" featurette on the *Nightmare* DVD, Selick credits Burton with the design of the main characters, the tone, and the look. He specifies that the art direction was based on what the crew thought a Tim Burton film should look like—that is, a combination of "German Expressionism and Dr. Seuss." Selick describes himself as "from the same planet, if not the same neighborhood," as Burton. Of Selick, Burton says: "He's someone who's got a lot of talented passion, and he knows a lot of people who do this work and do it well."

Burton was also primarily responsible for the story, as he worked it out scene by scene with Danny Elfman, who would then compose a song for each major scene. Shooting on the songs began before Burton's story was adapted by Michael Powell, a horror-novel writer, and the screenplay was written by Caroline Thompson, who had worked with Burton on *Edward Scissorhands*.

Even so, a lot of the look developed under Selick's supervision while Burton was elsewhere directing live-action films. Rick Heinrichs showed the animation team films by Ladislas Starevitch. Starevitch was born in Poland but did most of his work in France in the early twentieth century. He made stop-motion animation films using the carcasses of real insects such as grasshoppers and beetles, as well as the corpses of birds and other animals. His 1911 film *The Cameraman's Revenge* consists of a love-triangle story involving insects, which also commented on the voyeuristic aspects of cinema itself while making fun of the more melodramatic aspects of American cinema. Starevitch later began to work with puppets and continued to make animated films into the sound era. What stands out about his animation is the convincing emotional performance of his insect carcasses and later of his puppets and models. Starevitch's techniques of imbuing an otherwise lifeless figure with a lifelike performance is applied in simulated animation figures to this day.[38] Selick also credited the influence of the German animator Lotte Reiniger, who worked with shadow puppets, and Wilfred Jackson's "Night on Bald Mountain" sequence in Disney's *Fantasia* (1940). The *Nightmare* animators consciously imitated the delicate cross-hatching textures of the drawings of Edward Gorey and Charles Addams; some of the characters also seem to owe a debt of inspiration to cartoonist Ronald Searle.

Selick supervised the production of the storyboards. Once they were completed, the storyboard for the entire film was filmed, creating a story

To take over Christmas, start by taking
Santa hostage. From *Nightmare
Before Christmas.*

reel. Each storyboard shot was edited to run the same length as the final shot in the film and synced to a temporary dialogue track. As each scene was created in stop-motion, the storyboard scene was removed and the stop-motion version was inserted, so that the film was essentially made twice.[39] Burton approved of the "storyboard film," but that didn't stop him from shutting down the production for a week when he decided that Halloweentown needed to have a darker look.[40]

Nightmare is sometimes credited with being the first feature-length stop-motion theatrical musical, but that credit should go to Rankin-Bass's *Mad Monster Party* (1967), a film that inspired Burton when he did *Nightmare*.[41]

Although he would have been willing to make *Nightmare* as a TV Christmas special when he was first shopping the project around Disney, by the time *Nightmare* finally went into production, Burton felt the only way to do justice to the story was as a stop-motion theatrical. The fact that so few other feature-length stop-motions had been made illustrated why Disney had initially hesitated to take up Burton's and Heinrich's suggestion that stop-motion would revitalize their brand. As Burton's coproducer, Denise Di Novi, pointed out: "Usually you do stop-motion for a one-minute commercial, but we needed to build a whole studio from scratch. And we had to comb the world for animators."[42] The production required over a dozen animators and 100 other artists of different types, 40,000 square feet of space, 230 sets, and 74 characters, each of which had several puppet versions of themselves and separate parts that constantly needed replacing. The replacement technique had been modeled on that of George Pal, whose "Puppetoons" of the 1930s and '40s were a model for Nightmare. The Puppetoons were made from wood and had dozens of replacement heads for different facial expressions and lip movements. Nightmare had puppets made of plastic, with replaceable heads for Jack and a replaceable face mask for Sally, along with a whole set of eyelashes, eyepieces, and other individual parts.[43] In spite of the unusual, elaborate production, the film cost $18 million to make (much less than the equivalent cel-animation film) and eventually earned $70 million, inspired more animated cuddly monsters such as those in Shrek (2001) and Monsters, Inc. (2001). It is still a cult favorite today. But did it bring about the renaissance of animation, with Disney leading the way, that Burton and Heinrichs had originally envisioned?

When asked this question, Henry Selick gave a positive response:

It really is happening. This is the golden age of animation—it wasn't 1939–41. There's far more production going on, there are more independent animators, though it's not easy for everyone. Disney wants to do everything in-house and gobble up the rest of the world. They want to own anyone who is doing great animation. I think they have a deal with [the British stop-motion animation company] Aardman Studio. I hope they leave them alone and let them do what they do so well, though I wouldn't trust them to do so. They are also doing a film with Pixar [Toy Story], which is a company that does computer films with John Lasseter.[44]

Selick went on to mention MTV as a showcase for independent work, such as the Olive Jar Studio, Jon Lemmon Films, Sculptoons, Colossal Pictures, Cosgrove Hall, and his own. In addition to MTV, Paul Reubens's Saturday morning TV show, Pee-wee's Playhouse (1987–1990) was a showcase for stop-motion, including work by Aardman (whose short Creature Comforts, won the Oscar for Best Animated Short in 1990), to New York Broadcast Arts, to the work of independent animators. Stop-motion animation was used by companies such as ILM for certain special effects in Star Wars (1977), The Terminator (1984), and Robocop (1987). There was also Claymation (stop-motion with clay figures) by Will Vinton, who made the California Raisins commercial as well as the feature-length Claymation film *The Adventures of Mark Twain* (1985). In addition to such theatrical and artistic shorts, there was *The New Gumby*, a ninety-nine-episode TV series from 1988 produced by Art Clokey, who had brought us the original Gumby and Pokey in the 1950s. According to Frank Thompson, *Nightmare* benefited from the audience for stop-motion generated by *The New Gumby* as well as from the fact that several *Nightmare* animators learned their craft on the TV show.[45]

Selick and Burton technically did not break new ground with *Nightmare*. As Selick described it: "We took an old technique and did the highest-quality stop-motion that has ever been done for that many minutes. I think we moved stop-motion to a high level of performance in timing, lighting and computer-aided camera moves. We made it a serious contender rather than things that look like toys on a table top with two glaring lights."[46]

The computer-aided moves that Selick refers to are really a wonder to behold. There were two ways to film the moving shots on *Nightmare*: by blocking out the scene for the puppets with tape, marking the different camera positions for the tape, and as each frame is exposed, by moving the camera forward one notch. This system was used mostly for simpler moves such as camera pans and tilts. When a more elaborate move was needed, such as a flying move, a motion-control camera was used. This is a camera hooked up to a computer. The length, speed, and direction of the shot are programmed, so that every time a frame of film is exposed, the camera moves forward a fraction.[47] *Nightmare* is unusual for stop-motion in that almost every shot has a moving camera, and some of the moving shots run for as along as 540 frames. The crane shots, tracking shots, and long, elegant takes are Selick's particular touch.

The difficulty, patience, and length of time needed to make the film, not to mention the sizable number of specialized animators, made *Nightmare* a prime example of its genre, one unlikely to be improved upon, although both Selick (who would go on to make *James and the Giant Peach*, 1996, and *Monkeybone*, 2001, and is currently working on *Coraline*, 2005, for the Will Vinton Studio), and Burton would continue to try. Burton, for example, began working on another stop-motion feature, *The Corpse Bride*, in 1993, just after *Nightmare* was released. This film, which is slated for an October 2005 release, is the result of a collaboration between

Will Vinton Studios, Tim Burton Animation Co., and Warner Bros. Feature Animation. Both cast and crew are Burton regulars: Caroline Thompson, who wrote *Scissorhands* and *Nightmare,* worked on the screenplay (along with Pamela Pettler, who worked on the script for *Charlie and the Chocolate Factory,* though the first screenwriter to work on the project was Michael Cohn in the early 1990s); Danny Elfman is doing the score; Helena Bonham Carter is the voice of the Corpse Bride; and Johnny Depp, the voice of Victor, the man who abandons his real-life wife (Emily Watson) in favor of the Corpse Bride. Other characters are voiced by Albert Finney, Richard E. Grant, Christopher Lee, and Joanna Lumley. Burton codirected with Mike Johnson, who worked as an animator on *James and the Giant Peach.* This movie is based on a nineteenth-century Russian folk tale that apparently has some basis in fact, as anti-Semitic gangs would often attack Jewish wedding parties, killing and burying the bride in her wedding gown.[48] The story is about Victor, who is engaged to Victoria. On his way to his wedding he stops to rest in a clearing in the forest. To practice for the upcoming ceremony, he slips the ring onto what appears to be a twig growing out of the ground and says his wedding vows. It turns out that the twig is actually the bony finger of the Corpse Bride, who arises from her grave and declares herself married to Victor. Victor flees, but she chases him. Complications ensue.

Although star directors like Selick and Burton both have stop-motion features in production, it seemed that their original vision, that stop-motion would change animation as we knew it, was not to be. This was partly because a new method of producing three-dimensional animation was about to take precedence.

Jurassic Park

At the same time that Burton and Selick were putting the finishing touches on *Nightmare,* Universal Studios released *Jurassic Park,* directed by Steven Spielberg. Coincidentally, Burton had been one of four serious contenders (along with Joe Dante and Richard Donner) for the project when Michael Crichton's novel was put up for bid. However, Spielberg won Crichton's confidence and the right to develop the film.[49]

One of the reasons for this was that Crichton had wanted to "make a dinosaur story that really worked, that wasn't *One Million Years B.C.*"[50]

Spielberg and his creative team shared Crichton's concern for realistic dinosaurs. According to Rick Carter, Spielberg's production designer,

> What we tried to do . . . was find the animal in the dinosaur as opposed to the monster in the dinosaur. The idea was not to make them any less threatening, but rather to keep them from doing as much monster "schtick." For our human characters, we wanted their situation to be more like they were being stalked by an animal that is a carnivore, as opposed to something that is psychopathic and just out to get them. That's one of the reasons we wanted to have herds of dinosaurs, to show that dinosaurs were just like any other life-form and that they lived out their lives in a somewhat naturalistic manner.[51]

As we shall see, this concern with a "realistic" dinosaur performance is key.

Traditionally, realistic animals in a film of this type would be accomplished using stop-motion animation, but Spielberg wanted to go with full-scale animatronics so that interaction between actors and dinosaurs would be more realistic. Because Stan Winston had such success with the monster in *Alien,* Spielberg gave the Stan Winton Studio a $65 million contract to produce a variety of animatronics that would make it easier for actors to interact with them, as he had done in different ways with *E.T.* and *Jaws.*[52] Winston and his team were also very concerned about making the dinosaurs come across as animals rather than monsters. He and his artists based their drawings on the latest research that showed that dinosaurs were probably descended from prehistoric birds and were believed to have behaved in a birdlike manner.[53]

Creating the *Tyrannosaurus rex* was obviously the biggest challenge. Using traditional animatronic techniques, Winston's team built a 5,000-pound animatronic robot. Once built, the problem was how to animate it so that it would move with convincing fluidity. It was decided to divide the T rex into an upper and a lower half and have different hydraulic platforms, designed by a company that built flight simulators, run the motion. But how was the motion to be programmed? Winston decided to use a telemetry suit, a device that electronically links a human controller to a robotic figure, so that any movement the controller makes while wearing the suit is replicated, almost instantly, by his robot counterpart. "In the middle of the night I woke up with the idea of creating a small T-rex puppet that would link to our full-size one," said Winston, "so that every axis of movement would be covered—about forty of them in all. With four puppeteers we could move the small puppet around manually, and every movement would be translated to the hydraulics and duplicated by the big dinosaur."[54] In other words, the puppeteers' performance would be motion captured and replayed by the animatronic.

An animatronic version was also built of the velociraptor, but because of its smaller size, there was also a low-tech approach for the upper-body shots: a suit that a human operator could wear, not unlike the way Godzilla had been actuated in countless Godzilla pictures. "It's always an advantage to have a people-powered character because of the range of movements the human operator can produce,"[55] said Michael Lantieri, who had the privilege of wearing the suit.

Another body suit was built for the raptor's lower half. Because the raptor was supposed to be light on its feet, Lantieri had to be suspended from above so that there was just enough weight on his feet to allow him to feel where he was going.

Spielberg recognized that not everything he needed could be accomplished with animatronics, so he hired Phil Tippet, one of the developers of go-motion, to do about fifty go-motion shots for *Jurassic Park*. Introduced in *The Empire Strikes Back* (1980) and perfected by Tippet for *Dragonslayer* (Matthew Robbins, 1981), go-motion uses puppets with rods that extend from their extremities and are attached to computer-controlled stepper-motors. The result is a kind of motion control for puppets—the choreography of movements can be stored in the computer and repeated with variations. Although traditional stop-motion animators did not like the high-tech variation, it did have the advantage of eliminating strobing, a jerky look caused by the lack of blur in traditional stop-motion. (Some stop-motion traditionalists claim that instead of proper blurs, the "images merely lose overall clarity during broad movements," which they find more objectionable than strobing.[56])

Tippet and his team spent four months creating two brief animatic sequences (animatics are moving storyboards used as a guide for subsequent animation), almost fifty shots, using the go-motion technology.[57] The two sequences were of the T rex menacing jeeps that are stranded outside an electric fence and the two raptors hunting the children in the kitchen. These and other bits of footage were compiled in a "dinosaur bible" and later used as the basis of pantomime by the on-set dinosaur operators. The animatics were produced by Stefan Dechant, using an

Amiga personal computer and Video Toaster Effects software to construct a 3-D representation of the T rex, which was then animated.[58]

While all of this development was going on, Dennis Muren and his team over at Industrial Light and Magic (ILM) had used a combination of computer-generated imagery and advanced morphing techniques, which, along with some puppet creations by Stan Winston's shop, had gone into creating the shape-shifting robot of *Terminator 2: Judgment Day* (1991).

Spielberg had asked Muren if he could create a stampede sequence for *Jurassic Park* using computer graphics, as it would be difficult to achieve the effect using stop-motion. Two of ILM's veteran animators, Mark Dippe and Steve Williams, thought they could do more than the stampede, and secretly built a computerized T rex skeleton using images sent to them from the dinosaur repositories in Calgary.[59] Once they had a skeleton, they animated it in a brief sequence. They showed this to Kathy Kennedy, Jerry Molen, and Lata Ryan, the film producers, and piqued everyone's interest, then were given the go-ahead to try something more ambitious.

For their second attempt Dippe and Williams took a model of the gallimimus dinosaur designed by Stan Winston, and computer graphics artist Eric Armstrong fashioned a gallimimus skeleton and developed an animated running cycle for it. "After we built the skeleton," said Muren, "we animated about ten of [the dinosaurs] running along in a herd. For the background, we picked some photos out of a book on Africa and scanned them into the computer. . . . [W]e did two angles . . . one looking down over a prairie on these animals running along and the other . . . a view right down at ground level as they run past. It was the same animation in both cases, so we got two shots for the price of one."[60] Although the animals were in skeletal form, everyone at Amblin Entertainment was very impressed, and Steven Spielberg commissioned half a dozen shots: the stampede sequence he had asked for originally and a few grand vistas of dinosaurs dotting the countryside.

Still, the animators at ILM thought they could do more. Specifically, they wanted to take a shot at the T rex. For their next test they had to use film. They used a Cyberware scanner, which focuses a revolving laser beam on objects or persons and records the topographical data in the computer, on Stan Winston's fifth-scale prototype, then animated it against a still image of rolling hills. "The shot started out with the T-rex maybe a hundred feet away, about two-thirds of the size of the frame. Then it just walked toward camera, step by step, and we sort of tilted up at the head as it passed by," said Muren.[61]

Just as it had been an animated dinosaur that had impressed audiences in Willis O'Brien's *The Dinosaur and the Missing Link* (1914), and especially his stop-motion version of *The Lost World* (1925), so now it would be another animated dinosaur that would change animation in Hollywood forever. As Spielberg described it:

> My intention had always been to use full-size dinosaurs as much as I could, but I knew that my long shots or wide-angle shots would need to be done with stop-motion or go-motion, just like Willis O'Brien and Ray Harryhausen had done. None of us expected that ILM would make the next quantum leap in computer graphics—at least not in time for this picture. We had seen the gallimimus tests . . . but they were just skeletons and they were on video. The T-rex was complete and on film and walking in daylight, making full contact with the ground. It was a living, breathing dinosaur, more real than anything Harryhausen or Phil Tippet had ever done in their careers. At the showing, Phil groaned and pretty much declared himself extinct.[62]

It was clear that the go-motion from Phil Tippet would not be needed, and neither would any more animatronics have to be built by Stan Winston's shop. Instead, those contracts were reassigned to ILM. However, Spielberg discovered that he needed Tippet's expertise in generating convincing animated animal performances to guide the computer animators. Tippet had to get some crash computer training, which alternated with his training the computer animators in pantomime to help them block out the shots.[63] Furthermore, Tippet's animatics remained the definitive guide for the dinosaur movements.

Tippet had developed a system called dinosaur input devices, or DID (later renamed direct input devices), in which stop-motion movements on a dinosaur armature were recorded by a computer using encoders. This information would then be used by an animator to generate the CGI footage. The CGI thus was motivated, when the DID system was used, by stop-motion.[64]

The realistic dinosaur behavior that Steven Spielberg was so concerned with was achieved by numerous processes that all accomplished one goal: the breaking down of a performance into various elements that then could be remixed and matched at the will of the film's animators and, ultimately, the director. As we have seen so far, telemetry, motion capture, and direct input devices were all used to capture performances that originated in another format, whether in a physical performance by an actor, a puppeteer, or stop-motion animation, and translated to CGI. Various forms of scanning, from a still photograph of a valley setting or a dinosaur bone to the Cyberware background, fed images that could be manipulated by computer graphics artists and then animated.

This process has become a concern, especially for actors, since the release of films like *Star Wars Episode I: The Phantom Menace* (George Lucas, 1999), *Final Fantasy* (Hironobu Sakaguchi and Motonori Sakakibura, 2001), and *The Lord of the Rings: The Two Towers* (Peter Jackson, 2002). Synthespians such as Gollum from *Two Towers* are a great concern, at least to actors, because they alter our notion of a performance. Who can claim credit for a particular performance when we are talking about a character created out of digital imagery designed by a series of computer graphics artists, a character whose motions come from those of an actor's movements (in the case of Gollum, the voice and movements came from Andrew Serkis), and whose voice might be dubbed in from yet another actor? This debate was highlighted in the 2002 Academy Awards race, when New Line Productions tried to have the computer-animated Gollum nominated for a best supporting actor role.[65]

However, when Spielberg was working on *Jurassic Park,* his stated concern was realism. As we have seen, from the author of the original novel, to the director, to the production designer, to the effects artists, "realistic" dinosaurs were a key concern. But what makes a dinosaur realistic? How do we know how dinosaurs really behaved? How do we know if they would be interested in eating people or not? We don't, and we probably never will. What Spielberg was really after was not realism, but credibility:

> I never thought I wanted to do a dinosaur movie better than anyone else's, but I did want my dinosaur movie to be the most realistic of them all. I wanted the audience to say, "I really believe this could happen today." *Close Encounters,* in a way, was based on both scientific and popular belief that UFOs have existed, or at the very least, *could* exist. And there was credibility in that film that I drew upon in attacking *Jurassic Park.*[66]

Spielberg accomplished his goal by changing genres: instead of making a monster film or a disaster film, or an homage to either of those genres, he looked to documentaries and the action-adventure genre he already knew so well:

What I was after was kind of like *Nova* meets *Explorer,* with a little bit of *Raiders of the Lost Ark* and *Jaws* mixed in. But if I had to aspire to a particular movie, it would be *Hatari.* To me, that was the high-water mark of man versus the natural in a feature film.[67]

Jurassic Park is primarily a horror film, but the combination of horror with action, more than anything else, made the dinosaurs seem so credible.

Mars Attacks!

Burton was surely aware of the success of CGI in *Jurassic Park,* but he had a real loyalty to stop-motion; in particular, he seemed to like the way stop-motion captured an individual animator's energy:

When [stop-motion] is done beautifully, you feel somebody's energy. It's something that computers will never be able to replace, because they're missing that one element. For as good as computers are and as incredible as [CGI] will get and is right now, it goes back to painters and their canvases. This project [*The Nightmare Before Christmas*] and these characters and these visuals, the only way that it could have been done was with stop-motion. Therefore, it's very specialized. I remember getting shots and each time I would see a shot I would get this little rush of energy; it was so beautiful. It's like a drug. And I realized if you did it in live-action it wouldn't be as good; if you did it in drawing it wouldn't be as good. There is something about stop-motion that gives it an energy that you don't get in any other form.[68]

Burton made this statement to Mark Salisbury before 1995, and he went on to plan his next film, *Mars Attacks!* accordingly. The initial idea came from the 1962 *Mars Attacks!* Topps trading cards, which were included in nickle packs of bubble gum. Read and considered together, the fifty-five cards had a story that was inspired by 1950s B movies, pulp magazine fiction such as that of *Amazing Stories,* and the films of Fritz Lang and other movies such as *War of the Worlds.*[69] Burton and his screenwriter, Jonathan Gems, were also inspired by another set of Topps cards produced in 1988 called *Dinosaurs Attack!,* written by Woody Gelman and Len Brown, who also had written the *Mars Attacks!* series. This series had been withdrawn from circulation in the 1960s due to parental cries of outrage, but it was reissued in 1994. That was when Burton convinced Warner Bros. to buy the rights to both sets of cards.

Having just come off the production of *Ed Wood* (1994), Burton and Gems had the same goal: to make a big budget B movie using the cards as a basis, the way they thought Ed Wood would have made it if he had had the resources.[70]

In an interview in the London *Sunday Times* of February 9, 1997, Burton said that he had originally planned to use a great deal of stop-motion animation for his sci-fi satire *Mars Attacks!*[71] According to Burton, when Warner Bros. realized that his film would not play to the lucrative sci-fi audience, they forced him to switch from stop-motion to CGI—and shave $20 million from the budget. Burton fought the change, until ILM showed him what they had done on *Jurassic Park* and *Jumanji*. Burton was impressed with how good it looked—"better than stop-motion." Burton's decision-making process basically replicated Steven Spielberg's on *Jurassic Park* just six years before.

Burton had already hired Ian Mackinnon and Peter Saunders, owner-partners of a special effects company based in Manchester, England, and given them the job of making stop-motion Martians. Burton specified that he wanted the battle scenes between humans and Martians in *Mars Attacks!* to be reminiscent of the skeleton fight in *Jason and the Argonauts* (Don Chaffey, 1963), in which Ray Harryhausen had brilliantly combined live-action and stop-motion special effects. Burton had originally seen the film as a youngster at the Avalon Theatre on Catalina Island, a theater that featured an underwater motif, with art deco shells and so on. For Burton, the theater, its location, and the movie, with the mythology it evoked, seemed to be as one, and it made a strong impression on him.[72]

Burton also wanted the "hub-cap-like flying saucers" to be produced using stop-motion, and the visual design of many of the saucer elements echoes Harryhausen's work in *Earth vs. the Flying Saucers* (Fred Sears, 1956). Harryhausen had given his saucers a revolving inner section, time

The Mars ambassador and his cohort, originally intended to be stop-motion figures, ended up as CGI in *Mars Attacks!*

consuming to animate, but the result is that the saucers seem electrically alive. Harryhausen's saucers also fly in formation, raise and lower themselves on central stems, dip and swoop as they fly, and have an animated ray gun that emerges from beneath and turns to aim at its target. The screenplay also copied some elements of *Earth vs. the Flying Saucers*, such as the Martians' attempt to send a satellite signal from outer space. Other images from the Harryhausen film that Burton paid homage to were the gathering of people in front of the destroyed U.S. Capitol, the composite image of the saucer in the lake, with actors in the foreground, the pace of the scenes of destruction in general, and the destruction of the Washington Monument.[73]

To facilitate the stop-motion work for *Mars Attacks!,* Mackinnon and Saunders moved to Los Angeles and began to arrange a collaboration with the Skellington group in San Francisco, the company run by Henry Selick that had produced *The Nightmare Before Christmas*. However, Selick and forces were too busy with *James and the Giant Peach*. Mackinnon and Saunders got to work on their own, setting up a facility in L.A. and producing various models of Martians for Burton's approval. After viewing their models, Burton made two key decisions: that all the Martians should look the same and that they should never blink. According to Karen Jones, in her book on the making of *Mars Attacks!,* Burton made these changes to make the Martians more frightening.[74] However, these are also the types of decisions made by someone working in stop-motion who is trying to cut costs.

When Larry Franco, the producer of *Jumanji* and *Mars Attacks!,* saw the first stop-motion tests of the Martians, he was reminded of the early phases of the CGI animation for *Jumanji*. He asked Burton to meet with the people at ILM. Burton agreed, but with trepidation: he didn't like the look of *Toy Story* (designed by John Lasseter, who had been at Disney with Burton), and that's what he thought he was going to see. At ILM, Mark Miller, who had been the visual effects producer on *Jumanji* and would soon be playing the same role for *Mars Attacks!,* and computer graphics supervisor Jim Mitchell spent a month preparing a screen test of digital Martians against a real background, with a flying saucer and soundtrack.

When Burton saw the ILM test, he was finally convinced:

> When I first saw it, I was amazed. Every type of animation has a different vibe, and it's not something that you can really analyze or verbalize. But

there was SOMETHING about the computer medium that seemed to work with these characters, because they were all the same, because they had a certain quality in their movement.[75]

Also, because we needed so many [Martians], that would have been much more difficult with stop-motion. To animate ten of them in a room would have been a much more difficult task. . . . At the root of it, animation is animation. Each form requires its own special set of circumstances and expertise.[76]

As a result, just as Mackinnon and Saunders were ready to go into full Martian stop-motion puppet production, in November 1995, Burton pulled the plug. Karen Jones gives a more detailed description of the problem:

Faced with the incredibly demanding production schedule, the marriage of live action and animation proved too difficult. Due to the extremely time-consuming nature of stop-motion, Burton would have had to film the live-action plate shots—the background shots into which the animation puppets would be composited digitally—months before the other scene elements even could have been conceptualized, particularly those starring the live actors who would be filmed playing opposite the Martians.[77]

The only actor playing a Martian was Lisa Marie, Burton's then girlfriend (the two had been introduced by Jonathan Gems, the screenwriter for *Mars Attacks!*). Because the mayhem in the film required life-size Martian bodies, Mackinnon and Saunders were asked to produce fifteen full-scale Martians for use as corpses in the film. Their design work was passed on to James Hegedus at ILM, who inherited the job of creating 3-D Martians. Hegedus had worked as visual art director for Joel Schumacher on the Tim Burton–produced *Batman Forever* (1995). The digital architecture for *Mars Attacks!* kept some influences from its stop-motion incarnation: many of the sets were round, as round sets made it easier for stop-motion animators to reach in and make adjustments.[78]

The switch to CGI had certain benefits: the realistic interaction between Martians and live actors that Burton wished for would be easier to achieve, and Burton could now film the rest of the movie in an anamorphic format, which would not have been possible if he were still working with stop-motion.[79] Burton was able to return to some design elements, such as the teardrop-shaped Martian helmets, he had wanted but had to drop for stop-motion.[80] The ILM animators even offered to leave off the motion blur that is added toward the end of the computer animation process, to make the images look more like stop-motion and to keep Burton's original idea of an homage to the work of Ray Harry-hausen. But Burton refused: if they had the ability to make the Martians look real, then that is what they should do.

Like any animation format, CGI has a long lead time, and with a December 1996 release date, time was tight. A team of sixty at ILM was responsible for around two hundred shots, mostly involving the Martians in such a way that they would match with the live-action footage and interact with the live actors. Warner Bros.' own digital company, Warner Digital Studios, was responsible for the remaining 130 effects shots, including the Martian robot, the flying saucers, and the scenes of exterior destruction. An in-house model shop built exact replicas of such monuments as the Eiffel Tower, Big Ben, and the Taj Mahal to be exploded on film. None of these model shots ever stood alone; all required computer graphic additions, like flying saucers and death rays. The visual effects division at Warner Digital was run by Michael Fink, who had previously earned an Academy Award nomination for Best Visual Effects for the penguins and bats he had produced for *Batman Returns*. Fink commented on Burton's photoreal but completely stylized look for the animation:

> Unlike other films, where the effects you create are entirely photorealistic and completely modern, *Mars Attacks!* has a very different kind of production design. What we tried to do was re-create the feel of the fifties science fiction invasion from Mars kind of movies, but make it contemporary and modern, and completely photorealistic. It's a very fine line to walk.[81]

The appearance of the Martian robot, like the style for most of the film, was based on the 1960s Topps trading cards, with their "violent subversive images" of Martians firing ray guns at semi-naked blondes. The Martian robot is closely modeled on Topps Card 32 (Robot Terror), as well as related denizens of '50s sci-fi movies. For its movement, Warner Digital took cues from other Tim Burton characters, such as Edward Scissorhands and Jack Skellington. The robot, which Fink described as "a two-legged army tank," was transported directly from the page to the screen. "We had the reference from the trading card #32 (Robot Terror), and we also had a reference from Wynn Thomas (Production Designer), who had an illustrator draw a proposal for a robot. Based on these, we actually created a robot in our computer. Quite often, we'll actually sculpt a creature in three dimensions and then digitize it, but in this case, we started from scratch on the computer."[82]

By the time they had built and designed a robot model, the production company was already in Burns, Kansas, to shoot the robot sequence. There they filmed all the background footage or plates. Through computer-generated prestidigitation, these would eventually include the robot running down the road chasing Richie (the film's hero, played by Lukas Haas) in his pickup truck, demolishing the trailer park, getting caught in the power lines, and finally, crashing to the ground. According to Fink:

> We photographed all those plate shots and, as carefully as possible, measured the road, the camera position, and any other things we thought we would need to know in order to re-create that world in the computer. We re-created—with computer graphics—the power lines that the robot gets tangled in and the structures that tear down or that bend as he falls, so we had to decide where those things went.
>
> We took all the data and the background plates and brought them into our computers to re-create the environment. Texture-map artists were working on developing the proper textures and contours that were painted on the surface of the robot.[83]

The animators themselves accommodated details like shadows cast by the robot and the clouds of dust that erupt as the machine runs down the road. Explained Fink: "The robot weighs about one hundred tons, so when its foot hits, it *must* shake the ground. We jiggle the camera a little bit and added the dust it would raise and the dents it would make in the concrete."[84]

The thirty-second sequence took three months of effort. Warner Digital also created many of the effects featured in the desert landing sequence, in which the Martians first descend on Earth. Warner Digital designed and animated the spaceship from which the Martian ambassador emerges. But the ambassador was animated by ILM. Real helicopters were used in the scene, but the helicopters that were destroyed by the Martian spaceships' death rays were animated.[85]

Many of the visual elements of *Mars Attacks!* are in homage to the work of Ray Harryhausen, especially in *Earth vs. Flying Saucers.*

In addition to Card 32, (Robot Terror), other cards were specific sources of inspiration: Card 22 (Burning Cattle), for the opening scene; Card 2 (Martians Approaching), for the appearance of the Martians; Card 19 (Burning Flesh), for General Casey being disintegrated by a Martian ray gun; Card 21 (Prize Captive), as the source for Natalie's abduction; Card 5 (Washington in Flames), for the Martian attack on the Capitol building; Card 13 (Watching from Mars), for Martians gleefully watching the destruction of Earth from their ship (Burton also showed the Martians watching Godzilla destroy Tokyo); Card 4 (Saucers Blast Our Jets), for a brief scene in which a jet gets blasted out of the sky; Card 50 (Smashing the Enemy), with soldiers breaking open the skulls of Martians (who have red blood in the cards and not green, as in the movie); Card 40 (High Voltage Electrocution), for the destruction of the Martian robot (although in the cards it was a giant insect that was destroyed); Card 36 (Destroying a Dog), for the destruction of the presidential pet; Card 11 (Destroy the City), for Martians running amok; Card 41 (Horror in Paris), for the destruction of the Eiffel Tower; and Card 24 (The Shrinking Ray), for General Decker's shrinking end.

From the *Dinosaur Attacks!* card series, Card 43 (Business Lunch), Card 45 (Anchorman's Peril), and Card 30 (A Kid Strikes Back) were also influential.[86]

Hollywood's Transition to CGI

These two high-profile cases—*Jurassic Park* and *Mars Attacks!*—are indicative of a change that has taken place throughout the industry, where much work that would have once been done with stop-motion and animatronics is now done with computer-generated graphics. Some critics, such as Mark Langer, in his article "The End of Animation History," have pointed out that both practitioners and scholars need to come up with a new definition of animation, a definition that doesn't describe it as "not live-action cinema," but puts animation and live action in a new relationship. Langer goes as far as to say that "a hybridization of animation and live-action . . . [a] collapse of the boundary between animation and live-action . . . can no longer be viewed as an aberration, but as a major trend of contemporary cinema."[87]

We can put the relationship of animation and live-action cinema today in perspective by looking back at the relationship between the two at the very beginnings of film history. In film studies we have seen animation as a subset of live-action cinema. But if we compare the relationship between the two at the beginning of film history, we will see the aberration is not that the boundary between animation and live-action cinema is collapsing now, but that the two were ever seen as separate to begin with. Langer mourns the loss of film's indexicality (the link between an image and what it refers to, a link live-action cinema is assumed to have naturally) and connects it to an overall cultural fear that we can no longer distinguish between simulation and reality. But film has always been about simulation; even live-action cinema is staged, arranged, carefully lit, filtered, and manipulated in countless other ways. Furthermore, live-action cinema gives the viewer a sense of photorealism. Until recently, we have associated photorealism with realism, but our thinking of it that way does not make it so. In fact, I would go as far as to argue that live-action cinema and animation were never really distinct mediums, and that live-action cinema should be seen as a subset of animation.

I believe that we have misunderstood the primary drive behind changes in film production and exhibition. The primary drive is not toward increased realism, based on audience demand, but to mechanization. In my book on the first woman filmmaker, *Alice Guy Blaché, Lost Cinematic Visionary,*[88] I argued that processes such as the impulse toward color and synchronized sound in the cinema, which have usually been interpreted as responses to audience demand for increased realism, were really the result of an industrial drive to mechanization—to put it simply, the need of film manufacturers to standardize production and exhibition in order to define markets more reliably.

The drive to mechanization in live-action cinema made itself felt in animation as well, from the Taylorization of animation studios initiated by John Bray to the use of techniques like rotoscoping.[89]

When I looked more closely at this drive to mechanization, it struck me that, in many cases, whether I was looking at examples from live action or from animation produced at the turn of the twentieth century, the drive to digitization was already apparent. The mechanization of cinema in the twentieth century and the digitization of cinema in the twenty-first are related drives, therefore, acting on live-action cinema and animation in related ways. So it is not that "improvements in animation technology make it impossible to tell animation from live-action,

[and] improvements in special effects have made it impossible to tell live-action from animation," as Mark Langer claimed in the article already mentioned, but, rather, that we ever saw the two as separate at all.[89]

I will illustrate my point by taking three cases from early cinema: cases of early motion capture, early rotoscoping, and early digitization as represented by trick films, in the work of film and animation pioneers Etienne-Jules Marey, Emile Reynaud, and Georges Méliès.

Marey, and his associate Georges Demeny were peers of Eadweard Muybridge and pioneers in motion studies. In the pursuit of a better understanding of how the human body moves, Marey used an early version of motion capture: Demeny and other test subjects would wear black body stockings marked with white dots, so that only the dots were recorded by the camera as the subject moved. When filmed, all that was visible were the white lines and the white dots that marked the subject's joints, creating a skeleton dance version of the movement.[90]

Emile Reynaud, better known as an early animator, also applied a form of digitization. In 1896 he adapted Marey's proto-motion picture device, the chronophotographe, to develop a motion picture camera projector and made a handful of films. The first of these was a classic vaudeville act by two clowns, Footit and Chocolat, loosely based on the story of William Tell: Chocolat has an apple on his head (and takes bites out of it), and Footit shoots the apple off Chocolat's head with a water rifle, soaking Chocolat in the process. Once Reynaud had the film (shot at sixteen frames per second), he took a few frames from one part and a few frames from another. These short selected sequences were then reproduced on transparent celluloid, improved by coloring applied by hand, then strung into a sequential loop. Reynaud repeated this process with two other early digitizations, one entitled *Le premier cigare (mimodrame comique)*, in which a university student tries his first cigar and finds it comically sickening, and another vaudeville act featuring a pair of clowns, called *Les clowns prince (scène comique)*, made in 1898, which was never shown to the public. Unfortunately, these early efforts did not survive.[91]

A similar method was developed in 1899–1900, by the brothers Ignatius and Adolph Bing of Nuremberg, along with German manufacturers, Planck and Bub and Carette, and the French firm Lapierre. These companies, which manufactured toy filmstrip viewers, made cartoons for use in the viewers that were based on live-action films. These early animators invented a form of rotoscoping, which traced its roots from early live-action films such as *L'arroseur arrosée* (Lumière), *The Serpentine Dance (Loie Fuller,* 1901), *Skiers* (1900), and *Jumping Clowns, Clown and Dog,* and *Rider* (all by Ernst Planck, all from 1910).[92] Rotoscoping continued to be important in animation films until the advent of digital motion capture. (Films such as *Snow White,* 1943, relied extensively on rotoscoping, although the Disney animators were reluctant to admit it.)

A closer examination of trick film techniques shows that they also can be considered a mechanical version of modern computer simulation techniques. These techniques were then applied to animation using puppetry and models.

Trick films made before 1908[93] by Méliès, working in his own studio, and Zecca and Segundo de Chomón, working for Pathé, included techniques such as stop-substitution (stopping the camera and replacing a beautiful princess, for example, with an old hag, or a horse with a toy); filming in slow motion, so that when projected at normal speed, the film would appear speeded up; combining fast-motion through superimposition with a regular-speed sequence, so that some characters moved at comically fast speeds and others at normal speeds; cutting alternate frames out of a sequence to speed it up; shooting with the camera hanging upside down so that the film, when projected normally, would play the action backwards; fade in and fade out of a figure in superimposition to simulate the apparition and disappearance of a ghostly figure; and the use of props such as removable limbs and miniature sets. This incomplete list gives an indication of the creativity of early film directors working in live-action cinema.[94]

Let's look closely at some of these techniques. First of all, we have stop-substitution. In one film from 1904, for which no title has been found, a man appears to be run over by a car. In actuality, the camera was stopped before the man was run over, and a substitute with fake legs was put in his place. The car then runs over the fake legs, which are separated from the substitute's body. The film concludes with the driver of the car, a doctor, replacing the legs, and instantly the injured man (through another stop-substitution) is able to rise and walk.

The effect achieved through stop-substitution in this early film is thus similar to that achieved through digitization in *Forrest Gump* (Robert Zemeckis, 1994), in which actor Gary Sinise appears to have both legs amputated from the knee down. In both cases the goal was the same: to simulate an amputee when in fact the actor is whole-bodied. The difference is the means used to achieve the effect: in 1904, the process was mechanical; in 1994, it was digital.

Matthew Solomon, in his essay "Twenty-Five Heads under One Hat: Quick Change in the 1890s," made a connection between the turn-of-the-century illusions of the quick-change artistry type, such as "the rapid alteration of character through costume changes; chapeaugraphy, the manipulation of a piece of felt to form different hats; and shadowgraphy, the use of the hands to create human and animal figures in a beam of light,"[95] and digital morphing.

> Placing metamorphic performance within a longer history of transformation that includes not only the emergence of cinema but also the contemporary proliferation of digital media. . . . Foregrounds a significant set of continuities. Viewed one hundred years later, when the cinematic is being increasingly replaced by the digital, quick-change, chapeaugraphy, and shadowgraphy take on added significance, appearing not so much archaic as visionary.[96]

One example of such a performance is the film *Le roi du maquillage* (*Untamable Whiskers,* 1904) by Georges Méliès. This film is prescient, in that it is not simply a record of a quick-change performance—the transformations are too detailed for that—nor is it simply a series of repeated cinematic tricks; rather, it combines both, much in the way that morphing combines performance and digital trickery today. As Solomon concludes, cinema abandoned these early attempts at morphing, though the tradition could still be found in certain animated films; it reappears now with the possibilities of digital media.[97]

Most of the tricks I listed above are based on some kind of stop-motion technique used in live-action films, and it might seem a stretch to talk about trick films in the same discussion as 2-D animation. In fact, most film historians generally focus on the influence of early trick films on animation films in terms of content. But we must not forget that animation itself is a product of stop-motion animation, as each drawing is substituted by the next, shot on another bit of film, until the whole gives the impression of movement.

There is no question that the paths of cinema and animation were joined at the beginning of their history. It appears that their paths diverged after 1907, when live-action trick films using stop-motion such as those made by Méliès fell out of favor, though live-action films to this day rely on the techniques of animation for their special effects sequences. Trick sequences in live-action films are an area of overlap between cinema and animation, an area where we can see that what we thought were two mediums are really one.

We can discuss J. Stuart Blackton's *Haunted Hotel,* for example, as both live-action cinema and a trick, or animated, film. The mechanical techniques for making film move, animating objects, or imbuing line drawings with life were essentially the same until 1907 or so. As trick films lost their popularity, live-action cinema and animation went separate ways, though we can still find areas of overlap, such as Ray Harryhausen's stop-motion sequences in otherwise live-action films.

Many of these effects are still used in live-action cinema today, but increasingly, the effects are achieved digitally, by manipulating the image as part of a computer sequence. Because digitization was difficult and expensive, it was used only sporadically from around the mid-1980s until 1993, when Spielberg made the switch for *Jurassic Park.* Since then other Hollywood directors, even those deeply attached to stop-motion animation like Tim Burton, have followed suit. With films in the twenty-first century, it is becoming increasingly difficult to see where the digitization or animation ends and the live action begins. Think of all-digital films like *Final Fantasy* and films with almost-all-digital sets like *Star Wars Episode II: Attack of the Clones* (George Lucas, 2002). Even films we think of as live-action dramas, like *A Beautiful Mind* (Ron Howard, 2001), have numerous digital or animated sequences.

Through digital movies, cinema and animation are coming back together, and this forces us to reconsider the true nature of both mediums, I have argued here that animation has been the dominant paradigm since the advent of motion studies. If we give the animation paradigm its due, we should be able to develop a better understanding, not only of moving picture media, but also of the drive to mechanization and digitization that our culture is caught up in today.

Notes

1. Burton in Mark Salisbury, *Burton on Burton* (London and Boston: Faber & Faber, 2000), p. 5.

2. Produced by Joe Hale. Disney first bought the rights to the books in 1971. The film was ten years in the making, with a $25 million budget.

3. David Coleman, "Vincent," *Cinefantastique* 13.4 (April–May 1983), quoted in Jim Smith and J. Clive Matthews, *Tim Burton* (London: Virgin Films, 2002), pp. 21–22, n. 255.

4. Ibid., 24–25.

5. Ibid., p. 23.

6. It is interesting to note that Burton's dogs, whether live-action or animated, are always very similar in appearance. Even in the monstrous shadowy figures on the cave walls in *Aladdin*, the dog shape was the same.

7. Smith and Matthews, *Tim Burton*, p. 20.

8. Burton in Salisbury, *Burton on Burton*, p. 19.

9. First published in *Burtons* in 1839 and revised for Poe's collection *Tales of the Grotesque and Arabesque*, vol. 1, in 1840.

10. First published in *Dollar Newspaper*, July 31, 1844.

11. Published in the *Saturday Evening Post* in 1843.

12. Smith and Matthews, *Tim Burton*, p. 20–21.

13. First published in *The Raven and Other Poems*, 1841.

14. Smith and Matthews, *Tim Burton*, p. 19–20.

15. Burton, in the commentary on the *Edward Scissorhands* DVD, 10th Anniversary Edition, 20th Century Fox Home Video, 2003.

16. Smith and Matthews, *Tim Burton*, p. 23.

17. Burton in Salisbury, *Burton on Burton*, p. 17.

18. Gary J. Svehla and Susan Svehla, eds., *Vincent Price* (Baltimore: Midnight Marquee Press, 1998), p. 295.

19. Smith and Matthews, *Tim Burton*, pp. 22–23.

20. Burton in Salisbury, *Burton on Burton*, p. 24.

21. Svehla and Svehla, *Vincent Price*, p. 296.

22. Taylor L. White, "Vincent," *Cinefantastique* 20.1, 20.2 (November 1989), p. 67.

23. Smith and Matthews, *Tim Burton*, p. 26.

24. *The Nightmare Before Christmas* (Special Edition) DVD, Touchstone Video, 2004.

25. Taylor White, "Aladdin's Lamp," *Cinefantastique* (November 1989), p. 77.

26. Jody Duncan Shannon, "Cheap and Cheesy and Off-the-Cuff: The Effects of Beetlejuice," *Cinefex* 34 (May 1988): 13.

27. For an in-depth explanation of forced perspective, see Raymond Fielding, *The Technique of Special Effects Cinematography*, 4th ed. (London and Boston: Focal Press, 1985), pp. 262–265.

28. Shannon, "Cheap and Cheesy . . . ," pp. 10, 14.

29. Ibid., p. 41.

30. Neil Pettigrew, *The Stop-Motion Filmography: A Critical Guide to 297 Features Using Puppet Animation* (Jefferson, NC, and London: McFarland & Co., 1999), p. 105.

31. Ibid., p. 106.

32. Burton in Salisbury, *Burton on Burton*, p. 115.

33. Ibid., p. 116.

34. Ibid., p. 118.

35. Gerri Hirshey, "Welcome to His Nightmare: Weird Genius Tim Burton Goes Back to His Roots in Animation—and to Disney, His Old Employer—to Put a Creepy-Crawly Spin on the Kiddie Christmas Movie," *GQ*, November 1993, pp. 227.

36. Burton quoted in Andy Carvin, "An Interview with Tim Burton" (October 1993), *EdWeb*, http://sujnsite.ust.hk/edweb/nightmare.burton.html.

37. Harry Selick is an animator and director of animated films. He is best known for *The Nightmare Before Christmas* and *James and the Giant Peach*.

38. Paul Well, *Animation: Genre and Authorship*, Short Cut Series (London and New York: Wallflower Press, 2002), p. 115.

39. Frank Thompson, *Tim Burton's Nightmare Before Christmas: The Film, the Art, the Vision* (New York: Hyperion, 1993), p. 98.

40. Smith and Matthews, *Tim Burton*, p. 137.

41. Burton in Salisbury, *Burton on Burton*, p. 121.

42. Thompson, *Tim Burton's Nightmare Before Christmas*, p. 13.

43. Ibid., pp. 16–17.

44. Leslie Felperin, "Animated Dreams" (an interview with Henry Selick), *Sight and Sound* (December 1994). Reprinted in Woods, pp. 106–107.

45. Thompson, *Tim Burton's Nightmare Before Christmas*, 17–18.

46. Felperin, "Animated Dreams," p. 107.

47. Thompson, pp. 147–148.

48. Because the film is still in production as of this writing, all of these details are preliminary. My information is from Greg's Preview, http://movies.yahoo.com/shop?d = hp&cf = prev&id = 1808513469&intl = us, and International Movie Data Base (IMDB) professional details.

49. Don Shay and Jody Duncan, *The Making of Jurassic Park: An Adventure 65 Million Years in the Making* (New York: Ballantine Books, 1993), p. 7.

50. Ibid., p. 8.

51. Ibid., p. 14.

52. Ibid., pp. 16–17.

53. Ibid., pp. 20–21.

54. Ibid., pp. 28–29.

55. Ibid., pp. 32–33.

56. Shannon, "Cheap and Cheesy," p. 29.

57. Shay and Duncan, *The Making of Jurassic Park*, pp. 38–39.

58. Ibid., p. 47.

59. This is a reference to the Dinosaur Provincial Park in Calgary, Alberta, Canada, where huge repositories of dinosaur skeletons have been discovered.

60. Shay and Duncan, *The Making of Jurassic Park*, pp. 49–50.

61. Ibid., pp. 50–51.

62. Ibid., pp. 51–52.

63. Ibid., p. 53.

64. Pettigrew, *Stop-Motion Filmography*, p. 385.

65. I am grateful to Mary Desjardins and Mark Wolf, whose papers at the 2003 Society for Cinema and Media Studies Conference gave me a better understanding of the way synthespians are regarded by actors.

66. Shay and Duncan, *The Making of Jurassic Park*, p. 15.

67. Ibid., p. 16.

68. Burton in Salisbury, *Burton on Burton*, p. 119.

69. Smith and Matthews, *Tim Burton*, p. 173.

70. Ibid., p. 176.

71. "The Critters Who Gave Hollywood the Jitters," (London) *Sunday Times*, February 9, 1997.

72. Burton in Salisbury, p. 2.

73. For an excellent analysis of Ray Harryhausen's stop-motion work in *Earth vs. the Flying Saucers*, see Pettigrew, *Stop-Motion Filmography*, pp. 205–210.

74. Karen Jones, *Mars Attacks! The Art of the Movie*, New York: Ballantine Books, 1996.

75. Ibid., pp. 123–124.

76. Ibid., pp. 135–137.

77. Ibid., pp. 47–48.

78. Ibid., p. 67.

79. Ibid., p. 125.

80. Ibid., p. 133.

81. Ibid., pp. 141–142.

82. Ibid., p. 46.

83. Smith and Matthews, pp. 177–178.

84. Ibid., pp. 147–149.

85. Ibid., p. 149.

86. Ibid., pp. 149–151.

87. Mark Langer, "The End of Animation History," http://asifa.net/SAS/articles/langer1.htm.

88. Alison McMahan, (2002), *Alice Guy Blaché, Lost Cinematic Visionary* (New York: Continuum, 2002), pp. 49–52. See also Alison McMahan, "The Quest for Motion: Moving Pictures and Flight," in *Visual Delights: Essays on the Popular and Projected Image in the Nineteenth Century*, ed. S. Popple and V. Toulmin (Trowbridge: Flicks Books, 2000), pp. 93–104; and Alan Williams, "Historical and Theoretical Issues in the Coming of Recorded Sound to the Cinema," in *Sound Theory/Sound Practice*, ed. Rick Altman (New York: Routledge/AFI Film Readers, 1992), pp. 126–137.

89. In the 1880s Frederick Taylor, management consultant, proposed a "science of systems," or work efficiency for factories, and the philosophy that became known as Taylorism became popular in the United States. Louis Brandeis went on to apply scientific

management to the railroads with great success in 1910. This was when animation studios were being established in the United States, and John Bray, an animator with a regular production contract with Paramount, patented a series of inventions and, most importantly, a system of scientific management for animation studios. The idea was to automate the process so that a maximum number of unskilled laborers could be used for smaller tasks, as well as to plan the work of skilled laborers in such a way that their time was used to the fullest extent. Bray established a strict hierarchical chain of command, spelled out the daily tasks for everyone on his staff, penalized those who did not finish the assigned work, and rewarded (with bonuses) those who finished ahead of time. This was in sharp contrast to the earlier workshop arrangements. Because animation studios were just getting established, the system of scientific management became the norm and remains so to this day, even though scientific management fell out of favor in other industries by the late teens. Scientific management of the animation studio spread to France with Lortac (the pseudonym of Robert Collard, independent French animator who worked in the 1920s and 1930s) in 1921, who had observed the process at work in New York. See Donald Crafton, *Before Mickey: The Animated Film 1898–1928* (Chicago and London: University of Chicago Press, 1993), pp. 162–167.

90. Langer, ibid.

91. Marta Braun, *Picturing Time: The Work of Étienne-Jules Marey (1830–1904)*, (Chicago and London: University of Chicago Press, 1992).

92. Laurent Mannoni, *The Great Arts of Light and Shadow: Archeology of the Cinema*, trans. and ed. Richard Crangle, introduction by Tom Gunning, preface by David Robinson (Exeter: University of Exeter Press, 2000), p. 385.

93. David Robinson, Introduction, *Griffithiana* 43 (December 1991): 18.

94. For example, in 1897 *A Visit to the Spiritualist*, from Vitagraph, cofounded by Albert E. Smith and J. Stuart Blackton, used stop-motion animation. That same year *Humpty Dumpty Circus* featured stop-motion animation using small jointed figures and moving objects. In 1898, for *The Cavalier's Dream,* the Edison Company patented a stop-motion animation sequence in which an environment changes while a man is sleeping.

In 1899 Arthur Melbourne Cooper in the United Kingdom produced one of the first 3-D animated advertisements, *Matches: An Appeal.* In 1900 Georges Méliès made *Le livre magique*, in which drawings appear to become human beings.

In 1900 Albert E. Smith and J. Stuart Blackton used stop-motion to enhance "lightning cartooning" in *The Enchanted Drawing,*which showed a man smiling while drinking and smoking.

In *A Trip to the Moon* (1902), Méliès used stop-motion animation as part of his armory of fantasy effects. Also in 1902, Edwin S. Porter used stop-motion animation in *Fun in a Bakery* to show loaves made from clay being sculpted into the faces of famous people, and in *Humorous Phases of Funny Faces,* J. Stuart Blackton showed the ways animation could enhance the principles of the "lightning sketch." Vitagraph's film *The Haunted Hotel* (1907) also used stop-motion object animation to great effect. In *The Sculptor's Nightmare*, (1908) Billy Bitzer featured stop-motion animation of busts of political figures laughing and smoking.

From Paul Wells, *Animation: Genre and Authorship,* Short Cut Series (London and New York: Wallflower Press, 2002), p. 114.

95. Frederick A. Talbot, *Moving Pictures* (New York: Arno Press, 1970, facsimile of original published in 1912), pp. 211–214.

96. Matthew Solomon, "Twenty-Five Heads under One Hat: Quick Change in the 1890s," in *Metamorphing: Visual Transformation and the Culture of Quick Change,* ed. Vivian Sobchak (Minneapolis and London: University of Minnesota Press, 2000), p. 3.

97. Ibid., p. 4.

98. Ibid., p. 17.

4

BURTON'S *BATMANS*:
MYTH, MARKETING, AND MERCHANDISING

First came the posters, hats, and T-shirts, then the number one Prince single and the bats shaved onto teenagers' skulls. By the time Batman *swooped into theaters three summers ago, it was less a movie than a corporate behemoth, and nobody was warier or wearier of the hype than Tim Burton. The only problem was that Burton was the movie's director.*

"It was so weird," he says today. "To be working on something—it's your baby, you get very emotional about it, and then you keep hearing about it. You go, 'God, enough about this damn thing!'"

He tried to escape to the desert, only to run into people wearing Batman merchandise.

—David Handelman[1]

Movies like Planet of the Apes *are basically businesses, and they involve words like franchise and saturation that make my skin crawl. This one will be heavily merchandised, but that's not something that I have any control over. They ask my opinion, of course, but sometimes I feel like the film gets in the way of the merchandising. There were people over in Taiwan making* Planet of the Apes *swords before we'd even shot the thing, and the film is being aggressively presold. Personally, I don't want to know too much about a movie before I go to see it.*

—Tim Burton[2]

The two extracts above, from interviews with Tim Burton as he promoted his films *Batman Returns* (1992) and *Planet of the Apes* (2001), respectively, illustrate issues that frequently emerge when discussing blockbuster films:

1. The high-concept (and frequently myth-based) structure of the blockbuster film
2. Vertical integration, synergy, and ancillary markets
3. Total merchandising and how it interrelates with the high-concept blockbuster and vertical integration

In this chapter we will examine each of these issues in turn, focusing on Burton's blockbuster film *Batman* (1989).

The High-Concept Blockbuster Film

The most commonly accepted definition of the term *high concept* is Justin Wyatt's, from his book on the subject:

> [a] striking, easily reducible narrative, which also offers a high degree of marketability. This marketability might be based upon stars, the match between a star and a premise, or a subject matter which is fashionable. In practice, the locus of this marketability and concept in the contemporary industry is the "pitch." . . . [According to] Steven Spielberg: "If a person can tell me the idea in 25 words or less, it's going to make a pretty good movie. I like ideas, especially movie ideas that you can hold in your hand."[3]

Wyatt credits Barry Diller, a programming executive at ABC, with inventing the concept (though Diller did not use the term) in the early 1970s. Diller helped bolster his network's poor ratings by introducing the made-for-television movie format. He then promoted these television movies using thirty-second promotional spots. To sell a movie in thirty seconds, he had to be able to summarize it in one sentence. As a result, he tended to approve those projects that could be sold in a single sentence. This sentence would then appear in advertising spots and TV listings.

Wyatt also notes that Jeffrey Katzenberg[4] credited Michael Eisner, a creative executive at Paramount at the time, with coining the term *high concept* to describe a unique idea whose originality could be conveyed briefly. Columbia Pictures entertainment president Peter Guber defined *high concept* in narrative terms. Rather than stressing the uniqueness of the idea, Guber said that high concept could be understood as a narrative that is very straightforward and easily communicated and comprehended. Just as Diller worried about marketing a TV movie in a thirty-second spot, Katzenberg, Eisner, and Guber were concerned with selling the idea for a project in an initial short pitch to get it made, then pitching the finished film to the public. The initial one-sentence pitch is seen as equivalent to the logline, or one-sentence ad, that appears in campaign posters. Put another way, a film concept that cannot be summarized in one sentence will be difficult to market. As Dawn Steel[5] has pointed out, high-concept films are easily marketed, especially to youth audiences, and are critic-proof.

High concept is not related to the terms *high culture* and *low culture*; indeed, it means the opposite. *High culture* refers to cultural artifacts, such as classic opera, that require a certain degree of sophistication to comprehend; *low culture* refers to popular culture that does not require much intellectual sophistication to comprehend and enjoy. When scholars like Wyatt and film executives like Diller, Eisner, and Steel use the term *high concept*, they are referring to the high marketability of a film. The hook can be as simple as basing the film on an already well-known franchise, such as a popular book (think of the *Lord of the Rings* and *Harry Potter* franchises), comic book series, or television show.

There is often more to a high-concept pitch than brevity and narrative simplicity. Adding star power improves a film's marketability, as long as the star's persona is directly linked to the genre of the project under consideration. Wyatt gives the example of Clint Eastwood in a cop film: this is high concept, because we already know Eastwood in that role. However, a star working against his or her image can also turn out to be high concept, such as Arnold Schwarzenegger as a tooth fairy.

High concept can also imply "trendy," which generates cycles of similar films. Sometimes this trendiness can work against a film if it is released after the subject has been exhausted in other media. High-concept films rely heavily on the replication and combination of previously successful film plots, such as "Robocop = Terminator meets Dirty Harry," or revitalizing past successes by a shift in emphasis: Guber was sure *Flashdance* (1983), for example, would do well because it was a *Rocky* for women.[6]

Wyatt identifies certain stylistic elements that make up a high-concept film. He claims that such films with a particular look and packaging (the hook, the look, and the book) represent one clear postclassical trend in Hollywood cinema. The aesthetic and economic characteristics are entwined. Although I will examine each aspect in turn, we must not forget that they are inseparable forces.

Stylistic Elements of the High-Concept Film

Wyatt lists five major stylistic elements of the high-concept film, each of which is driven by the film's marketing: the look, stars, music, character, and genre. He defines the look as

> [a] set of production techniques composed of extreme backlighting, a minimal (often almost black-and-white) color scheme, a predominance of reflected images, and a tendency toward setting of high technology and industrial design. At times these techniques combine to freeze the narrative, creating an excess within the film. . . .[7]

Some of these stylistic elements, separately or in combination, can therefore create moments of excess that lift the viewer out of the film's fictional world.

An actor's appearance constitutes an important part of the look of the high-concept film, whose narrative and character development tend to be oversimplified. This means the spectator has to rely more on the actor's appearance than on exposition or character development for understanding. As a result, the character's fashion sense becomes extremely important. In turn, fashionable images from the film are lifted out as print ads to promote the film.

This reliance on visual style is emphasized by a strong match between the image and music soundtrack, either at key moments in music video–like sequences, which fragment the narrative even further, or throughout the film. Wyatt uses Jack Nicholson's character (The Joker, also known as Jack Napier) in *Batman* as an example:

> Nicholson's star persona is the iconoclast, the nonconformist whose energy and mischievousness are infectious and appealing. . . . By the 1980s this image had become so established that Nicholson could offer self-parodies in supporting roles in such films as *The Witches of Eastwick* (1987). *The Shining* (1980) can be considered as a transition in Nicholson's career in which the tendency towards self-parody begins to undermine a coherent, naturalistic leading performance.[8]

Wyatt suggests that casting Nicholson as The Joker was designed to match Nicholson's parodies of his own star persona to the character. This casting made it easier to presell the film, as this match between the star's persona and the character was easy for spectators to grasp. Once spectators actually went to see the film, the casting invited them to read it in multiple ways.

The same is true for musical devices. Again, Wyatt uses *Batman* as an example: in addition to the score by.Danny Elfman, Prince composed an album of nine songs for the film, of which two actually appeared in it. One of these was "Party Man," in which The Joker destroys museum art. (This scene was intended to function as a standalone music video, but in the end Prince made a separate video using the song.) The other songs are sung from the perspective of various characters and tend to focus more on their sexuality and less on the narrative.[9]

Finally, high-concept films rely heavily on the spectators' familiarity with genre. This partly results in "the placement of generic icons in altered contexts offering burlesque" and "characters and other icons [being] telegraphed with broader and broader brush strokes."[10]

Yet this combination of a generic, oversimplified narrative and an excessive visual and musical style does not always guarantee success at the box office: *Dick Tracy* (1990) and *Cocktail* (1988) are two examples of box office duds.

Wyatt dates the advent of high-concept films to 1975. His sample list starts with *Jaws* (1975) and ends with *Batman Returns* (Wyatt's book was published in 1994). Now that we have an additional ten years' perspective on blockbuster films in general and high-concept films in particular, it is useful to reexamine the high-concept film, designed to be a blockbuster, especially how the narration works. Also, it is still useful to use Burton's *Batman* films for this examination because those films started or cemented several industry trends, such as reinterpreting a comic book franchise (which actually started with the *Superman* films but became an industry trend after *Batman*) and advances in soundscape design.

Many critics, including Wyatt, assume that high-concept blockbuster films are characterized by an oversimplified narrative and flat characters. But this is true only for spectators who see a film in isolation and are completely unaware of the other types of media and other cultural production working on (or with) the same story, or sequence of stories. Most high-concept films are based on a myth cycle, and their sources of meaning, and hence the spectators' ability to dialogue with a particular film, extend well beyond the film itself in both space and time. In addition, these films mean in a new way, an intertextual or even a hypertextual way: they are meant to be read as one part of a larger discourse involving multiple types of texts, both past and present, from comic books to visual art, to novels, theater, and television, to print media and other films. Of these three characteristics of high-concept blockbusters—the linear narrative with little in the way of subplot, the myth-based foundation, and the interstitial references—the last two are shared with pataphysical films. Let as look in turn at each of these aspects of meaning.

The Mythic Basis of High-Concept Films

Burton cast Michael Keaton as Batman and Jack Nicholson as the Joker because he envisioned a psychological drama about split personalities, but the producer wanted an action movie; it ended up neither. Batman scored thanks to scattered shards of Burton's trademark comic-opera visuals and whacked out humor, but actually, once you got past the hype and Anton Furst's Oscar-winning production design, the movie was mostly a big snooze. Burton himself . . . told the LA Times: "I liked parts of it. But parts of it are boring to me. . . . It's OK. But I think it was much more a cultural phenomenon than a great movie."[11]

What are the ingredients of a cultural phenomenon? This is exactly what the discipline of film studies is about: to examine how films are rooted in their culture and what they can tell us about ourselves and that culture.

One school of thought says that for a film to become a real cultural phenomenon, it has to be myth-based. Joseph Campbell is credited with initially defining the elements of myth stories and outlining the key myth stories of Western culture, in his book The Hero with a Thousand Faces.[12] In Hollywood, people like John Truby and Robert McKee[13] applied Campbell's principles to screenwriting, although the best book on this subject is Christopher Vogler's The Writer's Journey: Mythic Structure for Storytellers and Screenwriters.[14] The main message of these teachers is this: almost all Hollywood movies are genre films, and genre structures are myth-based.

What is a myth-based structure? Generally, the hero of a myth-based story is someone who was meant to lead his (these heroes are usually male, although there are some females) society through a time of crisis. Usually the hero resists being given this messianic role when first asked, but eventually he comes around. This leads to the beginning of the heroic journey: leaving (or being thrown out of) home, then having a series of episodic encounters with archetypal figures, including guides or mentor types, and people who test the hero in either battles of strength or battles of wit.

But the real test comes from the internal confrontation. The hero's greatest struggle is not with his enemies, but with himself. In a well-written myth-based movie, the hero has some kind of internal flaw, sometimes called the tragic flaw, in a nod to Aristotle, and his flaw is somehow connected to the tangible challenge he has to overcome. (What this means in terms of production design is that the context of the film is a visible reflection of the hero's inner torment or problem.)

From the beginning of his film career, Burton drew parallels between his main characters and the world they live in, but never so much as in his first *Batman* film. "I like it when the set [is] a character and not just a set," Burton said during the filming of *Batman*.[15] Designer Anton Furst's sets for Gotham immediately received a lot of attention and were often credited with catapulting the film into the box office stratosphere by setting a new tone and look for Batman's world on screen: more like Fritz Lang's *Metropolis* (1927) and less like the pop-art look of the 1960s television series; more like Frank Miller's comic book vision of Batman from the '80s and less like the original comic book incarnation from the '40s and '50s. The look of *Batman* still defines Burton's approach to design for most audiences.

> Now, in *Batman Returns*, Burton has created a film that composer and regular Burton collaborator Danny Elfman describes as "almost operatic in tone" by borrowing visual themes from several of his previous films. Enlarging on the German Expressionism of *Batman*, Burton has incorporated some of the hyperrealism of *Edward Scissorhands* and the Felliniesque anarchy of *Beetlejuice* into the film to create disparate worlds inhabited by the three protagonists—Batman [Michael Keaton], Catwoman [Michelle Pfeiffer] and the Penguin [Danny DeVito].[16]

This means that once the hero has acknowledged his own character flaw and made an attempt to overcome it (if he ever does), then the environment of the film has to change along with him.

Anton Furst's set for *Batman* inspired the design of many subsequent films.

To say a film is based on a myth usually means it is based on a well-known epic tale; since most of us grow up with these stories, we recognize them, even if only subconsciously. For example, *Star Wars* is based on the *Iliad*: a group of soldiers band together to rescue a princess. Many writers begin by choosing a myth or fairy tale when they get a writing assignment. The most popular epic narrative is the life of Christ, in which an underdog takes on the establishment and wins, even if he himself is sacrificed in the process. Some films, such as *Hook* (1991), are quite clear about the story they are imitating, either in the film itself or in its marketing.

However, a film does not have to be taken from a story in *Bullfinch's Mythology* in order to be myth-based. Every culture creates its own myths; *Urban Legend* (Jamie Blanks, 1998) is a perfect example of a modern film based on modern myths. In this particular case, the myths are very specific to the United States, so the film is not intelligible on the same level to people from other cultures. This is one reason why warrior myths keep getting recycled in the form of action films: at the global market level they are the most accessible.

The *Batman* cycle is another example of a modern myth. *Batman* and the stories of other superheroes who are closely associated with him, such as *Superman*, were born out of mid-nineteenth and early-twentieth-century culture. Most of the inspiration came from comics and other films. Let's look at Batman's history.

Batman, the Myth

Beginnings

In February 1936, Harry Donenfeld, the future publisher of DC Comics, published an issue of *Spicy Mystery Stories* called *The Batman*. This story was about a man who believed his brain had been transferred to that of a bat, and as a bat he terrorized women (who were, inevitably, half naked). This tale had nothing to do with Batman as we came to know him, but it was the first use of the name.[17]

Comics were just making the transition from short newspaper strips to comic book form in 1938, when Superman debuted in Action Comics. Editor Vin Sullivan asked artist Bob Kane to come up with a similar concept for Detective Comics (both titles would eventually be united as

DC Comics). Kane worked with writer Bill Finger to come up with an idea. Kane started by drawing a figure similar to Superman's, muscle bound, wearing tights and a cape, then drawing over these elements with tracing paper to test out variations. His inspiration for the scalloped cape came from Leonardo da Vinci's sketches of a flying machine; the wings greatly resembled those of a bat. Kane was further inspired by two films. One was *The Bat Whispers* (1930), a talkie remake of *The Bat* (1926), both directed by Roland West, and both adaptations of Mary Roberts Rinehart's novel *The Circular Staircase* (1908), which inspired innumerable stories about fiends in animal disguise.[18] In addition to the figure of a detective who is also a killer known as The Bat, the silent film may have inspired the Bat signal, as one of the more memorable images in the film was of a moth trapped in an automobile headlight, its shadow magnified on the wall, looking like a giant bat. The film also featured a secret passage to a hidden room and a character wearing an eyepiece mask.

The 1926 version of the film centered on three women who have to solve the mystery of The Bat (the 1959 version, directed by Crane Wilbur, starring Vincent Price and Agnes Moorehead, followed the same plot), but when Roland West remade his version as a sound film in 1930,[19] he shifted emphasis to the male characters, who solve the mystery. West's "camera movements have a fluidity remarkable in a sound film of that era, achieved partly through the use of a gigantic scaffold 300 feet long and 30 feet high from which the suspended camera could zoom vertiginously through space, imitating the Bat's movements."[20]

Kane's other source of inspiration was *The Mark of Zorro* (Fred Niblo, 1920), starring Douglas Fairbanks Sr. Details such as entering a hidden room through an old grandfather clock, as well as the premise of a hero who pretends to be a wealthy fop but wears a mask and cape at night to bring justice to the oppressed, were inspired by *Zorro*.[21] Kane then turned to Bill Finger, who added the ears to the Bat mask to match the scalloped edge of the cape, a triangular motif that is recognizable to millions today.

Inspired by The Phantom (introduced in 1936), Finger suggested that Batman's eyes be glowing white spots behind the cowl and that the tights be gray (originally the colors we now associate with Robin were going to be Batman's colors), and instead of wings to have a flowing cape with scalloped edges that would look like wings when he moved.

This image was presented to Vin Sullivan and was immediately approved. Now the two artists needed to find a story. Finger was inspired by Alexandre Dumas' swashbuckler from *The Three Musketeers* (1844) and Sir Arthur Conan Doyle's detective Sherlock Holmes, who first appeared in 1887.

Finger was also inspired by pulp fiction, in which characters like Zorro and Tarzan had received their start, as well as The Shadow, which continued to be an inspiration, especially in its radio version. The Shadow was a wealthy playboy who had the ability to "cloud men's minds" so that they couldn't see him. Other pulp inspirations were The Spider (not the same as Spider-Man), and the Phantom Detective. Most of these in turn were inspired by *The Bat* of stage and screen (Superman was also inspired by Fairbanks in Zorro, especially his characteristic posture of arms on hips), so we can see here that a lot of cross-breeding of similar iconography was going on in the 1930s and '40s.

The early plots of Batman comics, and the first villain, Dr. Death, were inspired by many themes from the stories of Edgar Allan Poe, such as

"The Murders in the Rue Morgue," 1841 (the hideous, inhuman culprit)

"The Mystery of Marie Roget," 1842 (scientific analysis of clues)

"The Gold Bug," 1843 (the deciphering of hints ingeniously left by a criminal)

"The Black Cat," 1843 (The Insane Killer)

"Thou Art the Man," 1844 (the apparently supernatural intimidation of the guilty party)

"The Purloined Letter," 1845 (the hero's admiring assistant)

According to Les Daniels, Poe's detective, C. Auguste Dupin, also served as inspiration for Sherlock Holmes and Dick Tracy. However, Batman is probably the most famous character.[22] In turn, Batman was influenced by Dick Tracy: the style of line drawing in the comics, the gadgets, and the spectacular array of bizarre villains.

The most often-cited source of inspiration for The Joker is the joker playing card. Bob Kane even designed a new card, which showed up in the first Joker story. Bill Finger provided photos of Conrad Veidt in the German Expressionist film *The Man Who Laughs* (Fritz Lang, 1928, based on the novel by Victor Hugo). Finger's son said his father was also influenced by George C. Tilyou's Coney Island attraction, the Steeple-chase (a roller-coaster ride), which for decades featured a billboard of a man with a gigantic grin. Others said that The Joker looked like Bob Kane himself.[23]

Batman made his first official appearance in the May 1939 issue of Detective Comics (DC). Robin first appeared in April 1940; Batman's own series began in April–May 1940. The first film adaptation was the Columbia film serial *The Batman*, released in 1943.[24] Another serial, *Batman and Robin*, with thirty-one episodes, was released in 1948.[25] Batman did not return to the screen until the airing of the television series starring Adam West, from 1966 to 1968,[26] and a movie, also starring Adam West, in 1966.[27] Tim Burton's film *Batman* appeared in 1989, and his sequel, *Batman Returns*, in 1992. Burton produced the next sequel, *Batman Forever*, directed by Joel Schumacher in 1995. The series contin-ued without Burton with *Batman and Robin* (1997), also directed by Schumacher.

The success of these films spawned two animated series and several animated films: *Batman: The Animated Series* (1992–1993), a TV series directed by Kevin Altieri et al.; *Batman: Mask of the Phantasm* (1993), directed by Eric Radomski and Bruce W. Timm; *Adventures of Batman and Robin* (1994), directed by Kevin Altieri et al.; *Batman and Mr. Freeze: SubZero* (1998), directed by Boyd Kirkland; *Batman/Superman* (1998) and *Batman Beyond* (1999–2000), TV series, which spawned a movie, *Batman Beyond: The Return of the Joker* (2000).

The Warner Bros. Batman film series continued with *Catwoman* (2004), produced by Denise Di Novi, Burton's longtime associate, and starring Halle Berry. Basically, this *Catwoman* is not a sequel for the Selina Kyle character from Burton's *Batman Returns* but rather a new telling of the story. The character is named Patience Philips (Halle Berry), and the plot is the *Batman* creation story, except in *Catwoman* Patience learns that the cosmetic company she works for is selling an addictive poison in the form of face cream. To prevent her from reveal-ing this to authorities, she is murdered by the company's directors (played by Lambert Wilson and Sharon Stone) but brought back to life by feral cats. Her main goal once she is reborn is to punish and expose the company, but she also has time for some romance with Detective Tom Lone (Benjamin Bratt). In spite of a plot that adheres too closely to the overall *Batman* story (and also owes something to *The Crow*, 1994), the film holds interest because of its role reversal: Bratt's detective plays the role usually assigned to female love interests, which leads to one of the best, and most erotic, scenes in the film, in which the detective fights Catwoman without realizing she is the same woman he just spent the night with. Like *The Scorpion King* (2002), which brought a myth told until then (illogically so, given that it is set in Egypt) using all white characters, *Catwoman* expands the world of the *Batman* myth to include people of color, a long overdue step. It's a pity that Berry (and the scriptwriters, and the director, Pitof (Jean-Christophe Comar), who otherwise provide a stunning visual storyworld) could not communicate the character's deep rage, a rage that made Michelle Pfeiffer's Selina Kyle so powerful.

In spite of *Catwoman*'s poor performance at the box office, Warner Bros. is continuing the Batman franchise with *Batman Begins* (2005), directed by Christopher Nolan and starring Christian Bale as Batman. This version is based on the *Batman: Year One* comic series and shows how the boy Bruce Wayne turns himself into Batman. (Another iteration of the film, to be directed by Darren Aronofsky and scripted by Frank Miller and entitled *Batman: Year One*, was scrapped.)

One of the most amazing things about the Batman myth is how fixed the character of Batman himself has been despite the proliferation of Batman texts. Batman is always a one-man crime fighter who dresses in an iconographically specific costume (cape, cowl, and logo). He has great physical abilities enhanced by numerous incredible devices of his own invention. He maintains a secret identity. In his real life he is Bruce Wayne, a successful business tycoon and playboy who lives in Wayne Manor in Gotham. Although his creation story (the story that justifies his philosophical approach to life) wasn't written right away, once it was written it has never been altered: he chose to fight crime because his parents were killed when he was young. He has a supporting cast of costumed allies, principally Robin, but also Batwoman and Batgirl, as well as his butler, who in a sense is also costumed, because he never deviates from his role or his costume. He has a cast of costumed and fantastical enemies, indlucing The Joker, Catwoman, Penguin, Two-face, Mr. Freeze, and The Riddler. In spite of this fixity, the character has been unfailingly popular, a lightning rod for a host of cultural meanings and discourses.

It should be clear by now that Batman is a myth, with its origins not in ancient Western culture but in modern mystery stories, pulp fiction, comic books, and other films. We have seen that the characters in *Batman* are archetypes, flatter than the well-rounded characters we expect in drama, for example, and that Batman's adventures are episodic, with a focus on action, although sleuthing is also a part of it. His opponents are even less rounded than he is and equally colorful. Unlike Zorro in many of his permutations, the Batman saga does not recommend a change in how our society is structured. Batman does not use his wealth and intellect and political connections in Gotham to organize for change; rather, he works as a vigilante, taking on street thugs and organized crime on a one-on-one basis. This is part of Batman's appeal: his political philosophy does not require social systemic change; he is essentially a moral and compassionate hero, just one with a sinister side, and it is precisely this that appeals to us (whereas Superman comes across as too righteous, a problem the producers of the current television series *Smallville* have to deal with constantly). According to Les Daniels, ever since the attack on Pearl Harbor, Batman's fans have realized that the world is a very dangerous place: "For these millions [of fans], there is a certain satisfaction in imagining what it might be like to be Batman, to be alone in the dark and not afraid, because everyone else out there in the dark is even more afraid of you."[28]

Will Brooker, author of *Batman Unmasked: Analyzing a Cultural Icon,* believes that part of Batman's popularity is the result of the character's functioning as a "rigid and consistent template, which specifies not just the character's appearance but his location, associates, motivation and attributes." Yet this fixed template also functions as a "yielding, malleable figure of a man in a bat-mask": "[T]he character seems to become merely a name and logo adopted by a multitude of different 'Batmen,' each representing a different facet of a specific cultural moment and taking on the concerns of a period or the tastes of an audience."[29]

Brooker divides Batman's history into four periods, each with a focus on a particular set of cultural meanings. The first is the period of Batman's origin in World War II, in which his loner-vigilante character was established. According to Brooker, during this period Batman resisted being adapted to wartime propaganda use, unlike other superheroes such as Superman. In the 1950s Batman was given a "gay reading" by psychiatrist Fredric Wertham, a reading Brooker argues is supported as well as resisted by the texts, a reading to which Brooker himself is partial. The Batman of the 1960s, especially as manifested in the TV series, alternated between fully embracing and reviling the campiness always present in the original comic books.

Finally, there is the Batman of Tim Burton's films. Brooker doesn't analyze the film itself; rather, he gives us a historical overview of fan response to the films, using a methodology established by ethnographers Camille Bacon-Smith and Tyrone Yarbrough.[30]

Because Batman has had so many incarnations, Bacon-Smith and Yarbrough are able to divide the fan base into four groups:

1. Long-term fans of the comic books, who added the graphic novels, novelizations, and other forms of presentation to their repertoire as they appeared, and who judged not only the movie but also the mass media hype and promotional clips based on prior knowledge of the characters

2. Short-term fans with less direct experience with the primary sources (the comic books, graphic novels, etc.), who relied on word of mouth and references in the metaliterature, such as *Comics Journal* and *Comic Buyer's Guide*, and some promotional material to fill out the understanding of the *Batman* characters they bring to viewing the movie

3. Fans of the television series, who filled out their understanding of the *Batman* characters with promotional pieces on screen and in the press

4. Audiences who were not fans of Batman in any sense, but who attended because the movie was touted as an event, and who derive all of their information about the characters from word of mouth and promotional materials[31]

Fans of the TV series were initially disappointed that Adam West, the star of the '60s hit, was not recast to play Batman in the first Burton film, and many were disappointed when they found out it was not to be a comedy. Neither Bacon-Smith and Yarbrough nor Brooker really characterizes Burton's *Batman*, except to note that the film diverged in certain "key" ways from the comic books: in Burton's take, Batman is not muscular and athletic (the casting of Michael Keaton caused much outrage, especially in comic book circles); The Joker is not tall and thin; Batman and Vicki Vale actually have sex, whereas Batman in the comics is generally depicted as celibate; and The Joker is identified as the murderer of Batman's parents. Brooker says these changes are as major as if director Baz Luhrmann had had Romeo and Juliet survive at the end of his 1996 version of Shakespeare's tragedy, or Ang Lee had decided that the heroines of *Sense and Sensibility* (1995) should have a lesbian affair.[32] Although Brooker tells us what the Batman of the Warner Bros. films is not, he doesn't go as far as to tell us what this new Batman is. Perhaps that is a task best left to Burton himself:

> "There's tension and insanity," says Burton. "We're trying to say this guy is obviously nuts, but in the most appealing way possible. I go back to what I thought comic books gave people. *People love the idea that once they dress up, they can become someone else.* And here you have a human being in what I would consider the most absurd costume ever created. The villain is the Joker, the coolest of all. And also the flip side of Batman. Here you [have] a guy [Batman] who is rich, and something bad happened to him, and instead of getting therapy, he fights crime. But it's still kinda schizophrenic—it's something he questions in his own mind. And the Joker, something happened to him too, but he'll do or say ANYTHING, which is another fantasy all of us have—it's total freedom. So you've got two freaks. It's so great."
>
> The split is pure Burton: one unhappy character dresses up to express something but still feels hopelessly out of place in the real world; *another, an extremist, creates his or her own demented reality.* Burton clearly identifies with the former, but the latter—Pee-wee, Betelgeuse, the Joker—charges him up, inspires him too [emphasis mine].[33]

Burton's description of his two key characters was part of a publicity campaign to prepare audiences for a *Batman* quite different in tone from the TV shows and the original comic book series. His comments, and those of others involved in the film, were also preparing audiences for a shift from the pataphysical films he had made until then (the films so often characterized as "children's movie[s] made for grownups"), with

Some fans of the *Batman* franchise complained about the casting of Michael Keaton as Batman, but no one complained once they saw his performance.

characters that are flatter in order to enable us to project ourselves onto them instead of the other away around. Says Burton:

> "I just love characters that are symbols for things. I used to read those old folktales of lizard boy and snake girl. They were symbols. That's the great thing about the Batman story. No one is really evil; they're a mix of psychological problems.[34]

We can see this approach reflected even in a bare-bones outline of the plot of Burton's first *Batman* film.

Plot Summary of *Batman* (1989)

Act I

We first see Batman through the eyes of two petty criminals, who have robbed a couple in the same place (as we will discover later) that Batman's parents were killed many years ago. The criminals associate Batman with vampire characteristics, such as bloodsucking. Batman apprehends them and commands them to tell everyone about him.

We meet the mayor, the district attorney, and the police commissioner of Gotham City, who are overwhelmed by Carl Grissom's criminal mob, which is responsible for the city's economic decline. The mayor is trying to organize a 200th anniversary festival to help revive the city's flagging economy.

We meet mob boss Grissom and his second-in-command, Jack Napier. Grissom is worried that the police will connect him to illegal activities at Axis Chemicals. Napier suggests staging a robbery at the plant to destory the incriminating evidence. Grissom reluctantly puts Napier in charge of the operation. Napier is also having an affair with Grissom's moll, Alicia.

The police (rather belatedly, it seems) arrest the muggers that Batman had delivered to them. One of them, Lieutenant Eckhardt, is also working for Grissom. Napier arranges with Eckhardt the details of the Axis plant "robbery," but Grissom separately instructs Eckhardt to kill Napier during the break-in. We meet Elliot Knox, a reporter who is obsessed with getting the Batman story despite the ridicule of his colleagues. His cause gets a boost when Vicki Vale, a beautiful, elegant, and renowned photojournalist, pairs up with him.

Act II

Knox and Vale's first step in getting the Batman exclusive is to accost the police commissioner at a fundraiser held at Wayne Manor, home of Bruce Wayne (Batman's real identity). We meet Alfred, Wayne's butler, and Wayne for the first time. Before Knox can get any information out of him, the commissioner is called away to handle the robbery at Axis Chemicals. Alfred alerts Wayne, who has to leave Vicki just when they are getting acquainted.

At the plant, Napier finds the key evidence gone and realizes that he has been set up. He manages to kill Eckhardt before Batman catches him and escapes temporarily, only to fall into a vat of acid, where he and is left for dead.

Wayne invites Vale to dinner at the manor. Conversation is difficult at first, but Alfred saves the day, and the two end up in bed. However, Wayne can't sleep unless he is hanging upside down from a perch. In the morning, when Vale tries to make another date, Wayne puts her off.

Napier has plastic surgery and emerges as the Joker. His first official act is to kill Grissom and to establish himself as the new mob boss, with Alicia as his moll. He kills one mobster who dares to stand up to him, then lets the others go.

Vale finds out from Alfred that Wayne has been avoiding her and doesn't really have to go out of town, so she follows him to an alley (the scene of his parents' murder), where he lays red roses. She catches up to him on the steps of city hall just as one of the mobsters comes out, having laid claim to Grissom's business. As the mobster gives a press conference, the Joker and his men kill him and his gang. Wayne recognizes that the Joker is Napier and rushes home before Vale can speak to him.

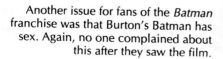
Another issue for fans of the *Batman* franchise was that Burton's Batman has sex. Again, no one complained about this after they saw the film.

The Joker plants poisoned cosmetics throughout the city and takes credit for the ensuing deaths in a series of bizarre commercials and broadcast messages. Batman works in his lab to figure out the source of the poison and ignores calls from Vale. Plans for the festival proceed. The Joker sees a picture of Vale and decides that she will be his next moll. He tricks her into meeting him at a museum by posing as Wayne, then makes a grand entrance by gassing everyone except Vale and defacing the artwork. He shows her Alicia's now ruined face, but before he can spritz Vale with acid, Batman rescues her. They make a grand escape in the Batmobile, with a chase through the city. Their way is blocked by the Joker's henchmen, and Batman fights them off. Vale takes pictures of the fight, but Batman takes the film from her after he brings her to the Batcave and gives her information about the source of the poisoned cosmetics. Alfred convinces Wayne to reveal his secret identity to Vail. Wayne goes to her apartment but finds himself tongue-tied. At that moment the Joker comes in, and there is a standoff. The Joker shoots Wayne, saying, "Did you ever dance with the devil in the pale moonlight?"—the same thing that had been said to Wayne's parents by their attacker. Wayne realizes that Napier aka the Joker is the killer of his parents. The Joker leaves Wayne for dead. When Vale regains consciousness, she realizes Wayne is gone.

Act III

In a broadcast message the Joker tells the citizens of Gotham not to cancel the festival because he will rain $20 million on the people and promises a showdown between Batman and himself. Vale and Knox learn about the murder of Wayne's parents. Vale puts two and two together and shows up at Wayne Manor to confront Wayne with the truth, and Alfred leads her to the Batcave. Vale and Batman are both relieved to have the truth out in the open, but Batman has to keep fighting the Joker and can't savor the moment. He drives the Batmobile to Axis Chemicals, where the Joker makes his poisoned gas, and blows up the plant. Meanwhile, the festival has started, and the Joker has unleashed a parade of gas-filled balloons there, killing onlookers. Vale and Knox survive by getting into a car. Batman flies down in the Batwing and takes the remaining balloons away, preventing further deaths. He then drives back to the festival in the Batmobile, but the Joker forces him to crash. Vale tries to rescue him, but the Joker takes her hostage and drags her into the cathedral. Batman follows and fights with the Joker. Each accuses the other of being responsible for what they have become. Finally, Batman pushes the Joker over a ledge, but he lands on the ledge below. He then attacks Batman and Vale, pulling them over the ledge. A helicopter approaches to rescue the Joker. Just as it seems that the Joker will get away, Batman connects a cable from a gargoyle to one of the Joker's ankles. The weight of the gargoyle causes the Joker to fall to his death. Batman and Vale fall too, but Batman uses a cable to interrupt their fall. An epilogue establishes that the city's leaders now see Batman as an ally and show the Bat-signal for the first time; Alfred takes Vale to meet Bruce Wayne, who will be "a little late." The last shot is of Batman on the rooftop admiring the Bat-signal.

Batman as a Pataphysical Film

Films like *Batman* are postmodern texts, with a heavy emphasis on intertextual references, linear plots, and slightly drawn characters, as well as special effects, high-level production design, and sound design.

Numerous intertextual references are readily visible in the film. To name only a few cinematic references, the stairwell climb at the end of the film is an homage to Alfred Hitchcock's *Vertigo* (1958). Having Napier kill one of his fellow mobsters while they are seated around a table is right out of Brian De Palma's *The Untouchables* (1987), as was Grissom's fear of being arrested because of a paper trail of evidence. The Batmobile's drive through the woods reminds us of Jack's trek through the woods in *The Nightmare Before Christmas*.

Although Batman is a comic book character, the plot of Tim Burton's *Batman* does not have the episodic feel of a comic book narrative. This is because, although myth-based and with certain fairy-tale qualities (especially in the character of Batman himself), in the multiple mix of genres that make up this particular blockbuster, the action genre is the anchor. This means that certain characteristics of the action genre will be prioritized over other genres—fantasy, horror, thriller—that are combined with it. Although the other characteristics of the high-concept blockbuster—the densely designed visual world, thinly drawn characters, and heavy reliance on visible special effects—are the same as in a pataphysical film, *Batman* is not pataphysical. For starters, *Batman*, like any good myth-movie, takes itself very seriously, with only Jack Nicholson's Joker providing a bit of black humor.

Batman Returns (1992) is a different story. Here we have a trio of characters, in outrageous outfits, with amazing gadgets, extraordinary ambition, bizarre creation stories, and deeply troubled psyches—Batman himself (Michael Keaton), the Penguin (Danny DeVito), and Catwoman (Michelle Pfeiffer). Adding to the complication, like Batman, Catwoman has a double persona that is in conflict with itself, with Batman/Bruce Wayne often at the center of that conflict. With the proliferation of leading roles there is also a multiplicity of stories, and the plot is multiheaded. Many fans count this as their favorite film in the series, in spite of the multitude of plots, probably because of the sophisticated layer of nondiegetic humor that was missing from the first instalment. On a narrative continuum with blurred boundaries, this film comes as close to being pataphysical as any other in the series, primarily because Batman and Catwoman have dual identities, each with a whole life, and their dual identities interact with each other. Most films with a complex narrative have multiple characters relating to each other at the same time, but this film has just two characters relating to each other with separate alter egos, in separate plots (which eventually come together), and simultaneously, at different levels of narration. It is this last characteristic that is the main source of the humor.

Batman Forever (1995), directed by Joel Schumacher and produced by Tim Burton, tried to replicate what was successful about *Batman Returns* by giving Batman (Val Kilmer) two enemies—Two-Face (Tommy Lee Jones) and the Riddler (Jim Carrey)—and two allies—Robin (Chris O'Donnell) and a new love interest, a psychiatrist (Nicole Kidman) who helps him understand his enemies' psyches as well as progress in his own self-healing. Although Two-Face is wonderfully conceived and created, the humor, the double entendres, and the hopping back and forth between different levels of narration seen in *Batman* are almost entirely gone in this film.

Burton did not participate in the next installment, *Batman and Robin* (1997), also directed by Schumacher. Now Batman (George Clooney) has three enemies: Mr. Freeze (Arnold Schwarzenegger), Poison Ivy (Uma Thurman), and Bane (Jeep Swenson). He also has two allies—Robin (Chris O'Donnell) and Batgirl (Alicia Silverstone). The loyal Alfred is now dying of a mysterious illness, and Mr. Freeze holds the key to the cure. With so many characters, no one is very rounded off, and the subplot between Robin and Batgirl and the backstories for Mr. Freeze and Poison Ivy make the narrative clunky and hard to follow. A layer of campy humor has crept back in (nipples on the Batsuit, anyone?), but it doesn't save a film that is widely acknowledged as a flop.

The genre of films I label pataphysical often lambaste established systems of knowledge, especially academic and scientific systems. These films follow an alternative narrative logic, closer to the logic of animation. They prioritize the graphic over the photographic (also a characteristic of animation), which leads to an emphasis on production design, costume, and special effects used in a blatant and visible way (as compared to "invisible" effects, which are meant to be read as live-action events). As I discussed in Chapter 1, pataphysical films have been made since the beginning of film history. With the separation of live-action cinema and animation into artificially isolated categories, pataphysical films faded from view, though they could be found in cartoons and avant-garde films and even the 1950s sci-fi films featuring giant insects. With the advent of postclassical Hollywood cinema and the digitization of movies, the artificial separation between animation and live-action films has come to an end. Many more recent pataphysical films, such as *Van Helsing*, are almost completely digital.

Pataphysical filmmakers are aware of this digitization process and the role that animation plays in it. They therefore make films that reflect this awareness. Burton's *Batman Returns* belongs to a specific trend or strand of pataphysical films—those based on comic books. In addition to the comic book films of the last fifteen years or so, such as *Spider-Man* (2002), *X-Men* (2000), *The League of Extraordinary Gentlemen* (2003), *Daredevil* (2003), *Hellboy* (2004), and *The Hulk* (2003), and their sequels, pataphysical films have been made by directors such as Joe Dante, Richard Donner, Henry Selick, Barry Sonnenfeld, Luc Bresson, George Lucas, Steven Spielberg, Guillermo del Toro, Roland Emmerich, Stephen Sommers, Jean-Pierre Jeunet, and Marc Caro. (Some of these films will be examined in greater depth in Chapter 7.) This doesn't mean that all comic book films are pataphysical. What makes a film pataphysical is not the source of the narrative, but how the story is told. A pataphysical film will make the audience conscious of the various levels of narration. A myth-based film will make the audience aware of the story's interstitial nature as a way of reminding spectators of its cultural importance. To put it another way, myth-based films work more like hypertexts and less like nonlinear narratives.

Films can work as hypertexts (texts that have a modular structure, where the individual modules, or lexia, can be read, or navigated, in almost any order), except that each lexia of the hypertext is actually a different media form. For the cycle started by Burton's *Batman* we find relationships, derivations, comments on, homages to, expansions of, and a variety of other texts: from the original comic books, to the films that inspired the original comic books, such as *The Mark of Zorro* and *The Man Who Laughed,* to later films such as *Metropolis* (1927), to radio shows such as *The Shadow,* to other comic book superheroes such as Superman, to Gothic horror films such as *The Bat Whispers* and the play that the film was based on, *The Circular Staircase,* to the serial film versions of *Batman,* to the 1960s television series of *Batman,* to the Frank Miller darker comic books of the 1980s, to the Prince music videos, and a miscellany of other media, trading cards, amusement rides, and so on. There is also the relationship to the ongoing cultural discourse on homosexuality and feminism.[35] Although they may not know the exact source of the reference, younger audiences especially watch films like *Batman* from a hypertextual perspective, that is, as one piece of many pieces that together form a myth cycle with almost endless permutations.

Evidence of the audience's hypertextual reading habits permeates Bacon-Smith and Yarbrough's ethnographic study:

> [T]he "raw" response of the audience with mixed expectations *and no guidance* [from film reviews] was very different from the response of later audiences. . . . Audience responses were primarily of two types: shock and intertextual recognition, with the latter being the most common.[36]

According to these researchers, audiences depended on intertextual guidance in order to know if the film was a comedy or a drama, if the Joker was frightening or humorous, the exact nature of the attraction between Batman and Vicki Vale, and even when the film ended. After reviews appeared, audiences were much less confused.[37] Comic book fans noted graphic matches between different poses adopted by Jack Nicholson's Joker and drawings of the Joker in comic books.[38] They also noted purloining from other comic books, such as Batman's straight-backed stance at the end of the film, more reminiscent of Superman than Batman's traditional gargoyle-like crouch.

Bacon-Smith and Yarbrough note that some of this intertextual reading is an aspect of "rehabilitation":

Fans, because they are fans, want to like the products that feature their interest. When the product falls short of fulfilling the fans' needs, viewers make use of an extreme form of traditional fill-in-the-blanks interpretation. Rather than fill in the action with what the movie has led them to assume would be there, fans substitute plot twists that change the meaning of the on-screen evidence.[39]

But the primary intertext for fans and nonfans alike is the publicity that precedes the viewing of the film, especially if the film is constructed as an event, as most comic book films of the last fifteen years have been. They are events because they are bringing beloved texts to the big screen, thus legitimizing them, promising to extend their textual life, and also threatening to alter them beyond recognition, because the films are almost always blockbusters; and because the films are either myth-based or pataphysical—with all that such films entail, especially the heavy reliance on "cool" special effects and the promise of a philosophical perspective, with its attendant zinging one-liners, that satirizes the status quo. Bacon-Smith and Yarbrough conclude with a very interesting appendix that lists audience's moment-by-moment intertextual and textual responses to *Batman*.[40] What their analysis reveals is that intertextual responses dominate the opening third of the film, and that the greatest textual response is elicited by Jack Nicholson's incarnation of The Joker. It is the fans' desire to make sure they catch as many of the intertextual references as possible that leads them to watch the film again and again and contribute to the film's runaway success. The film itself encourages this intertextual reading by gradually revealing its variations on classic Batman elements: we don't see the Batcave until halfway through Act II, the Batmobile even later than that, and the Batwing last of all. This is in contrast to a typical episode from the 1960s TV series, which trotted out all the gadgets early and often.

With the advent of pataphysical films, it would seems that the unifying idea of a "high-concept film" is eroding. Yes, *Batman* is high concept—a brooding, almost schizophrenic, Batman keeping watch over a dark, seamy, and corrupt Gotham, unredeemed by love but kept alive by the very devotion from which he distances himself. It has certain elements in common with a pataphysical film, with its emphasis on techno-science and graphics, from the comic book graphic matches to Anton Furst's set design to Batman's elaborate costume to the digital effects, and its thin, episodic plot that serves as a series of pointers to other texts. But the plot is linear, the relationships are straightforward, and the levels of narration are not played with; instead, there is an emphasis on hyper-textuality, which is the opposite of pataphysical. This emphasis on hypertextuality makes it easier for the film to work as a key cog in a merchandising machine.

These hypertextual links work in both directions: both to media that preceded the film and to media and other objects that come after it. In addition to sequels, the same story or cycle of stories will take on a life in other ancillary markets, such as television, computer games, and theme parks.

Ancillary Marketing, Synergy, Conglomerates, and Total Merchandising in *Batman*

Twenty years ago it was common that a hit film, or even a moderately successful film, like the original *Buffy the Vampire Slayer* (1992), led to a successful spin-off TV series. Because Batman was already a well-estab-lished myth, we have a TV series that preceded the film (the 1960s TV series starring Adam West) and various animated TV series that followed. Burton's *Batman* started the trend of producing movies based on old TV shows.

The '60s TV series had started out being fairly faithful to the hero of the comic books, but it soon deviated from them and began to take on its own look and rhythm. Probably the most unique thing about the TV show was its pop-art look, with psychedelic colors and dialogue balloons that spelled out sound effects. According to Lorenzo Semple, a writer on the TV series, "We [appealed] on two levels, to kids and grown-ups. On a sophisticated level the appeal [came] from inherent juvenility."

In his review of the music videos made by Prince for Burton's *Batman*, Armond White[41] argues that Burton's films have lost this subversive and anarchic element, both by dropping the pop-art approach and by being part of a corporate enterprise. White much prefers the Prince music videos, such as the "Partyman" video, in which Prince is the master of revels at The Joker's party, or Prince's songs from *Batman,* each one done in the voice of a different character, with a sampling of dialogue from the film. Though the Prince music videos are part of the film's ancillary marketing, they also comment on the film from which they are derived.

The success of *Batman* and its ancillary marketing has led to a new era, not just of ancillary marketing as a by-product of synergy, but of total merchandising on a global basis.

Most of the seismic shifts that shook the industrial landscape during the 1980s can be understood in terms of synergy, a concept that took on enormous importance in Hollywood during this period. Definitions of synergy include "the commercial possibilities of mutually locking commercial ventures,"[42] "tight diversification,"[43] and "a belief that one plus one could equal three."[44] More specifically, the *Harvard Business Review* outlined various aspects of synergy as follows: "In business usage, synergy refers to the ability of two or more units or companies to generate greater working value working together than they could working apart."

Most business synergies take one of six forms:

1. Shared know-how: sharing knowledge or skills by sharing information, documents, or manuals, or simply by getting together two groups of people with different skills.
2. Shared tangible resources: sharing physical assets or resources, such as a manufacturing facility or a lab. (Consider, for example, the relationship between George Lucas productions and ILM: companies that have to outsource their special effects cannot compete with Lucas because he gets his at cost.)
3. Pooled negotiating power: a recent example is the coordinated efforts of the Writers Guild of America and the Screen Actors Guild—when they proposed to strike together, the industry had to pay attention; when one guild decided not to strike, negotiations with the other was concluded quickly.
4. Coordinated strategies: having different companies or different parts of companies coordinate their response to shared competitors and so on. This balance is hard to achieve—and hard to distinguish from price setting or monopolistic practices.
5. Combined business creation: mergers and conglomerates practice this form of synergy. This is especially important in understanding contemporary Hollywood.

6. Vertical integration: defined as coordinating the flow of products or services from one unit to another.[45]

Point 5, linking synergy and the conglomerates, is crucial in understanding the industrial structure that made *Batman* and other blockbusters appealing. The conglomerate, a meta-company formed through a large company merging, taking over, and/or acquiring other companies, became a standard form of industrial organization after World War II. Tino Balio defines the conglomerate as "a diversified company with major interests in several unrelated fields of endeavor."[46] Of course, many media conglomerates now limit their diversification to several related fields of endeavor, especially different distribution channels for their product. Media conglomerates that own a film studio buy up not only theaters to distribute their films (reversing the Paramount Decrees[47] in the laissez-faire political atmosphere of the 1980s), but also cable TV channels, video and DVD distributors, book publishers for novelizations and behind-the-scenes books, and music companies to distribute soundtracks, then make licensing deals with toy companies, fast-food restaurants, computer game manufacturers, and so on.

In 1989, when *Batman* was released, 414 corporate deals were struck, totaling over $42 billion, the most notable of which were the Time-Warner merger ($14 billion) and Sony's acquisition of Columbia and CBS Records ($5.4 billion). Six vertically integrated multinational conglomerates engulf what we used to call the Hollywood studios, and the economy has undergone corresponding sets of shifts—from regulatory to deregulatory, liberal to conservative, and national to global capitalism/markets.[48]

The stakes in the film business have also become increasingly global, and with the industrial blueprint implemented during the 1980s, a new period ("post-Hollywood"?) has certainly begun.

In this global market, merchandising tie-ins have become increasingly important. If we want to look at how the total merchandising approach came about, the place to start is Disney. According to a 1962 *Newsweek* article, Disney hit on the total merchandising approach rather by accident, when the *Davy Crockett* TV series first aired in 1954. The *Crockett* phenomenon was relatively unplanned. At first, Disney made only a three-part television series in the fall of 1954, but the success of the series led to a feature movie, another TV series, and one of the most spectacular merchandising campaigns in history. Records, toy rifles, and buckskin jackets blanketed the country. In three short months, for example, the huge demand for coonskin caps pushed the price of coonskins from 25 cents to $3 each.[49]

After *Crockett*, total merchandising became Disney's standard approach to film marketing. Roy Disney, Walt's brother and financial mentor, noted that "once a decision is made to make a picture, the marketing starts. All of the moves are geared to publicizing the final product, and making money while you do it."[50] An example of Disney's early approach to total merchandising was the animated feature *The Sword in the Stone,* released in 1963. The film took four years to make, cost $4 million, but was expected to bring in returns almost indefinitely. The plan was for the merchandising to begin four months before the release date, when the first comic books and hard-cover books appeared. Then sheet music was printed, records were pressed, and songs from the movie soon were heard on the radio. At the same time, King Features released a comic strip, based on the movie, in one hundred newspapers. It was planned that six national manufacturers would use short scenes from the movie in TV ads for their products. The first signed manufacturer was a maker of Christmas tree lights, whose advertising would reach its peak just before the movie's premiere.

Disney took a synergistic approach to promoting the film. The plan was as follows: As release time approached, Walt Disney himself would plug the film in the end spot of his weekly *Wonderful World of Color* show. The afternoon show, *The Mickey Mouse Club,* aimed solely at children, would also find frequent occasions to refer to the movie. Shortly after the *Sword* premiere, some feature of the movie would be installed as part of the Disneyland theme parks. Finally, throughout the promotion, some one hundred manufacturers would be hawking merchandise. Arrangements were made for licensing items in fifty-six categories, ranging from masks to Arthurian shoe polish, underwear, and umbrellas. Each feature was designed to promote every other feature.

From the U.S.-based synergistic approach Disney used with *The Sword in the Stone* in 1963, total merchandising went global. The term *total merchandising* itself was generally adopted after George Lucas reduced his director's fee for *Star Wars* by $500,000 in exchange for the film's merchandising rights. The press at the time referred to it as "the biggest mistake ever made in Hollywood." But in the end *Star Wars* merchandise had grossed $5 billion. The studio executives who cut the deal thought they were in the movie business, but Lucas knew better. He was operating in the global entertainment economy. *Star Wars* was both a cultural phenomenon and a new business model, spawning T-shirt sales, computer games, and amusement park rides, along with the inevitable sequels.[51]

In a 1999 episode of *That's Entertainment,* Jay Carr referred to *Star Wars* as "one giant infomercial [that] set[s] up on screen all the stuff to be sold—posters, action figures, electronic games." In the same episode Mark Simpkin noted that the total merchandising return from the *Star Wars* films was $6.5 billion, twice as much as the series to date had made at the box office. Nancy Hass (a scholar from New York University) noted that entertainment "becomes something that infiltrates every level of your life—the scenery of your life—whether it be billboards or video games or the pencils you buy for your kids."[52]

Eileen Meehan has explored the role that economics plays in the formation of texts and intertexts in American culture. According to Meehan,

> corporate imperatives operate as the primary constraints shaping the narratives and iconography of the text as well as the manufacture and licensing of the intertextual materials necessary for a "mania" to sweep the country. This is not a claim that evil moguls force us to buy Bat-chains . . . rather, the claim here is that mass-produced culture is a business, governed by corporate drives for profit, market control, and transindustrial integration. . . . [T]he decision to create a movie is a business decision about the potential profitability of a cinematic product. Further, as film studios have been either acquired by companies outside the industry or have themselves acquired companies in other entertainment/information industries, decisions about movies are increasingly focused on the potential profitability of a wide range of products. The film per se becomes only one component in a product line that extends beyond the theater, even beyond our contact with mass media, to penetrate the markets for toys, bedding, trinkets, cups and the other minutiae comprising one's everyday life inside a commoditized, consumerized culture.[53]

One aspect of this economically driven culture is "recycling," for example, having a music sequence in the film double as a music video. What exactly will be recycled depends on what other kinds of companies make up part of the film conglomerate's holdings. According to Meehan, Warner Communications Inc. (WCI) acquired Detective Comics in 1971 as a source of licensing revenues and materials. WCI had tested the practice with *Superman* and its sequels and was ready to give *Batman* the same treatment, using the director who had already made a success of *Pee-wee's Big Adventure* and *Beetlejuice* for them. The first step toward the intertextual promotion of *Batman* was to release *The Dark Knight Returns*, first in comic book form and then as a book. *Dark Knight* was aimed at an adult audience, and with its success the process of audience building for a darker Batman continued with *Batman: Year One*, aimed at a younger audience. In 1988 WCI let readers vote on whether Robin should be killed or not; they voted for his death via a 900 number. Information on the audience was gathered from Marvel Comics, which described the average reader as a twenty-year-old male spending $10 a week on comics. Further advertising was obtained by articles in the press about the casting of key parts, which often elicited fan responses. The use of Prince songs and the attendant music videos was designed to reach middle-class white women, although Prince's music succeeded in crossing over to a black audience.[54]

Interestingly, despite *Batman*'s high earnings ($40 million in its first weekend), WCI was not sure that the images from the new film would sell, and so some of the merchandising followed the appearance of the characters in the comics and the '60s TV series. They needn't have worried: total merchandising can often bring in profits where a movie itself fails, as pointed out by E! newsreporter Ken Neville:

> In this day and age of nonstop commercialization, it was bound to happen: Inch-and-a-half plastic action figures have outperformed the big stars and big effects from the big-screen movie on which they were based.
> Recently released toy-industry estimates put the total merchandising take for tie-ins to *Batman & Robin* to be between $125 million and $160 million by year's end. Just take the total box office of the film, which petered out at $105 million after a huge opening weekend, add in Arnold Schwarzenegger's salary and the special-effects budget, and you're there.
> According to the Toy Manufacturers Association, the total take for action figures in '97 could reach $1.2 billion, a whopping 40 percent increase over last year's take. And with a new animated series on the WB network this fall, Bat-toy sales stand poised to continue strongly.[55]

What the sale of action figures, even with a lackluster box office, points to, is an increase in audiences' interactive engagement with myth cycles, even as the type of engagement is market-driven. What inch-and-a-half-tall action figures provide that the films themselves do not is the ability for the spectator to collaborate in the development and outcome of the story; the film now becomes a game. The exposition is provided by the film and ancillary media, such as television (even television ads), comic books, and print (it is now a normal part of marketing procedure for film novelizations, graphic novels, and how-to books on the animation and special effects to be released even before the movie itself comes out). Arcade, console, and computer games are now often produced in tandem with a film in order to satisfy this need. *Star Wars Episode I: The Phantom Menace* (1999) released no fewer than four computer games along with the movie, with the following language on the packaging:

LIVE THE SAGA. Take part in the epic events from the STAR WARS: Episode I story—and beyond.[56]

Some critics bemoan the fact that episodes like the pod-racing sequence in *Phantom Menace* were put there as a product placement for the computer games. And, in the age of total merchandising, it does seem that blockbuster movies are simply one long commercial for ancillary and merchandising product. However, as Janet Murray, one of the first writers to try to articulate the characteristics of interactive narrative, has noted, "Historically, spectacle tends to move toward participatory narrative in order to retain our attention, to lengthen the immersive experience."[57] Interactive narratives aim to satisfy two spectator desires: the desire for interactivity and the desire for immersiveness. A computer game can satisfy the desire for interactivity, but immersiveness is limited when all you have is the frame on your TV set.

For example, *Batman: The Animated Series* first aired in 1991. Unlike the earlier series, which had been made on an extremely low budget and was ghettoized in Saturday morning cartoon land, this series was well funded and well animated, and the actors were high-quality, recognizable names. In this series, Batman is now in his eighties, but he is training Robin to take over his role as the Caped Crusader. The series got new life with a computer game available for the Nintendo and Playstation2 consoles, using the same actors for voicing and the same animation look and style as the television show.

Throughout the history of cinema, movies have courted immersiveness in the form of wide screen and 3-D technologies, the most recent being Omnimax. But the most immersive form currently available is the theme park ride. Burton himself is aware of the importance of immersiveness, as part of his deal with super-agent Michael Ovitz when he moved from the William Morris Agency to Creative Arts Agency in 1992 was that he would get to design a theme park ride as well as a line of computer software.[58] Although Burton ended up returning to William Morris, he did design a ride for Disneyland based on *The Nightmare Before Christmas,* which is overlaid on the Haunted Mansion ride every fall.

Theme park rides don't offer spectators the kinds of choices and sense of control over the narrative that computer games do, but they do offer an almost complete visual and tactile immersion, an interpenetration of the worlds on and off screen, often achieved by using a combination of haptics (shaking floors, controls for the user to manipulate, etc.), 3-D or large 2-D visuals (the screen completely surrounds you), and live action (live actors play the screen characters and interact with spectators). Spectators in these theme park rides are often included in the narrative in some minimal way, even when they are waiting in line.

These developments have led scholar Thomas Schatz to argue that "the vertical integration of classical Hollywood, which ensured a closed industrial system and a coherent narrative, has given way to 'horizontal integration' of the New Hollywood's tightly diversified media conglomerates, which favours texts strategically 'open' to multiple readings and multimedia reiteration."[59]

Geoff King, one of the analysts of the blockbuster phenomenon, has pointed out that narrative in the blockbuster was always relatively "open," that is, loosely plotted.[60] As we have seen, Batman was a myth born of our times, with some of the accoutrements of earlier myth stories such as Superman and Zorro, but one that seems to remake himself over and over again to suit different audience needs while keeping his basic attributes intact.

Audiences have always loved to participate in the stories that really mattered to them, whether it was through fan activity, such as online chat rooms, playing with action figures, or simply wearing a Batman T-shirt.

What we have seen with Burton's *Batmans* is that high-concept films, especially blockbusters, are no longer stand-alone entities. Their meaning cannot be deduced solely from the text itself; audiences have to be clued in via other media, and in fact, this is part of the pleasure of the text, putting all of the pieces together, even if that requires repeat viewing. The experience does not end with this hypertextual mode of reading: for some portions of the audience, an interactive level of engagement will be added in the form of board games, action figures, computer games, fan-based discourse formats such as chat rooms, and theme park rides. Cinematic narrative seems to be turning in a new direction, a direction that focuses more on a mixture of immersiveness and interactivity. Like the pataphysical format, this is another alternative to classically driven narrative.

Notes

1. David Handelman, "Heart and Darkness: Even as the New, Improved *Batman* Sequel Continues His Unbroken String of Hits, Tim Burton Insists He's Not Cut Out to Be a Director," *Vogue*, July 1992, pp. 142–194.

2. Quoted in Kristine McKenna, interview with Tim Burton, *Playboy*, August 2001, p. 66.

3. Justin Wyatt, *High Concept: Movies and Marketing in Hollywood* (Austin: University of Texas Press, 1994), p. 13.

4. Started his Hollywood career as assistant to Barry Diller at Paramount Pictures (1975–1979), became President of Production under Michael Eisner. Followed Eisner to Disney in 1984 where he was CEO. Eisner fired him in 1994, and he then co-founded Dreamworks SKG with Spielberg and Geffen.

5. Steel is quoted in Justin Wyatt, *High Concept: Movies and Marketing in Hollywood* (Austin: University of Texas Press), 1994, pp. 9–10.

6. Ibid., pp. 8–13.

7. Ibid., p. 28.

8. Ibid., p. 31.

9. Ibid., pp. 49–50.

10. Ibid., p. 55.

11. Handelman, "Heart and Darkness," pp. 142–194.

12. Joseph Campbell, *The Hero with a Thousand Faces* (Princeton: Princeton Univesrity Press), 1972.

13. John Truby (www.truby.com) and Robert McKee (mckeestory.com) are Hollywood's two hottest screenwriting gurus.

14. Chris Vogler, *The Writer's Journey: Mythic Structure for Storytellers and Screenwriters* (Culver City, CA: Michael Weise Film Productions), 1992.

15. Hillary de Vries, "Ready or Not, It's Back to Tim Burton's World," *Los Angeles Times*, June 14, 1992.

16. Ibid.

17. Les Daniels, *Batman: The Complete History* (San Francisco: Chronicle Books, 1999), p. 18.

18. The first film adaptation of Rinehart's play was *The Bat* (1915/Selig Polyscope Co.), 5 reels, BW, silent, also known as *The Circular Staircase*, directed by Edward J. La Saint and

produced by William Selig, starring Eugene Besserer, Stella Razeto, Guy Oliver, and Edith Johnson. Then came Roland West's version *The Bat* (1926/Feature Prod./UA) 88 mins., BW, silent, directed by Roland West and produced by Julien Josephson, with a screenplay by Avery Hopwood and Mary Roberts Rinehart. Cinematography by Arthur Edeson; art direction by William Cameron Menzies.

From the novel *The Circular Staircase* by Mary Roberts Rinehart and the play *The Bat*, produced by Wagenhals and Kemper.

Cast: Tullio Carminatti, Sojin Kamiyama, Lee Shumway, Louis Fazenda, Emily Fitzroy, Jack Pickford, Charles Herzinger, Andre De Beranger, Jewel Carmen, Eddie Gribbon, Arthur Houseman, Robert McKim.

19. *The Bat Whispers* (1930/Art Cinema/UA), 88 mins., BW.

Credits: written and directed by Roland West; produced by Joseph M. Schenck, Douglas B. Murray, and Roland West; cinematography by Ray June, Robert Planck (65 mm version), and Charles Cline; edited by James Smith; designed by Paul Roe Crawley. Based on *The Circular Staircase* by Mary Roberts Rinehart and the play *The Bat*, produced by Wagenhals and Kemper.

Cast: Chester Morris, Una Merkel, Chance Ward, Grace Hampton, Gustav von Seyffertitz, Ben Bard, Maude Eburne, DeWitt Jennings, William Bakewell, Spencer Charters, Richard Tucker, Wilson Benge, Sidney D'Albrook, S. E. Jennings, Hugh Huntley, Charles Bow Clark.

20. See the Milestone Films Website at www.milestonefilms.com/pdf/batwhispers.pdf.

21. *The Mark of Zorro* (1920), 8 reels, B&W, directed by Fred Niblo.

Cast: Douglas Fairbanks Sr., Marguerite De La Motte, Noah Beery, Robert McKim, Charles Hill Mailes, Claire McDowell, George Periolat, Walt Whitman, Sidney De Grey, Tote du Crow, Noah Beery Jr., Charles Belcher, Albert McQuarrie, Charles Stevens, John Winn, Gilbert Clayton. Produced by Douglas Fairbanks Sr. Scenario by Eugene Miller, from an adaptation by Elton Thomas (Douglas Fairbanks Sr.) of the story "The Curse of Capistrano" by Johnston McCulley. Art direction by Edward Langley. Assistant director Theodore Reed. Cinematography by William McGann and Harry Thorpe.

22. Daniels, *Batman*, p. 31.

23. Ibid., p. 40.

24. *The Batman* (1943/Columbia), 30 reels, BW, 15 episodes (re-released in 1966 as *An Evening with Batman and Robin*).

Credits: directed by Lambert Hillyer; produced by Rudolph C. Flothow; screenplay by Victor McLeod, Leslie Swabacker, and Harry Fraser; director of photography James Brown Jr.; edited by Dwight Caldwell and Earl Turner; music by Lee Zahler.

Based on the comic book character created by Bob Kane.

Cast: Lewis Wilson, Douglas Croft, J. Carrol Naish, William Austin, Shirley Patterson, Eddie Parker, Charles Middleton, Gus Glassmire.

Batman (Wilson), and his assistant, Robin (Croft), battle the evil Dr. Daka (Naish), a Japanese gangster preparing the way for a Japanese invasion of America by using a unique machine that turns people into zombie slaves.

In 1965 this serial was edited as a four-hour feature titled *An Evening with Batman and Robin* to cash in on the renewed popularity of the Caped Crusader.

25. *Batman and Robin* (1948), 31 reels. BW, 15 episodes. Also known as *The Return of Batman and Robin, The New Adventures of Batman and Robin*.

Credits: directed by Spencer Gordon Bennet; produced by Sam Katzman; screenplay by George H. Plympton, J. F. Poland, and Royal K. Cole; director of photography Ira H. Morgan; edited by Dwight Caldwell and Earl Turner; music by Mischa Bakaleinikoff.

Cast: Robert Lowery, Rick Vallin, Lyle Talbot, Eddie Parker, John Duncan, Leonard Penn, Jane Adams, Ralph Graves, Don Harvey.

Batman (Lowery) and Robin (Duncan) are assigned by Police Commissioner Gordon (Talbot) to battle the Wizard (Penn), who can control cars and planes from a distance with a stolen, top-secret remote control device. The Wizard goes on to steal the Neutraliser, which, when used in conjunction with the remote control device, creates a zone of invisibility that allows him to commit further crimes.

26. *Batman*, TV series, directed by Robert Butler et al., ABC, January 1966–March 1968, 120 30-minute episodes shot on color film. Starring Adam West as Bruce Wayne/Batman, Burt Ward as Dick Grayson/Robin, the Boy Wonder, Madge Blake as Aunt Harriet Cooper (seasons 1–2), Yvonne Craig as Barbara Gordon/Batgirl (season 3), William Dozier as the narrator (also the series producer), Neil Hamilton as Commissioner Gordon, Byron Keith as Mayor Linseed, David Lewis as Warden Crichton, Alan Napier as Alfred Pennyworth, and Stafford Repp as Chief O'Hara.

27. *Batman* (1966), 105 min., color, directed by Leslie H. Martinson. Also known as *Batman: The Movie* (1966). Starring Adam West as Bruce Wayne/Batman; Burt Ward as Dick Grayson/Robin; Lee Meriwether as Catwoman/Comrade Kitanya "Kitka" Irenya Tantanya Karenska Alisof; Cesar Romero as the Joker; Burgess Meredith as the Penguin; Frank Gorshin as the Riddler; Alan Napier as Alfred Pennyworth; Neil Hamilton as Commissioner Gordon; Stafford Repp as Chief O'Hara; Madge Blake as Aunt Harriet Cooper.

28. Daniels, *Batman*, p. 201.

29. Will Brooker, *Batman Unmasked: Analyzing a Cultural Icon* (London and New York: Continuum, 2000), p. 39.

30. Camille Bacon-Smith with Tyrone Yarbrough, "Batman: The Ethnography," in *The Many Lives of The Batman: Critical Approaches to a Superhero and His Media*, ed. Roberta E. Pearson and William Uricchio (New York: Routledge, 1991), pp. 90–116.

31. Ibid., p. 91.

32. Brooker, p. 290.

33. David Edelstein, "Mixing Beetlejuice," *Rolling Stone*, June 2, 1988, p. 51.

34. De Vries, "Ready or Not."

35. This way of reading nondiegetic codes is not new. In fact, much feminist analysis has consisted of reading nondiegetic codes—also referred to as moments of excess—in classic Hollywood films. Take, for example, *All About Eve* (1950), starring Bette Davis, which contains both a story and comments on that story as it is told. See also the discussion on *Now Voyager* in Stanley Cavell's *Contesting Tears: The Hollywood Melodrama of the Unknown Woman* (Chicago: University of Chicago Press, 1996).

36. Bacon-Smith and Yarbrough, "Batman," p. 97 (my emphasis).

37. Ibid., p. 98.

38. Bacon-Smith and Yarbrough quote comic book artist Martin King: "I kept getting images templated over [Jack Nicholson] of comic book images . . . 'That's a Jim Aparo Joker drawing.' I shake my head and there's a Brian Bollan. Nicholson's amazing, he's all Jokers in one." Ibid., p. 103.

39. Ibid. p. 105.

40. Ibid., pp. 112–115.

41. Armond White, "Prince of the City" *Film Comment*, vol 25:6 November–December 1989.

42. Wyatt, *High Concept*, p. 70.

43. Thomas Schatz, "The Return of the Hollywood Studio System," in *Conglomerates and the Media,* ed. Erik Barnouw et al. (New York: The New Press, 1997), p. 84.

44. Tino Balio, " 'A Major Presence in All the World's Important Markets': The Globalization of Hollywood in the 1990s," *Contemporary Hollywood Cinema,* edited by Steven Neale and Murray Smith (London and New York: Routledge), 1998, p. 61.

45. Michael Goold, Andrew Campbell, "Desperately Seeking Synergy," *Harvard Business Review*, September–October 1998, p. 133.

46. Tim Balio, *The American Film Industry*, (Chicago: University of Wisconsin Press), 1985, p. 439.

47. The Paramount Decrees refer to the Paramount anti-trust case decision that took effect in 1948, the result of a Federal directive to all the major studios (not just Paramount) to break up their near-monopoly hold on film exhibition and to stop unfair trade practices such as blind selling, block booking and price fixing.

The aim of the Paramount anti-trust case was to protect small film businesses against the large studios, to allow more free market competition, and increase consumer choice. The case was initiated in 1938, but only became law in 1948. It then took the studios another 10 years to sell off their theatres, spelling the end of the classical Hollywood studio system, because the lack of an automatic exhibition space for films radically altered the industrial organization of filmmaking.

48. Calvin Sims, " 'Synergy': The Unspoken Word: New Bidding War Has Old Rationale 'Synergy': The Word Left Unspoken in 90's Bidding War," *New York Times*: October 5, 1993, p. D1.

49. "All of the Moves Are Geared to Publicizing . . . and Making Money," *Newsweek*, December 1962, pp. 48–51.

50. Ibid.

51. *That's Entertainment*, Australian Broadcasting Corporation, transcript of March 6, 1999, see http://www.abc.net.au/lateline/stories/s27923.htm.

52. Ibid.

53. Eileen R. Meehan, " 'Holy Commodity Fetish, Batman!' The Political Economy of a Commercial Intertext," in Person and Vricchio, *The Many Lives of The Batman*, p. 48.

54. Ibid., pp. 52–54.

55. Ken Neville, "'Batman' Toys Outperform Movie," *E! Online News*, August 25, 1997. See http://www.eonline.com/News/Items/0,1,1665,00.html.

56. Geoff King, *Spectacular Narratives: Hollywood in the Age of the Blockbuster* (London and New York: IB Tauris Publishers, 2000), p. 175.

57. Janet Murray, *Hamlet on the Holodeck* (New York: The Free Press, 1997), p. 112.

58. N/A "Art of the Steal" *Variety*, March 23, 1992.

59. Thomas Schatz, "The New Hollywood," *Movie Blockbusters,* edited by Julian Stringer (New York and London: Routledge, 2003), p. 40. Originally printed in *Film Theory Goes to the Movies*, edited by Jim Collins, Hilary Radner, and Ava Preacher Collins (New York and London: Routledge, 1993), pp. 8–36.

60. King, *Spectacular Narratives,* p. 188.

$$5$$

BURTON'S REIMAGININGS:
ED WOOD, PLANET OF THE APES, AND *CHARLIE AND THE CHOCOLATE FACTORY*

Ed Wood

With *Ed Wood* (1994), Burton shifted from pataphysical films, myth-based blockbusters, and animation to a new genre: the biopic.[1] The director Edward D. Wood Jr. is the perfect subject of a Burton biopic because Wood himself was a pataphysical filmmaker, like Burton, and a social outcast, like many of Burton's characters. Although the film made back only a fraction of its $18 million budget, many Burton enthusiasts consider it his best work. The film was shot in black and white by Stefan Czapsky, who had also shot *Edward Scissorhands* and *Batman Returns*. (Burton chose to shoot it in black and white to mimic Wood's own films.) Although it seemed tailor-made for him, Burton did not originate the project; rather, screenwriters Scott Alexander and Larry Karaszewski first brought a treatment to producer Denise Di Novi. Burton in turn asked for a script, which Alexander and Karaszewski wrote in six weeks; Burton liked it so much that he passed on *Mary Reilly* (1996) to do *Ed Wood* instead.[2] The writers credit Rudolph Grey's book *Nightmare of Ecstasy* (1992), a collection of accounts on Ed Wood, some rather contradictory. Burton liked the fact that not much was known about Wood, so that he wouldn't be hampered by a lot of well-known anecdotes. What was most important to him was that Wood, and everyone who worked with him, did everything with passion.[3]

The decision to shoot the film in black and white led Columbia Pictures to drop the project, but fortunately Disney picked it up. (Disney was hoping that Burton would stay with them, but he ended up returning to Warner Bros.) The film is actually shot on black-and-white stock and lit for monochrome, which gives it a real period look. It is also the only film Burton has directed since *Pee-wee* in which Danny Elfman did not provide a score, as the two had a falling out that was repaired in time for *Mars Attacks!* The honor went to Howard Shore, who used some themes from Ed Wood's own films for certain moments in the Burton film.

The movie is a loving look at Wood (played by Johnny Depp), the director of such B-movie classics as *Glen or Glenda* (1953), *Bride of the Monster* (1955), and *Plan 9 From Outer Space* (1959), hailed as some of the worst movies ever made. It also covers Wood's transvestism, his social circle which included transvestites; and his relationship with the aging, down-on-his-luck Bela Lugosi (played by Martin Landau, who won an Oscar for his performance). However, the film does not depict what being a transvestite meant to Wood, which he himself had explored in his novels *Killer in Drag* (1965) and *Death of a Transvestite* (1967). (*Glen or Glenda* proved to be autobiographical to a certain extent.)

Instead, the film focuses on Wood's emotional relationship with his work, as Wood himself depicted it in his guide to wannabe actors and filmmakers, *The Hollywood Rat Race*.[4] He was an avid salesman, wholly committed to his films, but his movies were bad, enough to be labeled "the worst films of all time." One reviewer sums up the value of Wood's efforts as follows:

> Still, at his best (which is to say, at his worst), Wood's mysterious illogic deforms the simplest narrative clichés so absolutely that you're forced to consider them anew. As the big lie of chronology is confounded by Wood's

Ed Wood making art out of the cheesiest special effects in *Ed Wood*. Burton saw *Mars Attacks!* as the film Ed Wood would have made if he had had the budget.

imperfect continuity, so the nature of screen acting is foregrounded by cloddish bits of business, the notion of originality undermined by the interpolation of library footage.[5]

Other authors, such as Ken Hanke, have made much of the psychobiographical elements in *Ed Wood*. The screenwriters did insert certain elements (such as gargoyles) that they thought Burton would approve of; Burton instead ended up taking most of these out. What does seem to be the appeal for Burton is Wood's love for what he did, his sense of self-definition by vocation. Burton has noted that "any of my movies could go either way, they really could, and so the line between success and failure is a very thin one. . . . [W]ho knows, I could become Ed Wood tomorrow."[6]

The emotional thread that runs through the story is Wood's relationship with Lugosi, although we also see the end of his relationship with Dolores Fuller (Sarah Jessica Parker) and the beginning of his relationship with Kathy O'Hara (Patricia Arquette), whom he later married. To preserve the focus on the relationship between Wood and Lugosi, certain details are omitted, such as the short marriages each of them had around this time. The meeting between Orson Welles and Wood is fiction, and it is not clear how Wood came to replace Dolores Fuller with Loretta King in *Bride of the Monster*. Lugosi had large dogs, not chihuahuas, and *Plan 9 From Outer Space* never had a theatrical run in Los Angeles, much less a premiere in a full Pantages theater, but otherwise the film sticks fairly closely to the facts.

Although Wood made some pataphysical films, this biopic is not pataphysical. Because it is based on facts, it is not a fairy tale, although Wood's story certainly has some fairy-tale elements. Although Wood has become a mythic figure, the story isn't structured as a myth, as Wood is never shown to have learned anything about himself. In fact, Burton has

Johnny Depp as Ed Wood, with a poster
for Wood's film *Bride of the Monster*.
From Burton's film *Ed Wood*.

noted that part of what attracted him to the character was Wood's passion and optimism, and the way they spill over into delusional denial.[7] Hoberman argues that the film canonizes Wood, but if anything, the film romanticizes the unrealistic, unheeding, undying love of filmmaking. Wood's eccentricities are depicted as the necessary accoutrements of his filmmaking passion.

In *Ed Wood* Burton seems to be moving away from pataphysical films. Although the movie was well reviewed and won numerous awards, it did miserably at the box office, and to date Burton has not tried to make another art house film. After *Ed Wood,* he made a committed move toward myth-based films, completing a transition begun with *Batman*.

Planet of the Apes

In Chapter 4, I discussed the *Batman* myth cycle. With *Planet of the Apes* (2001), Burton undertook a "reimagining," by adding his entry to the myth cycle initiated by Pierre Boulle's novel of the same title. At the time of the film's release, it was touted as neither an adaptation nor a remake, but rather as a new addition to a collection of stories revolving around a similar theme. *Planet of the Apes* represents a departure for Burton. Although it is part of a myth cycle, like *Batman,* it is not a fairy tale, nor is it a horror story (although the original novel is certainly horrific and the material could have easily lent itself to horror had it been handled differently); the International Movie Data Base (IMDb) classifies it as "action/adventure/sci-fi." Like many old-fashioned sci-fi films, it has some of the qualities of a morality tale, and like Burton's *Mars Attacks!* there is some political commentary.

The myth cycle began with Boulle's book, *La planète des singes* (*Planet of the Apes*), first published in 1963. In his introduction to the Penguin version, Brian Aldiss argues that the novel is a fairy tale, because in it animals behave like humans, as they do in so many fairy tales, and because the central events are things that could not possibly happen.[8] I prefer to follow the traditional screenwriting definitions of fairy tale and fantasy: fairy tales focus on the nuclear family and usually revolve around issues of maturation, especially from child to adult; myths deal with how societies should be run, often testing out various social programs by telling the story of the development of a single ruler, leader, or visionary.

Both story forms focus on chain-of-life transitions, such as the transition from adolescent to adult leader, and both often use unrealistic conventions such as magic. Finally, both can be told using a variety of genres, but we find Swiftian satire more often used in myth; Aldiss compares *Planet of the Apes* to *Gulliver's Travels* (1726) by Jonathan Swift and *The Island of Dr. Moreau* (1896) by H. G. Wells.

The novel begins as follows: "Jinn and Phyllis were spending a wonderful holiday in space, as far away as possible from the inhabited stars." It turns out the couple are on a vacation spaceship, much like a pleasure boat. As they sail along, they find a literal message in a bottle, which they fish in. The manuscript is in a language that Jinn happened to study in college, so he translates it for his wife. The manuscript was written by a journalist, Ulysse Mérou, who had traveled with several other astronauts to a planet they named Soror, to investigate radio signals coming from there. Ulysse's tale unfolds: After the astronauts land on Soror, they discover a lake, where they encounter a lovely naked woman, Nova, who is bathing, and her family group, who greet the astronauts by forcefully removing their clothes. The astronauts have brought with them some animals from Earth, including a chimpanzee named Hector, who has been taught to use diving equipment, but Nova promptly kills the chimp. The astronauts soon discover that the humans on Soror are prey to apes—gorillas, orangutans, and chimpanzees—who actually rule the planet. The apes have speech, art, culture, and fairly advanced technology, but the humans have no language, live in caves, and are incapable even of expressing emotion.

The apes capture many of the humans. One of the astronauts is killed immediately, another is sent to a zoo, while Ulysse is put in a lab with Nova, where simian scientists, including a chimpanzee named Zira, conduct experiments on them and encourage them to mate. Ulysse develops a physical attachment to Nova, but he quickly realizes that Zira is the most accessible of the apes and reveals to her that he can speak and think (by detailing the Pythagorean theorem for her). Zira teaches Ulysse the ape language, and he becomes a celebrity. However, Ulysse is admired more as an object of curiosity than as a fellow sentient subject. He tries to use his celebrity to rescue the other astronaut from the zoo, but by now the astronaut has become just like the other caged humans and has even lost his ability to speak. Ulysse gets involved in the research project of Cornelius, Zira's chimpanzee fiancé, who is doing anthropo-

logical and archeological research on the prehistory of the apes on Sor-
oro. A leading ape, Zaius, hates Ulysse and everything he stands for and
poses a constant threat to Ulysse and his chimpanzee friends. As Cornelius shares with Ulysse the discoveries he has made at his archeological
dig, they both come to the conclusion that Soror was once populated
and ruled by humans, who somehow met their decline and were replaced by apes that were descended from human pets or that were
otherwise trained by humans. (The key finds are a mechanical doll
shaped like a human that speaks and a human graveyard that shows
orderly thought and a concern for the afterlife.)

In spite of his friendship with Cornelius, Ulysse has trouble resisting
his attraction to Zira, based more on their common concerns and her
caring intelligence than on true physical attraction, but when he tries to
kiss her, a kiss she seems to desire, she pushes him away, saying, "Dar-
ling, it's a shame, but you really are too unattractive!"

At the same time Ulysse learns that Nova is pregnant with his child.
These two discoveries bring Ulysse out of his complacency; also, he
observes the experiments Cornelius performs on humans, which include
lobotomies and experiments that induce epilepsy. Most upsetting of all,
one brain experiment taps into the subjects' race memory, and though
unconscious, they speak and reveal the tales of "past lives," which include how they once performed such experiments on apes until finally
the apes rebelled. Ulysse cannot bear to be part of this anymore, but he
has more immediate worries: in order to suppress Cornelius's discoveries and the support that a talking human (Nova's baby has begun to
speak) provides, Zaius wants to have Ulysse, Nova, and their baby lobotomized or killed. Zira and Cornelius will not let this happen, and they
help Ulysse and his new family escape to the spaceship that the astronauts had first used to reach Soror. Now Ulysse guides them back to
Earth, and on the journey he teaches both his son and Nova to speak.
He manages to land the ship in sight of the Eiffel Tower, but once the
three disembark, they discover that Earth is now run by apes.

As Jinn finishes translating the manuscript, we have another surprise:
the wealthy couple on their space yacht are also chimpanzees, who treat
the manuscript as a work of fiction.

When the book was first published, Boulle was already well known
for his novel *The Bridge on the River Kwai* (1952), which drew on his
experiences as a prisoner of war of the Japanese during World War II.

He wrote many other novels after *Planet of the Apes* and apparently considered it one of his minor works. Joe Russo and Larry Landsman have noted that the book owes a large debt of inspiration to Swift's "Voyage to the Houyhnhnms" in *Gulliver's Travels*, in which Gulliver finds himself in a world where unemotional, intellectual horses rule and oppress a sordid race of mud-loving humans called Yahoos. Gulliver allies himself with the horses and identifies with them to such an extent that when he returns to his family, he cannot bear to be near them. The same authors also point out similarities to a novel by Aldous Huxley called *Ape and Essence* (1948), which had started out as a screenplay. The Huxley novel showed Earth in a postnuclear era. The hero, who is from a New Zealand untouched by the cataclysm, travels to California, only to discover that humans there have reverted to a bestial state and apes have reached an advanced level of evolution that emulates what they saw in Hollywood movies.[9] Boulle himself described being inspired by watching gorillas at the zoo.[10]

Producer Arthur P. Jacobs, who was a fan of *King Kong* (1933) wanted to make a film along the same lines. He acquired the rights to Boulle's novel in 1963, but he then struggled for several years to get funding. He hired Rod Serling to do a screenplay, and Serling worked on several drafts. From the beginning Jacobs and J. Lee Thompson, who was originally signed to direct, saw the film as a horror-thriller or horror-adventure. They considered Marlon Brando for the lead; when he turned them down, they approached Paul Newman, then Jack Lemmon, Rock Hudson, and even Gregory Peck, before finally reaching an agreement with Charlton Heston. Because of the delays, Thompson had to leave the project, as did Blake Edwards after working on it for a long time. The film was eventually directed by Franklin J. Schaffner, who had just collaborated with Heston on *The War Lord* (1965) and would go on to direct *Patton* (1970) and *Papillon* (1973). Schaffner was more sensitive to the cynical satire in the film:

> It isn't science fiction because it has something to say about our society, something about the cynicism of men who choose to exploit others. . . . The film is not intended as a mockery. It offers a parable, a moral lesson: Knowledge by itself is neither good nor evil. It is what you do with the knowledge that makes it one or the other.[11]

The film finally got the go-ahead from Richard Zanuck at Fox after a makeup test that proved audiences would not find the idea of a human engaging with apes laughable. There is some disagreement about the now iconic ending of the film, in which Heston's character discovers that the ape planet is postnuclear-apocalypse Earth when he sees the ruins of the Statue of Liberty. Most give credit to Rod Serling, as such endings were typical of his *Twilight Zone* episodes (Serling even wrote one episode entitled "I Shot an Arrow Into the Sky," in which three astronauts land on a planet, where one of them kills the other two for their food, then realizes they were on Earth all along). However, Jacobs claimed that he and Blake Edwards had the idea over lunch at a delicatessen that had a reproduction of the Statue of Liberty on the wall. (It is interesting to note that Boulle, when asked his opinion of the screenplay, hated the ending.[12]) The final script was a combination of Rod Serling's work and the efforts of screenwriter Michael Wilson, a blacklisted author who had done uncredited work on the screenplays for *The Bridge on the River Kwai* (1957) and *Lawrence of Arabia* (1962). However, Brian Pendreigh believes that art director Don Peters (not credited in the film because most of his work was not used) was the source of the original idea, though he was working from a series of concepts under discussion between Serling and Jacobs.[13]

Plot Summary: *Planet of the Apes* (1968)

Taylor (Heston), Dodge (Jeff Burton), Landon (Robert Gunner), and Stewart (Diane Stanley) are in a spaceship traveling at the speed of light. Their destination is not stated. Rather, the emphasis is on how relieved Taylor is to have left twentieth-century Earth and how space travel is moving them forward in time; in effect, eighteen months of space travel while they are in suspended animation is over 2,000 years of Earth time. The ship crash-lands in a lake, and the astronauts come out of their suspended animation, only to discover that Stewart died during the flight. As they explore the new world, Taylor's misanthropy becomes evident from his conversations with Landon. While they stop to drink from and bathe in a stream, some cavemen-like figures steal their clothes. They make chase to retrieve their clothes and discover a group of savage, speechless humans. Taylor is attracted to one he will later name Nova. The group is hunted down by apes, who are civilized, wear clothing, speak English, and hunt humans for sport. Dodge is shot in the back, and Landon and Taylor are taken captive, along with Nova (Linda Harrison) and others from her tribe. Taylor suffers a neck wound and loses consciousness. He awakens when he is being operated on by a veterinarian and getting a blood transfusion from Nova. He is in a behavioral science lab run by Dr. Zira (Kim Hunter), a chimpanzee. He can't speak, but he tries to communicate with Zira using sign language. Zira realizes that Taylor is more intelligent than the others, but her superior, Dr. Zaius (Maurice Evans), an orangutan who is the head of scientific research in the ape society as well as "keeper of the faith," doesn't believe her, and maintains that all humans should be exterminated. To make Taylor feel better, Zira puts Nova in his cage.

As he recovers, Taylor is allowed to exercise outside, and Zira brings her fiancé, Dr. Cornelius (Roddy McDowall), another chimpanzee, to see this human she considers intelligent. Taylor writes a message in the sand for them to see, as he still cannot speak, but Nova and another human erase his message, which enrages him and leads to a fistfight. As the apes subdue him with a water cannon, Zaius, apparently not surprised that a human can write, erases the rest of the message that Taylor had written. Later, Taylor takes Zira's pen and paper and writes further messages, trying to explain that he came from space and where his ship landed. This sparks a debate between Zira and Cornelius on simian evolution; as it happens, Cornelius believes that apes might be descended from humans. Zaius arrives to take Taylor away and have him castrated. Taylor manages to escape. In his flight he ends up in a natural history museum, where he sees his friend Dodge stuffed and positioned in a diorama with other humans. He is caught again by the simian police; but by now he can speak again, and Heston utters the famous line "Get your stinking paws off me, you damned dirty ape!"

Taylor is put back in a cage with Nova, but the two are then separated so that they won't breed. Taylor is forced to appear in front of the tribunal of the National Academy, which argues that Zira created a speaking human by interfering with his brain. Taylor is given the chance to prove his story by finding Landon, but when he does, he realizes that Landon has been lobotomized. Cornelius states his belief that Taylor is some remnant of an ancient culture in the Forbidden Zone, the geographical area that is thought to be the birthplace of the ape race, and both he and Zira are charged with heresy.

However, Zaius actually believes Cornelius, though he won't admit it, and privately threatens Taylor with castration, torture, and a slow death unless he reveals where he came from and where others like him could be found. With help from Cornelius, Zira, and other chimpanzees, Taylor manages to escape again, taking Nova with him. Cornelius and Zira lead them to the Forbidden Zone. They are chased by Zaius, but Taylor manages to take Zaius hostage, an act of violence that shocks the chimpanzees, who are pacifists. Taylor gets supplies, and they discover that Cornelius was right, from the evidence in an archeological dig of a talking human-shaped doll and artifacts left in a grave, that the Forbidden Zone was once a human city. Taylor kisses Zira goodbye, though she is repelled by him, and he and Nova go deeper into the Forbidden Zone in order to start a new life. Behind him, Zaius has the archeological dig blown up and arrests Zira and Cornelius.

Taylor and Nova reach a shoreline and see something ahead of them. As they near it, Taylor realizes that it is the Statue of Liberty, that he has been on Earth all along, and that this is a postnuclear world. Heston falls to his knees and says, "You maniacs! You blew it all up! Damn you! Goddamn you all to hell!"

The film was an incredible success, earning $26 million on a $6 million budget. It was followed by four sequels, a television series, and a cartoon series. Because Burton's *Planet of the Apes* was influenced by the sequels and the television series, I will summarize them briefly.

Plot Summary: *Beneath the Planet of the Apes* (directed by Ted Post, written by Paul Dehn, produced by Arthur P. Jacobs, 1970)

The film starts much as the first one did, with a spaceship from Earth crash-landing on the planet, two astronauts aboard, one dies from his crash wound, leaving Brent (James Franciscus) to make his way across the Forbidden Zone. He runs into Nova (Linda Harrison), who is looking for Taylor (Charlton Heston), from whom she has been separated. They travel to Ape City together, where Ursus (James Gregory), a gorilla leader, wants to invade the Forbidden Zone to eliminate a mutant human race known to live there. Zira (Kim Hunter) and Cornelius (David Watson), now married and expecting their first child, are now aligned with Zaius (Maurice Evans) in their agreement that this invasion should not take place. Brent and Nova find Cornelius and Zira, and they help him get back to the Forbidden Zone, where he finds the subterranean remnants of New York City ruled over by a race of telepathic mutant humans who worship a nuclear bomb. The mutants control others by implanting nightmarish images in their minds. Brent and Nova are jailed with Taylor, and Nova speaks for the first time, saying Taylor's name, but she is killed soon afterwards. The city is under attack by the gorillas (who had to fight their way through a demonstration of chimpanzees protesting the plan to exterminate humans), and the mutants want to retaliate by setting off their bomb. Brent and Taylor fight to stop them, but after Brent is killed and Taylor is mortally wounded, he sets off the bomb himself in disgust, thereby destroying the entire planet.

Plot Summary: *Escape from the Planet of the Apes* (directed by Don Taylor, written by Paul Dehn, produced by Arthur P. Jacobs, 1971)

With the help of a technologically minded chimpanzee named Milo (Sal Mineo), Cornelius (Roddy McDowall) and the pregnant Zira (Kim Hunter) have managed to escape in Taylor's original ship from their own planet, destroyed in the nuclear holocaust. The ship travels back through time and ends up on Earth at around the time Taylor had left it. Now we have a reverse of Taylor's experience: the apes land and are quarantined by humans in the Los Angeles Zoo, in a cage next to a gorilla. At first, they plan not to reveal that they can speak, but Zira loses patience with the same intelligence tests she once administered to Taylor and gives it away. However, the humans, or at least the president and his scientific adviser, Dr. Otto Hasslein (Eric Braeden), accept that the apes come from Earth's future rather readily, and Hasslein, like Zaius, sees them, especially Zira's unborn child, as the first step toward humanity's eventual downfall. Therefore, he plans to prevent the birth. A gorilla kills Milo, but Zira and Cornelius are interrogated by the CIA. Eventually Cornelius loses his temper and accidentally kills an orderly. The two escape, aided by a human doctor, who hides them in a circus. Zira gives birth there with the assistance of a kindly circus owner. However, Hasslein tracks them down. Zira switches her baby with that of a circus chimpanzee, and the circus owner promises to care for him. Though Zira and Cornelius keep running, they are eventually gunned down.

Plot Summary: *Conquest of the Planet of the Apes* (directed by J. Lee Thompson, written by Paul Dehn, produced by Arthur P. Jacobs, 1972)

It is twenty years since Zira and Cornelius's death, and their baby, Caesar (Roddy McDowall), is now grown up, still working in the circus with Armando (Ricardo Montalban), who treats him like family. In the meantime, a virus has made cats and dogs extinct. Humans have turned to small apes for pets and then, as human culture declined into a police state, for slaves. Caesar cannot stand to watch the torture of other apes, who cannot speak but can understand orders. He defends a gorilla who is being beaten, which leads to a riot and Armando's death. He escapes briefly but ends up at an ape retraining center, where he organizes the other apes into an uprising. His efforts are opposed at every point by Governor Breck (Don Murray) and the police, and aided by the governors aide, MacDonald (Hari Rhodes). The apes eventually win, with Caesar being the first to kill a human. (The ape revolution was originally filmed as very bloody, but this ending did not test well, so a new ending was shot. The apes overpower the humans with a minimum of killing, and Caesar ends by saying he hopes harmony between the species will be achieved once the war is over.)

Plot Summary: *Battle for the Planet of the Apes* (directed by J. Lee Thompson, story by Paul Dehn, written by John William Corrington and Joyce Hooper Corrington, produced by Arthur P. Jacobs, 1973)

This film is actually a story being told by a Lawgiver orangutan (John Huston). He tells about the benign chimpanzee dictator Caesar (Roddy McDowall), who overthrew human rule and enslaved humans in turn. Caesar has a mate and a son, Cornelius, still a child, when he decides to go to the Forbidden City (created by a nuclear blast that happened in a struggle between films) to trace his parents in the video archives. In the Forbidden City he finds his old enemy, the chief of police, who now leads a society of mutants who have a bomb. Caesar barely manages to escape after seeing a video of his parents. The mutants plot to attack the ape city, and the gorillas in the city plot to attack the human mutants. They are overheard by Caesar's son, who is then mortally injured by the lead gorilla. It soon comes down to a battle between human mutants and apes, which the apes win. After the battle, Caesar decides to release the human captives and decrees that apes and humans must live together as equals. When we see the Lawgiver's audience, we realize his vision has come to pass, as the children are an equal mix of different ape and human races.

Planet of the Apes, the Television Series (1974)

Although originally planned as twenty-four episodes, only fourteen were produced, and only thirteen of those made it to the air. The premise of the series was simple: three astronauts crash land on an ape planet, where humans are oppressed. One of the astronauts is killed early on. The other two team up with a chimpanzee (Roddy McDowall again). All three are on the run, trying to find a way to rebuild their spaceship and leave. In each episode they use their superior knowledge of technology to improve or help humans (and sometimes, though usually indirectly, apes). The relative subtlety of the early films in the cycle is completely lost here.

Return to Planet of the Apes, Animated TV Series (1975–1976)

This series replays many of the events from the films in a different timeline, with different levels of technological development than that of the films. In some ways it is closer to the world of the novel. Like the live-action series, it ended abruptly after thirteen episodes.

Planet of the Apes: The Political Content

Although the film cycle went steadily downward in terms of production value, it remains a classic because it touched a political and social nerve. More than a few books have been written on how the series comments on race relations in America. The depictions of racial tensions in the film are complex, as the apes have a strictly hierarchical society within themselves as well as a complex series of relationships with humans, with much tension between the chimpanzees, who are pacifists and intellectuals, the war-mongering gorillas, and the bureaucratic, power-hungry, controlling orangutans. Different analogies have been pointed out; for example, one Web site outlines it as follows: the gorillas represent a white supremacist view of African Americans; the chimpanzees represent Japanese Americans, whose constitution forbids military aggression (and who were the victims of American nuclear power); and the orangutans represent white conservative America and a stultifying adherence to tradition.

Alternatively, the chimpanzees represent southern white Americans, the orangutans represent northerners, and the gorillas represent American minorities in the army.[14]

The above interpretations highlight the function of film in general, and fantasy in particular: "Films are not simply indiscriminate reflections of society, nor are they disinterested . . . not just a mirror of the time, but a response to it."[15] Because of this, the Web author quoted above sees the film series from the perspective of someone who lives in the American South; reviewers in Great Britain, in contrast, saw it as a reflection of troubles with Ireland, and so on.

Eric Greene, in his book *Planet of the Apes as American Myth: Race and Politics in the Films and Television Series*, interprets the films' allegorical race classes as follows: "white gentile humans as orangutans, white Jews as chimpanzees [Rod Serling, the original screenwriter, was Jewish, and had written other programs on Jewish experiences in the Holocaust], and African-Americans as gorillas."[16] He also charted the changes in the balances of power from film to film as follows:[17]

Planet of the Apes	*Dominant: orangutans* *Mediator: chimpanzees* *Dominated: white humans*
Beneath the *Planet of the Apes*	*Dominant: gorillas and orangutans* *Mediator: chimpanzees* *Dominated: white humans*
Escape from the *Planet of the Apes*	*Dominant: white humans* *Mediator: Latinos, liberal white women,* *liberal white men* *Dominated: apes*
Conquest of the *Planet of the Apes*	*Dominant: white humans* *Mediator: Latinos, African Americans* *Dominated: apes*
Battle for the *Planet of the Apes*	*Dominant: apes* *Mediator: African Americans* *Dominated: white humans*

Each film is built around the conflict between a dominant and a dominated group. The mediating figures are from a group previously discriminated against who are still marginalized and at odds with the dominant group.

As Greene notes repeatedly, one reason why the *Apes'* cycle could go on for so long is that the filmic world is dystopian: the racial conflicts were similar to those in the United States in the late 1960s–early '70s, but intensified and escalated. No successful resolution was imagined. Greene considers resolution, even if only symbolic, as a form of suppression of social anxiety. He compares the *Apes'* refusal to compromise with the suppression of racial anxiety operating in *Edward Scissorhands:*

> In *Edward Scissorhands*, a white woman ventures into a dark and mysterious castle and finds the film's hero. Edward is brought back to the predominantly white community, and on the basis of physical difference is sequentially feared; fetishized; exploited; suspected and unjustly persecuted for a variety of crimes, most importantly the false charge of sexually assaulting a white woman; chased out of the neighborhood; and almost killed for daring to love a white teenage girl. His life endangered, Edward escapes back to his original home, with the aid of an African-American police officer who sympathizes with him and presumably identifies with his plight.
>
> The connection with the African-American officer is crucial, for the film recapitulates much of the experience of African-Americans in the United States and of the United States' history of racial conflict, even down to the belief that the demise of the community's most rabid racist can right the wrongs in which the whole community participated and from which the whole community profited.[18]

For Greene, *Scissorhands* is closer to *Within Our Gates*[19] than it is to James Whale's *Frankenstein*. Greene goes as far as saying that *Scissorhands'* solution to the race problem in America is a "back-to-Africa, or back-to-the-ghetto, style separation of the races."

Although Greene sees the *Apes'* saga as superior to films like *Scissorhands,* it is not without problems: it uses a white male as the icon of "civilized" humanity and characterizes the apes in such a way as to make the hierarchical separations appropriate (gorillas are brutish and therefore good soldiers, racist stereotypes associated with African Americans). The films try to avoid the issue of gender altogether, which only serves to highlight the gender divide, a reflection of the issues of the time. The first film, for example, puts a woman into space fifteen years before the the U.S. space program did, but she is killed off before the ship even lands on the planet. Greene notes:

> Of the three women characters in *Planet,* Stewart has violated male space in both name and body, and having spoken not a word, dies almost immediately, thus neutralizing her as a source of competition for power with the male astronauts. Zira, who is perhaps stronger and more committed to

"scientific truth" and interspecies understanding than anyone in the film, stands alone as the only female character in the film[20] who can talk and who does compete with males. . . . [T]here seems to be a logic at work that states that because she is intelligent, articulate, and assertive, she must therefore also be "ugly" by traditional standards. By contrast, Nova is beautiful, but literally and figuratively dumb.[21]

These are the flaws, or gaps, that Burton could have chosen to address or at least update in his "reimagining" of the first *Planet of the Apes,* and in some of the advance press for Burton's film it seemed that he intended to:

[T]his is not a remake or a sequel . . . there is a way to do it differently, exploring things thematically but in a different way. I think it can be revisited and re-imagined to a whole new generation and to people like me who are interested in other aspects of what the film said.[22]

In another interview, Burton expanded on what he saw in the series:

I think it's just the whole question of humankind. "What are we?" We relate to animals, and that's the funny thing about apes. When you're with them and you're looking at them, I get very disturbed by it. Because I get both this feeling of recognition—you know, "Oh, they're very close to us," which is something we're drawn in by—and at the same time they'd rip your head off in a second, and you don't know what they're thinking.[23]

One aspect Burton clearly wanted to explore was the violation of the miscegenation taboo, which Pierre Boulle dealt with rather directly in his novel but which had never made it into any of the *Apes* films apart from the goodbye kiss between Zira and Taylor. This could have been a powerful statement on the American bias against race mixing that goes back to colonial times and which was clearly articulated in the *Dred Scott* Supreme Court ruling of 1857:

A perpetual and impassable [legal] barrier was intended to be erected between the white race and the one they had reduced to slavery . . . which they then looked upon as so far below them in the scale of created being that intermarriages between white persons and negroes and mulattoes were regarded as unnatural and immoral, and punished as crimes.[24]

A romanticized and sexualized relationship in Burton's *Planet of the Apes* not only would have challenged the miscegenation taboos but would have led to further reflection of the evolution versus creationism debate, and with it some consideration of how racism is based on cultural projections, the fear of the "other's" difference and that the "other" might actually be the same. However, Fox studio executives squashed a love scene between the lead characters Leo and Ari from the beginning, worried about an NC17 rating for bestiality.[25]

So what did Burton do with the voluminous saga he had inherited? Let us look first at the story, in its first revision and final version.

Plot Summary: *Planet of the Apes* (Script by Sam Hamm, First Revision)

Earth is in trouble; all the babies born age and die within twelve hours, all from a virus brought to Earth by a visitor from the ape planet. In order to save Earth, a few scientists, including Dr. Susan Landis, retrofit the alien spaceship and fly back to its point of origin. Dr. Raymond Dodge recruits her, along with Alexander Troy, a hotshot pilot. With them are two other pilots, Stewart and Astor. Stewart dies in flight, Dodge and Astor die on the ape planet. The rest of the film is divided rather evenly between Landis and Troy, who quickly form a couple, as she tries to do research on the virus at its place of origin (helped by rebel apes), and he is treated as a specimen by the apes and develops a friendship with the female scientist ape Zira. Zaius, a religious leader, and Ursus, a military leader, try to hide the fact that these humans can speak. Troy never falls for a mutant human—his heart is with Susan. But Susan realizes she is related to a little girl that Zira has named Iocasta. She discovers that the virus prevents the mutant humans from speaking, but otherwise they are immune, the survivors of a similar epidemic that enabled the apes to gain control.

Upper-class orangutans know about Earth and human inventions and artwork, and use this advantage to claim their high social position. Troy ends up in a gladiator contest with another human—Dodge, who has been lobotomized. Susan is pregnant with Troy's child and is desperate to find a cure for the invidious virus. Once she finds the cure, it is a race to get back to the spaceship. The orangutans first promise that Susan and Troy can leave, but Susan, thinking that they will go back on their word, releases a virus that is similar to the black plague. In return for a cure, the apes allow Susan and Troy to get to their ship. Cornelius sacrifices himself to destroy the station where the orangutans steal art from Earth, so Zira leaves with the humans. The trip takes six years. Troy and Susan's child is six when they land on Earth, which is now populated by apes, as the epidemic has taken its toll, and the Statue of Liberty has an ape face.

Plot Summary: *Planet of the Apes* (directed by Tim Burton, written by William Broyles Jr., Lawrence Konner, and Mark Rosenthal, produced by Richard D. Zanuck, 2001)

After a very artistically designed credit sequence that shows us ape iconography, we meet Pericles, a chimpanzee in a space pod—he panics, and we realize it's a simulation. Captain Leo Davidson (Mark Wahlberg) is his trainer. They are on a space station, the *Oberon*, near Saturn. Leo plays a childish trick on Pericles, leading to the following exchange between him and his fellow trainer, Lieutenant Colonel Grace Alexander (Anne Ramsey):

> Grace: What? Was the *Homo sapien* mean to you again? We all know it's just rocket envy, don't we?
> Leo: Ever consider an actual boyfriend?
> Grace: You mean, do I enjoy being miserable? No thanks, I'll stick with my chimps.

The ethics underlying this exchange will set the stage for the conflict in the rest of the film. Just as Leo is watching a birthday message from Earth, which shows us that life is going on while he is stuck on the space station, forced to train chimps to fly but not allowed to fly himself, a space storm cuts communication with Earth. The station also gets a garbled mayday signal. Pericles is sent to investigate even though Leo wants to go himself; when the station loses track of Pericles, Leo disobeys orders, claiming he wants to "save his chimp." Leo gets blown forward in time and crash-lands into a lake on an Earth-like planet. He immediately encounters two humans in outfits right out of '50s Tarzan movies, the lovely Daena (Estella Warren) and her father, Karubi (Kris Kristofferson), who are being chased by gorillas. Leo discovers that the apes can speak when the gorilla Attar (Michael Clarke Duncan) says: "Get your stinking hands off me, you damn dirty human!" Leo, Daena, Karubi, and other humans are captured and paraded through the streets of an ape village, where the apes make fun of them, though one chimpanzee, Ari (Helena Bonham Carter), does not approve of treating humans this way. The captured humans are to be sold as slaves by Limbo (Paul Giammatti), the orangutan slave trader. General Thade (Tim Roth), a warrior chimp, brings his niece in to buy a human pet, a young girl, while the other humans are lined up for branding. However, Ari stops the branding and buys Leo and Daena. They become servants to Ari, who lives with her father, a powerful senator. A dinner at the senator's house, attended by Ari, her father, General Thade, Senator Nado (Glenn Shadix), and his companion, Nova (Lisa Marie—note the transference of the name of Taylor's mistress from the first film and novel to a chimpanzee mistress), tells us much about the relationship between apes and humans: Ari shows off a textile made by humans, which she claims proves their ability to be trained; the officials are worried that the humans outnumber apes four to one, which would make an uprising dangerous; and Thade violently pries open Leo's mouth to see "if there is a soul in there." His blasphemy is counterbalanced by Attar's insisting that they all say grace, a request the other apes go along with rather impatiently.

Thade leaves when two of his soldiers tell him that they have found something; they show him Leo's spaceship in the lake, and Thade promptly kills them.

Leo, whose understanding of technology is superior to that of the other humans, breaks them out of their cages, and they all escape. Daena insists on rescuing the young girl as well. They run through a series of rooms, past Limbo, who is grooming himself, past the senator and his concubine about to have sex, and straight into Ari, who decides to help them find their way out of the ape city after Leo promises to show her "something that will change her world forever." At this point, Daena is already showing signs of possessiveness and jealousy, while Ari acts entitled to her sense of ownership of Leo, all of her actions backed up by her gorilla bodyguard, Krull (Cary-Hiroyuki Tagawa). The party also includes Limbo, who tried to get his slaves back and was taken hostage instead. Once Ari gets them out of the city (in the process, Karubi is killed), Leo dives into the lake to get weapons and a homing device out of his ship. Daena, worried that he is in the water too long, dives in to rescue him, but she is startled by the dead gorillas that Thade has left in the water. Leo realizes the *Oberon* is nearby and decides to find it. The others are disturbed by his display of his weapon, and when he isn't looking, Krull takes it and destroys it.

The mixed party begins to travel toward the *Oberon,* with Ari questioning Leo intently on how humans related to apes on his world. Meanwhile, Thade convinces Ari's father to let him impose martial law so he can control the humans and "rescue" Ari, who is assumed to have been coerced into helping the humans. Thade and Attar organize an army, but Thade is called to his father's deathbed (an uncredited cameo appearance by Charlton Heston), who reveals to Thade an ancient gun and the knowledge that in the prehistory of their planet humans ruled over apes. This knowledge strengthens Thade's resolve, and he sets out to make a final, annihilating war on the humans.

The humans and Attar reach an ape military encampment on a lake edge just before "the holy grounds of Calima," which is also the area where Leo needs to go. They must get through the ape army, which is not expecting any trouble, though Attar tries to organize them. Leo shoots off a flare, which creates a distraction, and steals horses for his party. They rush through the camp, knocking over tents and starting fires as they go, disrupting Attar at prayer (Attar always prays to Semos, the First Ape and the founder of the royal ape line from which Thade is said to be descended). Daena's younger brother, a teenager named Birn (Luke Eberl), has become attached to Leo, much as the chimp Pericles was at the beginning of the film, and Leo treats him much as he treated Pericles, constantly telling him not to look up to him, not to expect much from him—in other words, Leo only wants to leave, not make a commitment to these people. Ari is more committed to her new friends, and she tries to protect them by offering herself to Thade, who has lusted for her, but he simply brands her as a slave, and she flees. The refugees make their way across the lake even though the apes are terrified of water, and Ari almost drowns Leo in her terror. Limbo has begun to indentify with the fugitives and stays with them.

When the band of refugees finally reach Calima, they quickly realize it is actually the ruins of the *Oberon*, from which the original humans and apes of the planet came. (The mayday in the beginning of the movie was actually from the *Oberon* itself.) For Leo, there now seems to be no hope, and everyone awaits the battle that is to come. Ari and Daena

Burton's primary alteration to the *Planet of the Apes* myth was the character Leo, the reluctant savior, played by Mark Walhberg.

have a moment of understanding, now that Ari is wearing the slave brand, and other humans come up, ready to fight and die if Leo will lead them. Leo at first resists the leadership role assigned to him, but he then realizes there are still some elements of the ship that can be used as weapons. By using the fuel cells that are still functioning on the ship, Leo manages to deflect the first wave of the ape attack, but after that it is hand-to-hand combat. Many die, including Krull. Thade tries to kill Leo, knowing that without his leadership the humans would fall back. Just as it seems the battle will be lost, Pericles lands in his pod, also apparently homing in on the *Oberon*'s signal through the time warp. The apes believe that Semos has returned (except for Thade, who tries to kill Pericles, but Leo succeeds in imprisoning him on the *Oberon* bridge, where Thade appears to have a nervous breakdown), and the battle comes to an end by common consent. Attar now fulfills his destiny as a religious leader. Leo clearly is needed to continue leading the humans, but he knows Pericles' pod can get him back to Earth, and he doesn't want to miss his chance. He kisses Daena goodbye perfunctorily and then Ari, a kiss that still manages to feel transgressive in spite of everything.

Leo does succeed in returning to Earth, and crash-lands at the Lincoln Monument. However, when he looks up, he sees the face of Lincoln is now that of General Thade, the inscription clearly identifying him as such, and the police that are approaching are all apes.

There are various ways to explain this ending. Mark Crawley, on the Web site Movieprop,[26] sums it up:

1. Leo does not land on Earth even though he thinks he does. Instead, he lands on the planet he has just left, only arriving in the future.
2. Leo arrives on a planet other than Earth or the ape world he left.
3. General Thade escapes his captivity and leads a group of apes via time travel to conquer Earth before humanity becomes stronger. Leo then arrives on Earth to see the results of this conquest.
4. The ending is a dream.

However you interpret the ending, Burton's *Planet of the Apes* has one thing in common with Boulle's novel: both are morality tales. Leo is being punished for his lack of commitment. He isn't committed to his job training chimps, because he wants to be a pilot himself; he doesn't commit to Ari, who risks life and dignity for him; he refuses to acknowledge his parental relationship with Birn, and as a result Birn is nearly killed; and worst of all, he refuses to acknowledge or accept the role he is fated to play as leader of the humans on the ape planet. Each time he refuses to commit he is punished in some way—he is separated from the *Oberon,* Ari almost drowns him, Birn almost derails Leo's battle plan, and when he manages to return to Earth (at least, he thinks it is Earth), in the end he is in a worse situation than he was on the ape planet. It doesn't help that Leo is given so many chances; the relationship with Birn, especially, takes away from his relationship with Daena, and probably should have been deleted from the film altogether so that Leo and Daena could talk to each other. As it is, although the humans in this film can talk (they just keep it secret from the apes), Leo and Daena have as little real communication as Taylor and Nova did in the original movie. By not having another character with whom to confide, Leo never has to confront his own tragic flaw. So Burton has put one of his trademark fairy-tale characters into an action-adventure picture—a character firmly wedded to his own postadolescent state spends the entire movie trying to get back to his spaceship, ignoring, as much as possible, the huge social upheaval going on around him and refusing to participate except when he absolutely has to. His greatest moment of revelation is the Calima sequence (outlined shot by shot below). Here, Leo realizes that this world exists primarily as the result of his decision to chase after Pericles. Leo is thus the real Semos of the planet, and not Pericles' offspring. This makes his decision to leave in Pericles' pod even more incomprehensible.

Although much is made of the differences between apes and humans in this film, the emphasis seems to be more on class differences than on racial tensions. When Burton made his film, it might have seemed that the racial tensions of the 1960s were a thing of the past, but that was

Helena Bonham Carter, as the chimp Ari, and Estella Warren, as Daena, along with Daena's tribe, ask Leo to lead them in a battle that will free them from oppression.

before September 11, 2001, created new lines of willful ignorance and hatred. Leo, the commitment-phobic white male, is a creature of the late twentieth century. He is a fairy-tale hero in a mythic story. Burton was conscious that he was making a fairy tale: "[The original *Planet of the Apes*] was a movie that had [an] impact on me as a kid. It's like a fairy tale, a folk tale to me."[27]

This is probably one of the worst flaws of Burton's project: a fairy-tale hero set in a story of mythic proportions, a story that the worldwide audience was very familiar with. Despite its obvious production values and its $140 million budget, Burton's fabulous designs, Danny Elfman's music, and Rick Baker's incredible ape makeup, this is merely the story of a postadolescent who refuses to accept the leadership role he is called on to play in society.

It could have worked as an overblown fairy tale, or maybe even as a fairy tale with a myth base, but it is derailed, not by tongue-in-cheek humor (noticeably lacking in this film except for a few blatant references to the 1968 version, which fall flat because they are ill-timed, such as Heston's repetition of his "Damn them all to hell!" line), but by a direction that takes for granted that the humans are naturally superior. What the original cycle of films accomplished so well is clearly missing here: we do not believe for a moment that the apes are rightfully ascendant (the satire of our own culture is missing), so we feel as if we are simply waiting for Leo to restore the correct order. The most blatant aspect of this is that the ape characters themselves, from Thade's father and Thade himself on down, also believe that humans can easily overwhelm them, and in fact, it is only a matter of time. Such nihilism kills satire, and with it, any suspense or direct engagement with the film. It doesn't help that Mark Walhberg and Estella Warren have no range in their performances. The actors who play the apes, especially Tim Roth, Helena Bonham Carter, Michael Clarke Duncan, Cary-Hiroyuki Tagawa, and Paul Giamatti, give such riveting performances, even under total body makeup, that they save the film from almost complete failure. However, even these performances are marred by moments that simply fall flat, such as Limbo's too-quick revelation that slavery is bad, and his easy transition to selling aspirin to children at the end of the film (how does he even know what aspirin is?).

Burton clearly meant for the important relationship to be between Leo and Ari, a relationship fully developed in Boulle's book though shied away from in the original series. He apparently aimed to show the two actually making love, but apparently that was one idea he was forced to drop. In this performance Leo seems almost asexual, especially given his phobia of commitment, paying no attention to Daena's beauty and engaging with Ari only to the extent he needs to in order to escape from the ape planet. Ulysse's original passion to understand is completely missing from this portrayal, replaced by some incredible apes-versus-humans battle sequences.

The Calima Sequence

That Leo's tragic flaw is his phobia of commitment is highlighted in the film's revelation scene, labeled "Calima" on the DVD version of Burton's *Planet of the Apes*).[28] The scene starts with references to western iconography. The location looks a bit like Monument Valley (although it is not), the setting for many westerns. The group rides in through a dust cloud and rounds a stone abutment, as the ruins of Calima gradually come into view. Multiple crane shots are used for this reveal, from different angles but mostly cut front and back on a 180-degree line, first showing the ruins alone and then framing the characters with the ruins in the foreground, completely dwarfing the characters and telegraphing that what they are about to see is very significant for them.

Visually, the Calima ruins look like Antonio Gaudi's cathedral in Barcelona, famous for its endoskeleton appearance. The camera comes off the crane to show Leo, but we are given another establishing shot after everyone has gone inside the ruins.

Leo consults his tracking device. In a close-up we see that the device has made contact—in a visual that matches the 90- and 180-degree cuts we have just seen, the angles on the tracking device flip around until the 90 degree and 180 degree lines match and it announces it has made contact. However, there is nothing different about the ruins, which are just as they have been for thousands of years, and the other humans around Leo are quickly losing faith in him. "They were never here," says one, and "You said they'd come for us," says Daena.

Leo spots a skull in the dust and pulls it out. It is a human skull. He looks around and sees the lettering from Ca Li ma. He dusts off the lettering. The real wording is "Caution: Live Animals." He realizes that these are the ruins of the *Oberon,* his mother ship.

Limbo, the slave-owning orangutan, is watching all of this in the background. The scene is really filmed from his perspective: the perspective of an ape realizing, for the first time, that his ancestors were brought here from Earth, that they were basically slaves on a spaceship. The whole logic of his world is collapsing as he watches.

Now that Leo knows where he is, he explores the ruins until he finds the control center. The cells are nuclear and still power on when he tries them. He cleans a computer screen and consults the ship's log. The message there is the same as the mayday he heard on the *Oberon*: it is the *Oberon*'s own mayday. The woman he flirted with earlier appears, now aged, and reports that a chimp she herself raised from infancy, Semos, has organized the other chimps against the humans. Sounds of an ape mob can be heard in the background, and then silence. We know the apes have killed the humans.

There are two revelations in this scene, both focused on Leo. The spoken one is by Leo: "They are all dead because they were out looking for me." Ari tries to console him: "We are all here because of you." In other words, Leo is as much the planet's Semos as the original Semos was.

Clearly, this is not a pataphysical film, but rather a myth-based film with a fairy-tale hero. There is a linear, fairly traditional action-adventure plot. Numerous characters are well developed, from Leo's fear of commitment, to Ari's human-rights activism, to Thade's race rage. The primary special effects work is Rick Baker's astonishing ape masks and makeup (Burton refused to use CGI for the apes because he wanted real actors to relate to each other.[29] It's an action-adventure movie that combines some aspects of classic sci-fi, western, and gladiator films. The fact that this film is not pataphysical might explain why a lot of critics find it to be Burton's worst, for, despite *Ed Wood,* they were not prepared for Burton's shift in tone.

The screenwriters, including Mark Rosenthal, were clear that they did not want to write an epic, because they believed we no longer live in a world of epic issues. According to Rosenthal:

> The first *Planet of the Apes,* and what [screenwriter] Rod Serling was interested in, was living in a world of epic issues. The first one wasn't just a generalized social question about the nature of man, it was about the Cold War. It was about whether or not we were going to be here in the future; do we have something inside of us so that the world will end with a bang? Which is an epic mode.[30]

Had the film not been a reimagining of a myth where Taylor, Leo's model, at least tried to raise the level of the humans on Soror (in *Beneath the Planet of the Apes*, he tells Nova he is going to raise a race of intelligent human children), then the implied commentary of Burton's version, which could be interpreted as white middle-class culture eroding due to self-absorption and lack of commitment to social group as well as family, as personified by the character of Leo, might have gotten more attention from the critics.

Given this uneasy balance between inspired and not-so-inspired film elements, and the contrast with the canonical position of the first film, it is not surprising that the reviews were neither overwhelmingly negative nor overwhelmingly positive. For Rita Kempley, the movie was an "astonishing new version" of the original story, "splendidly envisioned and boldly executed" by Burton.[31] Bob Graham of the *San Francisco Chronicle* is equally enthusiastic: "'Planet of the Apes' is not a remake, and it's not a sequel. It is an amazing display of imagination."[32] Frederic and Mary Ann Brussat of *Spirituality and Health* said: "Hits the bull's eye with its thematically relevant portrait of the clash between hostility and hospitality as the major challenge facing humans in the twenty-first century."[33] And Elvis Mitchell in the *New York Times* commented: "When Mr. Burton's *Planet* fixes on being entertaining as single-mindedly as the gorillas bearing down on homo sapiens, it succeeds. But the picture states its social points so bluntly that it becomes slow-witted and condescending; it treats the audience as pets." Roger Ebert in the *Chicago Sun-Times* acknowledged at the beginning of his review that he "expected more" from Burton, then wrote later that the director "had some kind of an obligation to either top [the original], or sidestep it. Instead, he pays homage. . . . He's made a film that's respectful to the original, and respectable in itself, but that's not enough. Ten years from now, it will be the 1968 version that people are still renting."[34]

The film did well at the box office, earning $359 million worldwide. There was much discussion of a sequel, but Burton categorically refused to direct one, bitter about his relationship with Fox (which insisted, for example, that any overbudget expenses would come out of the director's fee).

Charlie and the Chocolate Factory

As of this writing, Burton's remake of *Willy Wonka and the Chocolate Factory* (Mel Stuart, 1971) is scheduled to be released on July 15, 2005. It is unclear how much reference Burton makes to the original film by Mel Stuart, which was based on the book by Roald Dahl titled *Charlie and the Chocolate Factory*. He had two options: to make a pataphysical film with an emphasis on humor and special effects, or to make a dark, horror story. A review of the original film's plot may be helpful in anticipating Burton's take on the material.

Plot Summary: *Willy Wonka and the Chocolate Factory* (directed by Mel Stuart, written by David Seltzer, produced by Stan Margulies and David Wolper, 1971)

The film opens with a shot of children running out of school and into a candy store, where the owner sings "The Candy Man" song (just one number from the Anthony Newley–Leslie Bricusse score). Charlie Bucket, a sweet, quiet kid, doesn't run with the other children; instead, he picks up his allotment of newspapers and his first pay from his boss at the newsstand. He delivers the papers as any kid would: throwing them so that they land in the most out-of-the-way places. On his way home he passes the Wonka candy factory and stares through the gates. A peddler tells him ominously that "no one ever comes in, and no one ever goes out."

At home, Charlie's mother is feeding his four grandparents, all bedridden for twenty years. Charlie arrives and brightens up the place. With his first pay he buys bread and gives his Grandpa Joe, his favorite relative, money for tobacco. He tells Grandpa about the peddler, and Grandpa tells him about the competition between Mr. Slugworth and Willy Wonka and how Mr. Slugworth's industrial espionage led Wonka to fire all his workers and close down the factory, then reopen three years later without hiring new workers. The mystery is, who is running the factory?

Charlie is next seen in science class. Mr. Turkentine, his teacher, is demonstrating how to make a wart remover, but the chemicals cause a combustion. There is a commotion in the hall: Willy Wonka has announced that the finders of five gold tickets will get a tour of his factory and a lifetime supply of chocolate. A news bulletin announces the competition: there are shots of people around the world anxiously buying up all Wonka bars, and a man in therapy recounts a dream in which an angel tells him where to find a Wonka golden ticket.

The first ticket finder is Augustus Gloop, a glutton in a family of gluttons who can't stop eating long enough for the press conference. Mr. Slugworth, dressed as a waiter, whispers in Augustus's ear.

It's Charlie's birthday. The women in the family have all collaborated on a long red scarf for him. Grandpa Joe has used his tobacco money to buy Charlie a Wonka bar, which doesn't have a ticket.

The next scene shows Mr. Salt's peanut-shelling factory, where he and his daughter, Veruca, anxiously watch the entire factory staff as they unwrap Wonka bars, which they have been doing for a week at the rate of 19,000 a day. Veruca is having a tantrum because they haven't found a golden ticket yet, and Mr. Salt indulges her every whim. A factory worker finally finds one, and Mr. Slugworth pulls Veruca aside just as she is given the ticket.

Next are more scenes of people around the world searching for Wonka's golden tickets. One man has programmed a computer to find the chocolate bars, but the computer, more principled than most people in the film, refuses to tell because that would be cheating. Reprogramming yields no better results.

Violet Beauregarde, a gum-chewing girl from the American Midwest, finds the third ticket. Mr. Slugworth is seen next to her, too. In addition to her amazing gum-chewing habit, she is very rude to her parents.

Charlie meets his mother at work, where she is doing laundry by hand, and he tells her that the third ticket has been found. His mother tries to put the contest into perspective for him, but Charlie is starting to become resigned to his life of poverty. She sings a song, "Cheer up Charlie," which reveals that Charlie's cheerful nature has helped her and that she needs him to stay happy.

Mike Teevee, another American, finds the next golden ticket, but he is too busy watching TV to be polite to the press, though he does listen to Mr. Slugworth. A newscaster, reflecting on the fact that there is just one ticket left, notes that there are other, more important things in life, but he can't think of what they are. The last case of Wonka bars is auctioned off in Great Britain for thousands of pounds and purchased by the queen. A wealthy American woman cannot bring herself to give up her case of Wonka bars to kidnappers who are threatening to kill her husband.

The last ticket is found in Paraguay by an adult, a casino owner. This brings disappointment and some calm. Charlie is back in science class, where his teacher uses the Wonka madness to teach percentages. On the way home, Charlie finds a coin on the street and uses it to buy candy.

On a whim Charlie buys a Wonka bar for Grandpa Joe. As he comes out of the store, he sees his boss at the newspaper stand surrounded by a crowd—the last ticket has been declared phony, which means one more real ticket is still out there. Charlie unwraps his Wonka bar and finds that he has the last golden ticket! He is immediately mobbed by the crowd, but his boss rescues him and sends him home. As Charlie runs home, he encounters Mr. Slugworth, who asks him for an everlasting gobstopper, a new candy Wonka has in development, and offers him a lot of money for it.

Charlie runs home to tell his family. The tour of the Wonka factory is the next day. Charlie needs someone to go with him. He overlooks his mother and asks Grandpa Joe instead, which means Grandpa must get out of bed. He does, and by the end of a happy musical number, Grandpa is dancing.

The next day, the holders of the five winning tickets and their chaperones are gathered outside the Wonka factory. The other winners display their various bratty, disrespectful, and rude characteristics. Mr. Slugworth is also there. Willy Wonka himself appears, at first leaning on a cane, but then doing a somersault, a kind of ying-yang behavior that we will soon realize is typical of everything he does. He greets each child individually, then takes them into the factory, where mechanical hands grab their hats and coats. The children sign a contract with print they can't read, then crowd through two forced perspective spaces, where they (except for Charlie and his Grandpa) are very disrespectful of Willy Wonka, until they sail on the *Wonkatania* through a tunnel filled with scary visions. This is so frightening that the others calm down a bit and finally start paying attention to what Wonka is saying. He eventually leads them to the chocolate room, where everything is made of candy and a river flows with chocolate. There they see the diminutive Oompa-Loompas hard at work, and Wonka sings "Pure Imagination." He also speaks in German and French and often quotes Shakespeare and other authors. Everyone eats candy with delight. Augustus drinks from the river and falls in, then gets sucked through a tube. Wonka predicts dire results, and Augustus's mother is rushed off by Oompa-Loompas to retrieve him, his share of the tour clearly over.

Wonka then begins the tour of the factory proper. One of the first displays is the everlasting gobstopper machine, and each child is given a sample. Next is the gum machine that tastes like an entire meal. Violet takes one, disregarding all warnings. When she gets to the blueberry dessert flavor, she blows up like a large blueberry and has to be rolled out for decompression, her share of the tour over. They next pass a fizzy drink machine. Although they are told not to taste or touch, Grandpa suggests that he and Charlie do so anyway. They drink, then float up to the ceiling, almost getting sliced by a fan, but Grandpa and Charlie manage to lower themselves by burping. They rejoin the tour without, apparently, anyone noticing their absence. Next, they take a ride on a Wonkamobile to another part of the factory, where they reach the "Wonka vision" room. Here, anything can be transported—teleported—but, at the same time, reduced in size. Mike Teevee hops into the device, is beamed, and arrives safely back but much smaller, his part of the tour over.

The tour suddenly seems to be over for Charlie and his Grandpa, too, as Wonka shuts himself in his office. Grandpa confronts Wonka, and Wonka reveals that he knows that they had taken a sip from the fizzy drink machine. Grandpa decides he will get his revenge by selling a gobstopper, but Charlie stops him and gives the gobstopper back to Wonka. This causes Wonka to jump up in delight, declaring Charlie the winner. Apparently the whole contest was a test to find a successor for Willy Wonka, a child he could train to run the factory and care for the Oompa-Loompas. Mr. Slugworth is actually Mr. Wilkenson, who works for Wonka. Charlie, as Willy Wonka's hand-picked heir, can now ride with him in the Wonkavator, which floats over the entire town.

Differences between the Novel and the Movie

> [In the novel] [t]here was no drama in Charlie's victory. He won the prize simply because he made it through the day without causing trouble. Dave [Wolper], Stan [Margulies], and [Mel Stuart] realized that major changes were necessary if a successful movie was to be made.[35]

The original movie was meant to be a marketing tie-in for a chocolate bar to be made by Quaker Oats. Wonka bars were never produced, however, even though the company had invested $2.9 million in the film.

There were several differences between Dahl's story and the 1971 movie. For example, Dahl's novel called for Oompa-Loompas to be

Pygmy-like people from Africa, but Stuart made the Oompa-Loompas orange with green hair. (The illustrations in Dahl's book were later changed to little white people.) The title *Charlie* was also considered racist at the time, so the movie's title was changed to *Willy Wonka and the Chocolate Factory*.[36] To emphasize "moral fallibility," Stuart and his team came up with the everlasting gobstopper test, which is not in the book; this required creating Mr. Slugworth, only alluded to in the novel. The fizzy drink machine is simply mentioned in the novel, but this becomes Charlie's test, which he fails just like the other children. Veruca's punishment (to fall down a "bad egg" chute) is an alteration from the book, where she is beset upon by hundreds of squirrels that pound on her to see if she is a "bad nut." The strange rooms that Wonka leads them through before they get to the chocolate room were also added, spaces that Stuart refers to as "Alice in Wonderland rooms."[37] The songs by Antony Newley and Leslie Bricusse, of course, were an addition. Stuart had resisted turning the movie into a musical, but producer Dave Wolper, who was inspired by films like *The Sound of Music* (1965) and *Oliver!* (1968), insisted. Wolper also came up with the idea of adding animated lyrics to the Oompa-Loompa songs, which Stuart eventually agreed to.[38]

Some of the changes were scripted by Dahl, who wrote additional scenes, for example, those with Mr. Turkentine. Dahl at first resisted other changes to his script, but he eventually agreed to the final draft.

Regarding the special effects in the film, Stuart said:

> Someone once asked me if I wished I had been able to take advantage of the digital effects that are so prevalent today. Strange as it may seem, I told them that I felt that the Wonka effects, created with an ingenious use of more naturalistic resources, are part of what adds to the believability of the film.[39]

This is the sort of thing that Burton always says, so we can expect theatrical effects with "invisible" digital effects like digital mattes for location backgrounds and some establishing shots, a la *Sleepy Hollow*. Probably the most visible effect in Stuart's film is the ride on the *Wonkatania*, with various layers of projection combined to give the feeling of fast motion and visual scares. Some critics compared it to a drug trip, but Stuart has always vehemently denied that there was any intended analogy.

The story is a pataphysical one, with various cartoon aspects. According to Stuart:

> I saw Willy Wonka in the mold of the wacky inventor of cartoon mechanisms, Rube Goldberg: The manufacturing process in his factory should look bizarre and delightfully strange, but it should somehow work. The place to best express this concept was in the Inventing Room.[40]

Harper Goff, the production designer for the film whose drawings for the chocolate room were closely followed, had designed a sleek, stainless steel lab for the invention room, but Stuart insisted on something more chaotic. After an angry discussion, Goff returned with a design for a room with overtones of a junkyard.[41]

Stuart noted:

> The other important aspect of the film that may have enabled it to retain its popularity is that it is not only a clear-cut morality tale but one that is infused with a strong sense of irony . . . [tempered with] wit, occasional absurdity in the writing, and the superb portrayals, [which] provide a source of constantly sophisticated amusement.[42]

Burton's Version

The idea of a remake (or "revival," as it was referred to in one press release) started with the Dahl estate and Plan B, the company run by Jennifer Aniston and Brad Pitt. The Dahl estate especially wanted Burton to direct the film (Martin Scorsese was also discussed as a possibility) and approached him while he was finishing *Big Fish*.[43] Before Burton was attached to the project, heavy metal cult singer Marilyn Manson made it known that he wanted to play Wonka as Satan. Manson said, "I see Willy Wonka as Satan because [he] presents people with temptation of picking good and evil, and they all pick evil."[44] By July 2003, Burton was rumored to be considering Christopher Walken and Michael Keaton for the role of Willy Wonka. Other names bandied about were Steve Martin, Robin Williams, and Nicolas Cage. However, Burton ended up going with Johnny Depp. Depp convinced Burton to cast Freddie Highmore, who starred with him in *Finding Neverland* (2004), as Charlie Bucket.

As with *Planet of the Apes*, Burton faced an incredible challenge: to reimagine a film that several generations of children (and their parents) had grown up on, and who knew all the lyrics by heart. How could

Burton improve on a movie that is so secure in the canon of childhood films?

At the time of this writing (February 2005) certain details about Burton's film have come to light.[45] He is filming in Europe, and, by taking advantage of European production credits, has a $150 million dollar budget at his disposal (compare that to the $3 million budget Mel Stuart had). He has filmed episodes described in the book that were not depicted in the first version, such as Wonka's visit to Loompaland and the melting candy palace of Pondicherry. He has restored the nut-cracking squirrels, but these are not digital squirrels but real ones, bottle fed from birth and hand trained to do their part in the film. By contrast, the Oompa-Loompas will be digital clones of Deep Roy, who also appeared in Burton's *Big Fish*. The Oompa-Loompas still sing, but apparently no one else does. Mel Stuart's expansion of Slugworth's part into an assistant villain is gone, but Wonka has a new backstory: his father was a dentist who never let him eat candy, and as a result he became so obsessed with candy that he became a candy-maker. Estranged from his father, he is now looking to hand over the factory so he can go home and reconcile with his father.

More interesting is Depp's interpretation of the role created by Gene Wilder. His appearance, which Horn describes as "an asexual Anna Wintour, with a touch of Oscar Wilde," stands out, especially the over-bite. And Depp's performance has been described as inspired by Marilyn Manson.[46]

Horn describes the set, though inspired by the black and white urban photography Bill Brandt, as similar in feel to *Edward Scissorhands*, including a return to Burton's "signature curlicues." The town is set up like a medieval village, and Wonka's estate looks down on the village from above.[47]

In his article, Horn gives a wealth of detail about the path of the *Wonka* project to a green light. The film was in development for a decade before Burton was selected as director, with other directors, such as Tom Shadyac (*Bruce Almighty*) vetoed by Roald Dahl's widow, Liccy Dahl, who had approval over directors, screenwriters, and principle cast. It was only after she vetoed Shadyac that Warner Bros. suggested Burton direct. John August wrote the screenplay after many other drafts were produced and discarded, and is collaborating with Danny Elfman on the Oompa-Loompa songs. Christopher Lee plays Wonka's dentist father, Helena Bonham Carter plays Charlie's mother, and Missi Pyle (of *Big Fish*) plays Mrs. Beauregarde.

Although it took many years for Burton to be selected for *Chocolate Factory*, it now tantalizes with its potential to be another Burton classic, a true Gothic fable along the lines of *Edward Scissorhands* and *Sleepy Hollow*.

The poster for the film shows Depp in black coattails, his head tipped downward, his eyes hidden by his top hat.[48] The trailer shows Depp's Wonka as lithe and androgynous, with the high-pitched cracking voice of a boy about to enter puberty. He still comments on the activities of the misbehaving children, but it is almost as if he is one of them. The sets glimpsed in the trailer are all highly expressionistic, though the chocolate room is clearly inspired by the original. Most tantalizing is the allusion to Disneyland's It's a Small World After All ride, with the implication that in Burton's film Wonka's factory is a theme park. Between his version of *Wonka* and the animated *Corpse Bride*, 2005 should be an excellent year for Burton fans.

Notes

1. Burton has also made a documentary on the life and work of Vincent Price, which has never been released.

2. Jim Smith and J. Clive Matthews, *Tim Burton* (London: Virgin Films, 2002), pp. 150–151.

3. Ibid., p. 155.

4. Ed Wood's *The Hollywood Rat Race* was published for the first time in 1998 by Four Walls Eight Windows Press; it is not clear if the filmmakers had access to the manuscript.

5. J. Hoberman, "Ed Wood . . . Not," *Sight and Sound*, May 1995, p. 11.

6. Burton in Mark Salisbury, *Burton on Burton* (London and Boston: Faber & Faber, 2000), p. 131.

7. Hoberman, "Ed Wood."

8. Brian Aldiss, Introduction, in *Planet of the Apes*, by Pierre Boulle (London and New York: Penguin, 2001), p. v.

9. Joe Russo and Larry Landsman, with Edward Gross, *Planet of the Apes Revisited: The Behind-the-Scenes Story of the Classic Science Fiction Saga* (New York: St. Martin's Press, 2001), pp. 3–4.

10. Jean-Claude Morlot, "Interview with Pierre Boulle," quoted in *The Planet of the Apes Chronicles*, by Paul Woods (London: Plexus, 2001), p. 30.

11. Ibid., p. 26.

12. Ibid., pp. 19–20.

13. See the interview with Don Peters in *The Legend of the Planet of the Apes, or How Hollywood Turned Darwin Upside Down*, by Brian Pendreigh (London: Boxtree, 2001), pp. 46–47.

14. Mark Crowley, "Essay about the Racial and Anti-Slavery Message," http://www .movieprop.com/tvandmovie/PlanetoftheApes/racial2.htm.

15. Eric Greene, *Planet of the Apes as American Myth: Race and Politics in the Films and Television Series* (Jefferson, NC, and London: McFarland and Co., 1996) p. 10. This book was republished in 1998 as *Planet of the Apes as American Myth: Race, Politics, and Popular Culture* by Wesleyan University Press.

16. Ibid., p. 55.

17. Ibid., p. 24.

18. Ibid., pp. 146–147.

19. Directed by Oscar Micheaux in 1919, as an answer to the racism of *The Birth of a Nation* (D. W. Griffith, 1915).

20. This would remain true for the entire saga, including the television series.

21. Greene, *Planet of the Apes as American Myth*, pp. 37–38.

22. Paul A. Woods, *The Planet of the Apes Chronicles* (London: Plexus, 2001), pp. 161–162.

23. Ed Gross, "Re-Imagine That!" interview with Tim Burton, in *SFX Collector's Edition The Planet of the Apes* (Bathjuk: Future Publishing), 2001, p. 58.

24. *Dred Scott v. Sandford*, 60 U.S. 393, 15 L. Ed 691, cited in Derrick A. Bell, *Race, Racism and American Law* (Boston: Little, Brown, 1973), p. 8. Quoted in Greene, *Planet of the Apes as American Myth*, p. 34.

25. See "On-Screen Monkey Business Causes a Stir," *WENN*, August 8, 2000, and "Mark Wahlberg Gets His Gorilla," *World Entertainment News Network (WENN)*, August 4, 2000.

26. http://www.movieprop.com/tvandmovie/PlanetoftheApes/2001ending.htm.

27. Burton, quoted in Woods, *Chronicles*, p. 161.

28. *Planet of the Apes* (2001) DVD, released by Twentieth Century Fox Home Video in 2002.

29. "Digital Apes? No Way, Says Director Burton," studio briefing for July 25, 2001, http://www.maxfilmpro.com/insider/newsstand/Newshare/archive/2001/July/July-25.html.

30. Ed Gross, "Allegory on the Planet of the Apes," interview with screenwriter Mark Rosenthal, in *SFX Collector's Edition*, pp. 81–82.

31. Rita Kempley, "Grand Gorilla Theater," *Washington Post*, July 27, 2001.

32. Bob Graham, " 'Great Apes': Under Tim Burton's Hand, this sci-fi warhorse has evolved into something splendid," *San Francisco Chronicle*, July 27, 2001.

33. Frederic and Mary Ann Brussat, "Planet of the Apes," http://www.spiritualityhealth .com/nesush/items/moviereview/item_3102.html.

34. Elvis Mitchell, "Get Your Hands Off, Ya Big Gorilla," *New York Times*, July 27, 2001, Roger Ebert, "Planet of the Apes," *Chicago Sun-Times*, July 27, 2001.

35. Mel Stuart with Josh Young, *Pure Imagination: The Making of Willy Wonka and the Chocolate Factory* (New York: St. Martin's Press, 2002), p. 14.

36. Ibid., pp. 14–16.

37. Ibid., pp. 24–25. On pages 55–57, Stuart credits group sessions with Harper Goff, Han Wynands, and Stan Margulies as the origin for the ideas of the rooms, from the vestibule with the hands, to the psychedelic hallway, the Alice in Wonderland hallway, and, later, Wonka's cut-in-half office.

38. Ibid., p. 68.

39. Ibid., pp. 43–44.

40. Ibid., p. 48.

41. Ibid., p. 50.

42. Ibid., pp. 117–118.

43. "Aniston and Pitt to Revive *The Chocolate Factory*," May 23, 2003 (WENN), http://pro.imdb.com/news/wenn/2003–05–23#celeb2.

44. Stuart, *Pure Imagination*, p. 110.

45. All details in the following two paragraphs, except as otherwise noted, are from John Horn, "On the set: A Nuttier Chocolate," *Los Angeles Times*, February 6, 2005, pp. E1, E30–31.

46. N/A, "Depp's 'Creepy' Performance to Scare Audiences," February 15, 2005. http://pro.imdb.com/news/wenn/2005-02-15/celeb/4.

47. Horn, *Los Angeles Times*, p. E31.

48. The design of the poster is very similar in style to the Gaumont poster for Louis Feuillade's *Fantomas* (1913), about a band of thieves who plague Paris.

6

THE MUSIC OF DANNY ELFMAN

It is impossible to talk of Tim Burton's films without mentioning the work of composer Danny Elfman, who has scored all of Burton's films since *Pee-wee's Big Adventure,* with the sole exception of *Ed Wood.* It is only slightly less impossible to talk of pataphysical films without mentioning Elfman, who, in addition to Burton's movies, has scored eleven comic book films, making his style of composition the default for the genre. Finally, it is necessary to discuss Elfman because his music is the third key element (the other two being the screenplay and the production design) to what goes into Burton's auteur "brand." This book has referred repeatedly to the types of stories and screenplays Burton prefers and seems to do best with: the tone of production design, usually carried out by regular collaborator Rick Heinrichs; the "silent movie star" style of acting Burton prefers, often embodied by Johnny Depp; and the type of music. Each of these elements has an important role to play in the making of a film that we recognize as Tim Burton's. Elfman's musical brand is identified by the style of music he has written principally for Burton, music that is often called "dark" and "Gothic." It is characterized by an emphasis on "minor keys, low-pitched melodies and textures, and frequent use of dissonance both at melodic and harmonic levels. . . . [He] regularly applies atonality, dissonance, and sonic experimentation to [all of his], scores, not just those written for Burton."[1]

The goal of this chapter is not to do an in-depth musical analysis of Elfman's work, but to give the reader an overall sense of how film scores are produced, and in particular how Elfman's scores work with Burton's films.

Elfman was born in 1953 in Texas but grew up in the Crenshaw area of Los Angeles. He taught himself to play the organ, starting with the keyboard solo to The Doors' "Light My Fire." He fooled around with his Fender knockoff, imitating Jimi Hendrix licks. He took piano lessons when he was told he didn't have long enough arms for the trombone. As a senior in high school he settled on the violin.[2]

After graduating from high school in 1971, Elfman spent a year traveling through Ghana, Nigeria, Senegal, Upper Volta, and Uganda, hitching rides along the way. He took a violin with him and learned how to play it on the trip. In Africa he encountered and fell in love with Highlife, an African pop music style similar to a combination of salsa and reggae. A Highlife band usually had seven or eight members, on guitar, bongos, drums, bass, and a three-piece horn section, a musical setup that Elfman would imitate when he later formed the band *Oingo Boingo*.[3] Music professor Janet K. Halfyard describes Highlife as follows:

> Highlife is a twentieth-century African fusion of several different musical idioms that have been finding their way to Africa since the nineteenth century. The hymns introduced by the Christian missionaries during the nineteenth century produced a musical idiom that combines European harmony with African practices. The brass instruments of British military bands from colonial days led to the use of brass as the main melodic instrumental group in a typical Highlife band, with the usual regular 4/4 meter, not typical of traditional African music, reflecting the regular rhythm of military marches. This is then blended with polyrhythmic ideas from African traditional music played on percussion in an improvisational idiom that owes a great deal to jazz, which became as influential as dance music in Ghana and Nigeria from the 1920s onward.[4]

The Africa trip would affect Elfman's musical thinking. In fact, while in Africa he considered becoming an ethnomusicologist, with a particular interest in Java and Balinese gamelan.[5] It was also in Africa that he became interested in building instruments, especially percussion instruments. He built three percussion orchestras, one composed of West African–style balophones, which resemble xylophones. In Africa they are made of bamboo and gourds, too fragile for Elfman to take home, so he built his own. He had to invent ways to make huge gourdlike resonators, and ended up using weather balloons and fiberglass and resin. He also made an Indonesian–style gamelan, using metal tubes, and a "kitchen orchestra" made out of found objects such as brass pans and army surplus pots. His pride and joy is still the celeste he made out of Schlitz beer cans.[6]

While Elfman was in Africa, his older brother, Richard, spent several months in San Francisco working with a transvestite theatrical company called The Cockettes, directing and composing music for their shows.[7] On a trip to Canada, Richard had a chance encounter with an avant-garde musical theater group called Le Grand Magic Circus. He moved to Paris to work with the group. In 1971 he returned to Los Angeles, bringing with him a singer-acrobat, Marie-Pascale, whom he married. Together they formed a theatrical group he called The Mystic Knights of the Oingo Boingo. Richard invited Danny to join them. It started out as a twenty-person company, with several female vocalists, including Marie-Pascale and Miriam Cutler (who is now a well-respected film composer herself, scoring *Lost in La Mancha*, 2002, for example). Later Richard reformed it as a twelve-piece group and spent years playing on the streets as a kind of busker act, with Danny playing bongos, violin, and the trombone. Their money came from passing the hat. Richard was responsible for the staging and theatrical aspects, while Danny was responsible for most of the music. The Mystic Knights performed for eight years, during which Danny dutifully reenacted, reworked, and transcribed jazz numbers from the early 1930s. Their performances consisted of both original material and old jazz classics.[8]

In 1978 The Mystic Knights formally disbanded. Danny organized a few of the remaining musicians into a rock band, which he called Oingo Boingo. One of the continuing members was guitarist Steve Bartek, who would go on to become Elfman's orchestrator when he started composing for film. It was while working with The Mystic Knights that Elfman learned how to write music:

> That is where I learned my confidence in my ear. Cab Calloway's arrangements . . . could be very fast and complicated. I would listen to videocassettes of Betty Boop cartoons and old records, but I learned that if I listened hard, I could freeze it in my head and hold it there and write it down. It ended up being critical training for me, even though I didn't know it at the time.[9]

At first, Elfman composed by hearing a tune in his head, then picking it out on an instrument. Once he could pick it out on an instrument, he could write it down. Bartek would then transcribe the music for the other band members.[10] This is basically the method Elfman and Bartek still use when working together.

In 1982 Oingo Boingo contributed the song "Goodbye, Goodbye" to *Fast Times at Ridgemont High,* which led to the theme song for the short-lived TV series of the same name. The band also contributed several songs, including "Better Luck Next Time," for the film *The Last American Virgin* (1982). In 1985 the group did "Weird Science" for John Hughes' film of the same title. This would turn out to be the band's most successful song.

Oingo Boingo stayed together for seventeen years and made sixteen albums and numerous singles, as well as a handful of music videos. They never had a hit at the top of the charts and were never really accepted by the critics, but they had a loyal fan following, especially in California, and some international recognition.

Elfman wrote over one hundred songs for Oingo Boingo. He also did a five-minute piano concerto, Oingo Boingo Piano Concerto One and a Half, for piano and small ensemble. By the time he did the piano concerto, he had learned how to write music.

Writing music for The Mystic Knights, and later for Oingo Boingo was, in fact, good preparation for orchestral composition. Elfman has noted that The Mystic Knights had eleven or twelve individual instruments, and each one needed its own part. This is not so different from an orchestra, which might have ninety instruments, with between twelve and seventeen parts. The challenge is the same: to divide the themes among the various instruments. Elfman still occasionally writes material that, by his own admission, is "semi-impossible for the musicians to play,"[11] but this confession on the *Edward Scissorhands* DVD implies he does this on purpose to keep his musicians on their toes (he works with the same musicians as much as possible).

Pee-wee's Big Adventure (1985)

About six years after he wrote the "One and a Half" piano concerto, Elfman was asked by Tim Burton and Paul Reubens to score a film starring Reubens. Burton, it turned out, was a fan of Oingo Boingo and liked to see the group perform at the Whiskey A Go Go in Los Angeles, and Reubens liked Danny's brother Richard's first directorial effort, *Forbidden Zone* (1980), with a score by Danny. This was to be Burton's first feature, *Pee-wee's Big Adventure*. In the 1980s most scores produced for comedies were jazz-influenced or featured a synthesizer pop score, similar to Oingo Boingo's song for *Weird Science*. Elfman found a "different and effective" way to score a comic film, inspired by Nino Rota, especially by his work on Federico Fellini's films: a music with bright colors, which constantly switches between major and minor keys.[12] Elfman was given four and a half weeks to compose the score for the film, which he saw for the first time after it was completed (unlike his later collaborations with Burton, where he was brought in much earlier in the process).

Caught by surprise by Burton and Reubens's request, Elfman proceeded to teach himself film scoring by listening to the work of classical film composers:

> I still believe that the old school guys tend to be more talented than the new school guys, as a general rule. My heroes are all dead: Bernard Herrmann (Citizen Kane, Psycho, Taxi Driver), Nino Rota (La Strada, La Dolce Vita, 8½, Godfather Part II), Max Steiner (The Informer, Gone With the Wind, The Treasure of Sierra Madre), Franz Waxman (The Blue Angel, Sunset Boulevard, A Place in the Sun, Rear Window), Erich Korngold (Midsummer's Night Dream, Anthony Adverse, The Adventures of Robin Hood). I don't think anybody working today can hold a candle to just about any of those guys.
>
> And the people today I really like are Elmer Bernstein (The Ten Commandments, To Kill a Mockingbird, True Grit, Animal House), Jerry Goldsmith (Patton, Planet of the Apes, Chinatown, The Omen), and Ennio Morricone (Fistful of Dollars; The Good, The Bad, and the Ugly; The Mission; Cinema Paradiso), so again they tend to be the older guys. I still think they're the best, and of course John Williams (Jaws, Star Wars, Close Encounters, Schindler's List)—he really helped to re-open the door of orchestral composition for us all.[13]

The Pee-wee score has a few recognizable themes that are used and then reused in altered form according to the thematic need. The opening cue is chase music, which will be reused every time Pee-wee is chased in the film. It has a slight variation that plays with the breakfast machine and works as a "Rube Goldberg" theme,[14] which reappears when Pee-wee starts using the amazing gadgets on his bike to elude the people chasing him on the studio lot.

When Pee-wee sees two boys doing stunts on their bikes, a quick little melody in the form of the schoolyard taunt "na na na na na na" is heard. This is a Puccini-like device, to use leitmotifs that show us what people are thinking.[15] In this case, it is what Pee-wee assumes the boys are thinking of him, which leads him to try a few stunts of his own, with painful results.

A similar very direct cue is a series of descending scales, as Pee-wee drives a convertible over a cliff.

Because the film spoofed TV genres, Elfman's music also spoofs TV music, especially in the scene where Pee-wee goes shopping before his bike is stolen.

Elfman has said repeatedly that he learned much of what he knew by listening to the film scores of Bernard Herrmann over and over again. For him, Herrmann was a role model, the perfect composer. (Elfman's admiration for Herrmann is most manifest in his score for *Dolores Claiborne,* which in many ways is a tribute to Herrmann's *Psycho* score; he also arranged Herrmann's music for Gus Van Sant's remake of *Psycho,* 1998). There are some homages to Herrmann in *Pee-wee,* especially the shrieking violins when Pee-wee discovers his bike has been stolen and the dark, morose music that plays as Pee-wee wanders around dejectedly, while others on their bikes, unicycles, and so on, wheel around him. As his dejection turns to obsession, the music sounds more and more like Herrmann's score for *Vertigo* (1958), especially the sequences where Jimmy Stewart tails Kim Novak.

As a result of *Pee-wee*'s success, Elfman was asked to score numerous other comedies, including *Scrooged, Midnight Run, Hot to Trot, Big Top Pee-wee,* and *Beetlejuice,* all in 1988. In fact, Elfman did so many comedies that he thought "short little cues" and a lot of starting and stopping were normal for film scoring. It wasn't until he worked on *Dolores Claiborne* (1995) that he got a chance to write a twelve-minute cue.[16] Elfman discovered that there was more than the length of cues that distinguished comedy from drama: in comedy, the music has to follow the action very closely, "like close dancing" (he specifically compared it to a tango); the music can never stray too far from the action, unlike in drama.[17]

Over the length of his career Elfman has been somewhat averse to scoring romantic films, although he eventually did *The Family Man* (2000). It is interesting that the first time he wrote romantic music was for *Pee-wee,* in a scene where Pee-wee and a waitress, Simone, spend the night inside a dinosaur. Later, when Pee-wee sees Simone about to get on a bus to go to Europe, the music is a "twisted little waltz"—very similar to the waltz music that Paul Reubens liked so much in Richard Elfman's *Forbidden Zone.*

Elfman and Burton have such similar tastes that it is not surprising they decided to work together again. From his Oingo Boingo days it is clear that Elfman, like Burton, has a macabre interest in the more fantastical aspects of death. He loves monster movies, including the ones that

Burton likes—Hammer films, Roger Corman films, with a particular fondness for characters portrayed by Christopher Lee and Vincent Price (Elfman has stated repeatedly that he was very grateful for the opportunity to meet Vincent Price on Burton's *Edward Scissorhands*). Whereas Burton identified primarily with Vincent Price as a youngster, Elfman had a particular fondness for Peter Lorre. Furthermore, Burton fell in love with stop-motion when he watched *Jason and the Argonauts* and *The Seventh Voyage of Sinbad*, the same films that, along with *The Day the Earth Stood Still*, encouraged Elfman to become a composer.

Beetlejuice (1988)

For *Pee-wee*, Elfman had mixed major and minor keys, but for *Beetlejuice*, his commitment to working predominantly in minor keys became firmly established:

> The music [in *Beetlejuice*] is in a minor key and has an angular melody played by the brass, the sense of angularity being increased by the repeated use of an augmented fourth. This acts as a constant "wrong note" that upsets the expected melodic outline and is symptomatic of Elfman's use of dissonance in most of his scores. The dissonance in the melody is underlined by repeated augmented fourth chords from muted trumpets, and these elements would all suggest a sinister tone to the music. However, the rhythmic character of the piece is fast-paced, bright, and dancelike. It has a scurrying, klezmerlike clarinet line and the trumpet motif comes in on a jauntily syncopated offbeat. The juxtaposition of this exuberance with the sinister character implied by the harmonic and melodic material is one of the more characteristic features of Elfman's music. It would aptly describe much of the music he wrote for Oingo Boingo, as well as for *The Nightmare Before Christmas*, and this particular quality is something that has been exploited by directors in a line of films that combine various genres—including thrillers, dramas, fantasy and horror films—with blackly comic elements. The combination of the dark and quirky can be found in *Scrooged* (1988), *To Die For* (1995), *Freeway* (1996), *The Frighteners* (1996) and *A Simple Plan* (1998) as well as almost all of Elfman's scores for Burton, the main exception being *Planet of the Apes* (2001).[18]

When songs are mixed into the films, Burton usually chooses them. It was Burton, for example, who chose the Tom Jones song "It's Not Unusual" for *Edward Scissorhands* and also the "Day-O" song for *Beetlejuice*. In Burton's films, songs, like the Prince songs in *Batman*, are usually diegetic (emanating from the story world and heard by the characters), whereas Elfman's score is nondiegetic, outside of the story world (and not heard by the characters). Some of Elfman's music works as a score but is also diegetic, such as the '60s-style lounge music for the "waiting room in the beyond" in *Beetlejuice,* with a Polynesian sound but also a sense of menace. Elfman likes to parody other genres of music, especially television, a practice that works well for pataphysical films. For example, for *Pee-wee,* Elfman had written music inspired by '70s TV ditties.

Batman (1989)

In pataphysical films and comic book movies, the composer's contribution is close in importance to that of the screenwriter and director. The screenplays for these films are often thin and the characters archetypal rather than well-rounded, so the score adds a layer of emotional development that complements the dialogue and the actor's performances and supplements the camera's movement or its stillness. Elfman's approach to scoring the heroic theme for his comic book hero was a departure from the confident militaristic music with its regular beat and sense of action and optimism that characterizes the music usually used for action-adventure heroes, especially by John Williams in films like *Superman, Star Wars,* and *Indiana Jones.*[19]

Elfman's opening theme for *Batman* is darker, more "Gothic." Batman's theme is in a minor key, then leads to a pounding march with snare drum and brass punctuation, a martial sound that functions as a fanfare for the character.

Elfman came up with the particular heroic theme for Batman in an effort to impress producer Jon Peters: "I just took the same basic theme and turned it into this march, and did it a certain way—changed the key around a little bit—and all of a sudden [Peters] leapt up out of his chair and it was completely obvious that I had found the *Batman* hero theme."[20]

The title cue[21] for *Batman* is two minutes, thirty seconds long. It has an extraordinary number of key changes: it starts out in B minor, changes to A minor, then G minor, then F♯ minor, then D minor, all before reaching the one minute, nineteen second mark. At that point the sequence reaches its "faster" section, which goes from G minor to C♯ minor, then E♭ minor, ending in diminished 7, leading to a whole-tone cluster.[22] We will find out later in the film that C minor is the key most associated with Batman, especially toward the end of the film, when he has found his place as a man who is loved and is part of law enforcement in Gotham. This is in direct contrast to the love theme associated with Vicki and Bruce Wayne, which is usually in C major. The tension between the major and minor key emphasizes the tensions between the two aspects of Batman's personality.[23]

The title sequence is worth dwelling on because the title cue of any film, but especially of fantasy films, is extremely important. It is what enables the spectator to leave the real world behind and enter the story world of the film. It gives the spectator a sense of what the conventions of this new world will be. Burton is known for his trademark title sequences, but by the time he made *Planet of the Apes* (2001), he didn't seem interested in doing one. Elfman had to beg to do it, and finally Burton relented. As a result, Elfman ended up working with Bob Dawson to make the credit sequence, with Elfman writing some music, Dawson drawing some storyboards, and Elfman writing more music in reaction to Dawson's storyboards, until the sequence was finalized.[24]

Although Elfman establishes Batman's theme early on, Jack Napier (who will become the Joker by the end of Act I) does not have his own theme; instead, he has silence and some association with Batman's theme, to emphasize how much the two have in common and how easily Batman could have become like the Joker. Once the Joker emerges, he has his own melodies, all appropriations of some sort, especially his variation on Stephen Foster's "Beautiful Dreamer" and waltzes of all kinds, which have been "twisted" (as Elfman did for *Forbidden Zone* and very briefly for *Pee-wee*), mock versions of circus-type tunes and Strauss-type waltzes.[25] Elfman scores Batman's theme in various ways, so that it takes on different meanings, from heroic to loving, from a revelation to fate.[26] The difference in music for each character underlines the duality and opposition between them. Their relationship to power is indicated by their musical themes. The Joker's are all from songs that are so well known they are difficult to alter, and so the action has to comply with them; but Batman's music is part of the orchestral underscore, which is more flexible to the needs of the film. As K. J. Donnelly puts it: "One could almost say the Joker represents the triumph of musical logic over cinematic logic, while Batman represents the subordination of musical logic to cinematic logic, his image consistently invoking his musical theme."[27]

Donnelly also points out that this relationship was inverted in *Batman Returns*: only one pop song was used, "Face to Face," performed by Siouxsie and the Banshees, which was cowritten by Elfman, and it attains a degree of continuity with the orchestral score by using leitmotifs, or musical elements from the film's character themes.[28] Batman, Penguin, and Catwoman have their own leitmotifs that are heard whenever they are on screen.

Batman is 121 minutes long, with 10 minutes of songs written by Prince and 70 minutes of nondiegetic music composed by Elfman. A high proportion of screen time is therefore supported by music, reflecting the trend toward increasing use of music in contemporary films. In the 1960s and '70s, the standard length of a score was between forty and sixty minutes.

Batman was, and remains, Burton and Elfman's biggest success, a breakout film for both of them. Because of the success of *Batman*, the Elfman "sound" has become part of the genre of comic book films, whether Elfman composes the score (as he did for the *Darkman, Men in Black,* and *Spider-Man* series, as well as *Dick Tracy* and *The Hulk*) or not.

There is a lesson here about what it means to be a film auteur. In today's film world, an auteur is not an individual artist working on his or her own. Rather, an auteur name like "Burton" or "The Coen Brothers" or "Sam Raimi" represents a brand. It stands for a group of people who work together to create a consistent look. Burton works consistently with Elfman and with production designer Rick Heinrichs, and he often works with the same actors over and over again.

Elfman has described *Batman* as the hardest score he has ever worked on, and it was while writing it that he became comitted to his new identity as a film composer.

Batman Returns (1992)

Although *Batman* veered from Burton's usual pataphysical approach, with *Batman Returns* he circled back to it, but subtly. This shift is amply signaled in the music, which is overblown and consciously filled with musical clichés. Donnelly compares the film and its score to a classical

Hollywood musical such as *Seven Brides for Seven Brothers* (1954), "where design and music coalesce into a world of dazzling visuals and explosive musical sound." He relates this to the style of cartoons because, like cartoons, "*Batman Returns* constructs its own world . . . with a preponderance of 'mickeymousing' (where the music directly mimics the action)."[29] A key quality of this music is that it relies on the audience's familiarity and sense of recognition for its meaning.

The Elfman Myth

Since the fall of 1989 a rumor has circulated that Elfman does not know how to write music. Janet K. Halfyard deals extensively with this controversy in her recent book, *Danny Elfman's Batman: A Film Score Guide*. Apparently the rumor started when Elfman frankly admitted in an interview that he writes out twelve to sixteen staves of music, and his orchestrator, Steve Bartek, transposes and does the orchestral parts.[30] Ironically, it was Elfman's candor about how he worked with his orchestrator and his conductor (at the time, Shirley Walker,[31] who transcribed the Mantovani-style arrangement of "Beautiful Dreamer" that Elfman incorporated into the score, a musical idea that Elfman freely attributes to Burton) that enabled a composer (Micah D. Rubenstein, who was at that time a professor of composition at Kenyon College in Ohio) to respond to the article, castigating the author for glorifying Elfman's "musical ignorance." Elfman responded by defending his status as a self-taught musician. Halfyard credits the fact that the *Batman* score was not nominated for an Oscar to this exchange. In fact, none of Elfman's scores for Burton until *Big Fish* (2003) were nominated, although he did receive nominations in 1997 for *Men in Black* and *Good Will Hunting*. Halfyard quotes music critic Lukas Kendall's assessment of Elfman's abilities:

> [t]he similarity of style from score to score, the fact that he has continued to write large-scale scores without using Shirley Walker to conduct, who people at one point assumed really wrote *Batman*; that the scores . . . Steve Bartek has done on his own have been completely different from Elfman's music; and the sheer illogic to the assumption that Elfman could have hidden an army of ghost-writers somewhere without anyone naming names or coming forward.[32]

Bartek, in an interview with Kendall,[33] notes that Elfman has an "unorthodox" notation practice: "[H]e's not good at bass clef, but he does everything in treble clef with an octave marking so you know exactly where he wants it to sound. . . ." (Halfyard confirms this from her examination of the *Batman* score, which is now on deposit at the University of Texas at Austin.)

Halfyard also points out that the very nature of film scoring itself, poorly understood by people outside the industry, also added to the confusion. Most people assume that all film composers work like concert hall composers, who have six months to a year to complete a twenty-minute symphonic composition; the average film composer has two months or so to write seventy to one hundred minutes of music. In addition to producing the score, Elfman and his team have to produce the recording, with specific cues of music timed to specific events in the film (called "writing to cue"). The only way to accomplish that is to work with a team, consisting of one or more orchestrators and arrangers and a conductor, as well as the orchestra, in much the same way that a director relies on the skill of his or her director of photography, art production, and editor and their crews.

Halfyard notes that Elfman's working method echoes practices common in the golden age of Hollywood film, when the number of films being made and the speed at which they were turned around in production necessitated the existence of the studio music department, staffed by both composers and teams of orchestrators and copyists.[34] Thus the tight deadlines required of film composition lead to a need for a reliable, talented staff. Elfman's candor about the contributions of his colleagues, unfortunately, has called his credibility into question; however, there seems to be no evidence to support his critics' charges. Any remaining doubts would have been dispelled by Elfman's symphonic debut at Carnegie Hall in New York, where his twenty-minute "Serenada Schizophrana"—with six movements, rolling piano solos, and a female chorus—was performed by the American Composers Orchestra, conducted by Steven Sloane. The single performance was well reviewed.[35]

The Film Scoring Process

On his commentary for the *Pee-wee* DVD, Elfman described how he works with Burton. As with other directors he has worked with before, he often gets involved in Burton's productions early on and reads the script before anything is filmed, though for him the real work begins when he gets to visit the set during production. This is especially important on Burton films, where the production design is so critical to the overall tone of the piece. Elfman revealed that he would take a tape recorder with him on these set visits and start "laying down tracks"[36] by singing ideas for different orchestral parts into the tape recorder, the most direct way he could capture his first impressions and thoughts while on the set or on the way home from the set. For *Batman*, Elfman said that ideas suddenly started coming to him while he was on an airplane, so he had to keep running to the plane's restroom with his tape recorder to lay down tracks. The flight attendants thought he was either ill or in dire need of illegal substances, but Elfman knew that if he didn't get the tracks down before he landed, the Muzak on the plane would act as a "mind eraser." He came close to panicking when he got home, as the notes on his recorder weren't very clear because of plane noise—but after listening repeatedly to the tape, he was able to figure it out.[37]

Once at home, Elfman transcribes what is on the tape recorder and then starts building themes. He has described his process of finding themes as follows:

> I'll take the theme and figure out whether I can play half of it and still recognize it. Then, does it work in a major and a minor key: Can I turn it from funny to spooky? Can I cut it down to just three notes and still make it recognizable? These are some of the acid tests I put a theme through while I'm composing.[38]

He then composes the main themes, taken from key moments throughout the film, while watching a video with time code (a numeric indicator that gives the exact position of the scene within the film as a whole) burned into the lower frame of the image, so that he can match the timing precisely to the time-code numbers. The first step in composing is to "map the tempo" of a scene by writing out a map of the beat of every cue. This can be time consuming, but it has to be done before Elfman can write a single note.

Elfman often will do numerous variations of each theme. If Burton doesn't like the first attempt, Elfman will play one of the variations, until they agree on a basic set of musical ideas, which Elfman will then expand. He begins really composing often as early as the rough-cut stage of editing (at which point the film may already have a "temp track,"[39] some music thrown together by another composer or even by Elfman himself for screening purposes). He describes his greatest challenge as "writing to cues" or "the business of finding timings," which means having the music build up, be expressive, or come to a point in synchrony with a specific action on the screen—a door slams, a character throws up his hands, and so on. Comedies and action films have more points to hit and so can be harder to compose for. Elfman has worked out his own system of writing to the action and makes multiple notations to make sure that the precise bar of music will coincide with a specific action.

Elfman has often compared the process of assigning themes to key parts of the film to doing a jigsaw puzzle. Each puzzle piece will be three or four or even nine minutes of solid music, and he will write between three and eight pieces, which he uses as a resource throughout the scoring process. On the *Edward Scissorhands* DVD, he compares composing to assembling color-coded pieces. His job is to come to an understanding of what each color group does for the movie, then to divide the color groups into individual shapes that make up the various cues. These various pieces are then relinked, like a puzzle.

In describing how cues bridge different kinds of moments in a film, such as in the third act of *Edward Scissorhands* when the neighbors turn against Edward, Elfman compared scoring to knitting, as the thread holds together various sequences of the film that would otherwise feel separate. Even though the music will change in tone and tempo to bridge the changes in a scene, the melodic thread knits the disparate elements of the cue together.

Although Elfman usually has very little time to compose when doing comedies, for films like *Batman* he usually has three or four months. Because, at most, he can write about two minutes of music a day, the length of time he needs to do a score is rigidly determined; a large part of his job is negotiating how much time he will have to do the score.

Regardless of how much time he has had to compose, he often has only three to six days to record. The recording sessions run in three-hour segments, with a ten-minute break for each segment. During recording, a fast-paced, high-pressure process, he will listen to the performance with Burton in the sound booth and redirect his composer and musicians from there after getting notes from Burton or simply a sense of Burton's reactions. The two of them have now worked on so many films and television episodes together that this process has become intuitive. Elfman describes their communication as "almost telepathic." In an interview with Brian Lanser, he said the following:

> Lanser: What are you actually doing during a scoring session? You hire a conductor to conduct the score, and . . . ?
>
> Elfman: Conducting for film scoring is actually a very technical job. People really get confused about that because in a symphony orchestra the conductor is interpreting the piece. The conductor really is the director. But in a film score the conductor is really just moving things along very efficiently.
>
> BL: Do you ever conduct?
>
> Elfman: No, I never conduct. . . . I'm listening in the booth, which is where I prefer to listen anyway because I am hearing [the score] closer to the way it's going to sound. In the room it is a wonderful sound, but you really aren't hearing the balance in a real sense.[40]

Edward Scissorhands (1990)

Although *Batman* started a trend toward denser soundscapes, when scoring *Edward Scissorhands* Elfman found that allowing some scenes to play in silence, especially when a scene was well performed, would highlight the music in other scenes.

According to Elfman, *Edward Scissorhands* was the first time he thought of himself as a film composer.[41] Until then film scoring was only something he dabbled in (even though he had scored fifteen films by 1990). It was the only film he was sorry to be finished with once it was recorded, and as late as 1999 he was considering scoring a ballet based on *Scissorhands*. In 2005, he announced that he would work with choreographer Matthew Bourne, whose ballet of *Edward Scissorhands* will debut in London in November.[42]

The opening credit cue contains both of the key themes of the film: the storybook theme, carried primarily by a boy's choir with a lullaby feel to it, and Edward's theme, which has two aspects—a light, evanescent theme with voices, strings, and a bell-like xylophone, and the theme that represents Edward's emotions. Kim, Edward's love interest, does not get her own theme; rather, a variation of his plays over her. In other words, we see Kim only through Edward's eyes, a rather unusual choice—not in keeping with classical Hollywood practice.

The extensive use of voices, a practice Elfman would continue with *Sleepy Hollow* (1999), ties *Scissorhands* to Disney films such as *Pinocchio* (1940)[43] and *Sleeping Beauty* (1959), though the Disney scores favored major keys.

The opening theme is replayed, but more darkly, when Dianne Weist's character, Peg, goes to Edward's mansion for the first time. This is a packed cue with a lot of emotional variation.

There is another variation of Edward's theme in the scene where Vincent Price is teaching him about manners. Here his theme has been slowed down. Unlike in comedy, where, as noted above, the music has to match the action closely in both tone and tempo, in fairy tales or more dramatic material the music can diverge more from the action. Another difference between comedy and more dramatic scores, for Elfman, is that comedy scores have very short cues and the theme is often interrupted before it is played to completion. However, in films like *Scissorhands,* Elfman can almost always play the theme all the way through, and can choose to interrupt it for effect.

The "suburbia theme" in *Scissorhands* has a little bit of a Muzak feel to it, combining Edward's sense of wonderment and the way suburbia appears to us. The theme returns when we see the housewives approaching Peg's house, and a variation of it appears when we see their husbands driving home from work or leaving for work in the morning.

Elfman had written some '60s-inspired lounge music for *Beetlejuice,* and he used this idea again in *Scissorhands* for some of the suburban scenes, what he called "the ballet de suburbia," which had a Polynesian beat added as well as some sense of menace.

He used fast-paced gypsy music for scenes where Scissorhands shows his mastery with the scissors, whether for dog grooming or haircutting. The music sets the erotic tone as the housewives find his mastery stimulating, especially when he is working his magic on them.

The ice dancing scene was a major focus of the score early on. Elfman knew it would define how he would start the movie, and indeed the entire score. This is another trademark of how he works: he identifies three key emotional moments of the film, with one especially in the middle, and builds the score around the themes he writes for these moments.

Edward's musical theme is always live; it is the unifying melodic thread. Even in the theft and rampage scenes, his theme is distorted and twisted, but it is still there.

An example of the music "playing away" from the action occurs in the overlap scene where Edward cuts Vincent Price's face accidentally when he is trying to be tender, and when he cuts Kim's brother's face accidentally when saving him from an oncoming van. The music lets us know that his intent is not to hurt, that he is just trying to help.

There are two moments of Puccini-like leitmotifs that convey revelation, or at least describe a character. There is a kind of church organ refrain that appears with the pious housewife, and a variation of Edward's theme that plays briefly while Kim is watching him on the television talk show, indicating that Kim is warming up to him.

Eflman's music for *Edward Scissorhands* has been imitated more often than anything else he has done, in movies and especially for television commercials.

The Nightmare Before Christmas (1993)

Elfman's process for scoring *Nightmare* was quite different from standard animation practice. Burton described the film to Elfman while they were working on *Scissorhands*. To begin with, all that Burton had when the film went into production was a Seussian-like poem and numerous drawings.[44] This led to the two of them working on the songs before there was a script. Burton would describe each part of the story, and Eflman would write a song. He recorded the songs in his home studio, singing all the voices but Sally's on the demos. Elfman would later supply the singing voice of Jack in the finished film. The animators began to work by animating the songs before there was a script; screenwriter and associate producer Caroline Thompson actually had to write the script around the songs and flesh out characters who weren't fully formed. She likened it to designing a house after everyone was living in it.[45]

Usually the composer receives a black-and-white pencil version of an animated film, so the score can be composed while the animation is in the works, but in stop-motion "there's either footage or there's no footage."[46] Elfman couldn't start scoring until the film was done, though music editor Bob Badami created a temp track for screening purposes.

Because Elfman had already composed thirty minutes of songs for the seventy-minute movie, half of his job was already done, and he had three years to work on it, as compared to the usual six to eight weeks. Moreover, the main music themes already existed in song form, so he could adapt those themes to the dramatic needs of the underscore. The orchestra was midsized, of about fifty to sixty pieces. "I wanted a very punchy, old-fashioned sound on this," Elfman says. "I wanted it to sound as if it were recorded in 1951, even though it was in stereo."[47]

While working with the orchestra, it was important to keep the music in close sync with the picture, so a computerized metronome was used, creating the illusion that the sound and images were made together.

Sleepy Hollow (1999)

Elfman often describes the score's function as "narrative storytelling." This is clearly the primary function of his score for *Sleepy Hollow*. There is one main theme for the Horseman, but Ichabod's memories of his mother and his reliving of her death generates a second theme, which is used as contrast. As in *Batman,* the two themes are sometimes used interchangeably, underlining the connections between the two sets of events.

As Halfyard notes:

> It is quite possible to read this use of the "wrong" theme in a logical and meaningful manner. Both the main plot and the subplot are bound up with dark forces, witchcraft, and death. The Horseman theme is used for the Horseman, the supernatural threat he poses, and the fear he inspires. The second theme is associated specifically with Ichabod's memory of his mother's death but more generally with memory and mystery: things unknown and needing explanation, things that are not understood by those who see them, and things that are remembered and recalled, especially when those memories are not entirely revealing. As a result, it tends to be found in flashback sequences, but it also occurs in relation to the Horseman because the reason for the murders he is committing are mysterious, while the truth of his death is concealed, just as the circumstances surrounding how and why Ichabod's mother died are a mystery. The music is working to link narrative ideas at a level rather more sophisticated than simply having a theme to represent the Horseman and one to represent Ichabod, although they do work as character themes in relation to their orchestration. The Horseman's music, regardless of which theme is being used, is characterized by male-voice choir, brass, pipe organ, and low strings. When the memory

theme is used for him personally, it tends to be delivered with a brass *fortissimo*, compared to the delicate, ethereal orchestration and children's voices used for Ichabod's memories of his mother. There are some strong narrative ideas underlying why it makes musical sense to use the second theme for the Horseman's character.[48]

Elfman used the same kind of connection to narrative in *Men in Black* (1997), which was nominated for an Oscar.

Sleepy Hollow is also typical of Elfman's work from this period in that he had a typical orchestra, but giving particular weight to a certain instrument, in this case children's voices.

Planet of the Apes (2001)

The orchestra for *Planet of the Apes,* on the other hand, is highly unusual, consisting of a large brass section, no woodwind, no violins, six violas, four double basses, and twelve cellos. This ensemble is then augmented with an enormous amount of percussion, similar to Jerry Goldsmith's percussion-based textures in the original film of 1968.[49]

Elfman usually lays down about 20 percent of his scores himself in the form of percussion. The instruments include drums, hollow bamboos, PVC tubes, bass drums, and timpani. His first two weeks of work on *Apes* consisted of laying out a palette of percussion for the ape marches, which he then recorded on analog synthesizers.

For *Apes,* Elfman laid down much more than usual, seventy-two tracks,[50] or 50 percent of the score, leaving the percussionists (including Emil Richards, who had done percussion on the original film) very little to do. Elfman did not play his tracks for the orchestra. Since they did not hear his tracks, and were forced to play his tracks rhythmically, as they had to hit the beat precisely in order for their tracks to work with the percussion.

In this film Elfman returned to the connection between action and marches. His first visual inspiration for the film came on set after seeing apes in battle gear. Elfman used to record his tracks on tape, but beginning with *Apes* he recorded them digitally, so that he now can make changes either at the studio or at home (he has duplicated his home studio at the recording studio).

In spite of the change in instrumentation, the film is still scored narratively. On the commentary for the *Apes* DVD, Elfman says: "If you just watch the picture and hear the music, or close your eyes and listen to the music, you know what it going on—the classical Hollywood approach. The music was expected to carry everything and tell everything."[51] Elfman also discusses "exposed scenes," by which he means scenes in which the music is foregrounded, for example, during the charge of the apes, when Elfman switches tempos and goes to percussion.

One of Elfman's favorite cues was the scene in which Leo first enters the ape city. There Elfman used various layers of diegetic music, which was great fun to write, as was the "corny hip teenage bad ape music"[52] in the scene in which Leo and his friends escape. The scene in which Ari tries to exchange her favors for Thade's mercy for her human friends is a "sick, twisted version of the . . . music for the romantic scene," an inversion that Elfman loves.[53]

Stretching the Boundaries of the Frequency Range

In addition to considering the various aspects of the music itself, Elfman must be conscious of the fact that his music shares a frequency range with human voices and the sound effects.

> This is a technical aspect of Elfman's writing that breaks with some long-standing traditions relating to instrumental pitches and the voices of the actors. One of the reasons that it is more usual to find melodies in the higher ranges in classical Hollywood scores is the fact that they are further removed from the pitch of the actor's and actresses' speaking voices, [thus] avoiding the possibility that the music might either obscure the dialogue or be obscured by it. Concentrating on lower-pitched melodic lines effectively gives an alternative solution to the same problem, in that the melodic line is usually removed from the pitch area occupied by the voices but in the opposite direction to that dictated by convention. However, this is not always the case: in Batman's "Descent into Mystery," the musical material, in particular the choir, is pitched at exactly the same level as Kim Basinger's voice, and Elfman thins the texture considerably when she speaks to prevent one interfering with the other.[54]

As the trend toward denser soundtracks, begun with Batman, continues, sound effects play a larger and larger role in the soundscape. Sound designers now have to consciously work for moments of quiet, especially in comic films, which have a lot of "wham-bam-pow" sounds. In addition, these films tend to be so noisy that not all the sounds can be

Foleyed (re-created in the studio for the soundtrack), as there would be too many; sound effect designers focus only on those sounds that we need to hear for greatest emotional impact.

For *Spiderman 2* (2004), Elfman created a "template" of sounds before he started really composing. He refers to these sounds using texture names, such as "metal." As Kevin O'Connell, the sound re-recording mixer on the film, pointed out, in a comic book film there are no rules as to what things should actually sound like. For this particular film, sound effects carry about 50 percent of the emotional drive, with the rest carried by the music, a stark contrast to the practice of even the recent past, when most of the emotional impact was carried by the music.[55] We must wait and see if this is a development unique to comic book films or if it is an industry trend.

Notes

1. Janet K. Halfyard, *Danny Elfman's Batman: A Film Score Guide*, Scarecrow Film Score Guides, No. 2 (Lanham, MD: Scarecrow Press, 2004), p. 31.

2. John M. Glionna, "A Different Beat: Danny Elfman Pinged from Oingo Boingo Front Man to Prolific Movie Score Writer, Now This Oddball May Pong Into Directing His Own Scripts," *Los Angeles Times*, quoted in *Clowns of Death: A History of Oingo Boingo*, by Keith T. Breese (Xlibris Corporation, 2001) Philadelphia, PA, p. 24.

3. Ibid., p. 27.

4. Halfyard, *Danny Elfman's Batman*, p. 3.

5. Bryan Lanser, and Kevin Monahan, "Danny Elfman's Big Adventure Continues In Sleepy Hollow" (1999), http://www.emu.com/artist/d_elfman/elfman_interview.html (no longer available).

6. Elfman commentary on the *Planet of the Apes* DVD, Twentieth Century Home Video, 2002.

7. For more on The Cockettes, see the documentary *The Cockettes*, by David Weissman and Bill Weber, distributed by MDM Productions (USA) and Strand Releasing, 2002.

8. Breese, *Clowns of Death*, pp. 27–34.

9. Rick Clark, "Danny Elfman," *Mix Magazine*, May 2001, http://mixonline.com/ar/audio_danny_elfman/.

10. Breese, *Clowns of Death*, p. 76.

11. Certain DVDs of Burton's films have separate audio tracks that isolate Elfman's music and his commentary: *Pee-wee's Big Adventure*, *Edward Scissorhands*, and *Planet of the Apes*. Other DVDs include interviews with Burton. Unfortunately, no such commentary is included on the DVDs for the *Batman* films, *Big Fish*, or *The Nightmare Before Christmas*.

12. Halfyard, *Danny Elfman's Batman*, p. 22.

13. Lanser and Monahan, "Danny Elfman's Big Adventure."

14. Rube Goldberg was a cartoonist who routinely depicted people using elaborate devices to accomplish simple tasks.

15. Giacomo Puccini (1858–1924) wrote some of the best-loved operas of all time, including *Madame Butterfly*, *La Bohème*, and *Tosca*. Unlike other composers, who used leitmotifs (short melodic phrases) to indicate a character's presence, Puccini used them to give a sense of what characters were thinking.

16. Elfman, DVD Commentary for *Pee-wee's Big Adventure*, DVD (2004) distributed by Warner Studios.

17. Ibid.

18. Halfyard, *Danny Elfman's Batman*, pp. 23–24.

19. Ibid., p. 64.

20. Randall D. Larson, "Danny Elfman: From Boingo to *Batman*," *Soundtrack!*, September 1990, p. 20. Quoted in ibid., p. 27.

21. The cue sheet contains information for each piece of music, including the writer. The sheet is a document that is filed with the performing rights societies and contains a detailed listing of each piece of music used in a film or television production. Each of these pieces of music is called a "cue."

22. Halfyard, *Danny Elfman's Batman*, p. 114.

23. Ibid., p. 112.

24. Elfman commentary, *Planet of the Apes* DVD.

25. K. J. Donnelly, "The Classical Film Score Forever? *Batman, Batman Returns* and Post-Classical Film Music," in *Contemporary Hollywood Cinema*, ed. Steve Neale and Murray Smith (London: Routledge, 1998), p. 148.

26. Halfyard, *Danny Elfman's Batman*, p. 111.

27. Donnelly, "Classical Film Score," p. 149.

28. Ibid.

29. Ibid., pp. 151–152.

30. Robert L. Doerschuk, "Danny Elfman: The Agony and the Ecstasy of Scoring *Batman*," *Keyboard*, October 1989, 85. Quoted in Halfyard, p. 11.

31. Since Shirley Walker went on to her own composing career, Elfman has consistently worked with music supervisor Bob Badami.

32. Lukas Kendall, "Danny Elfman: From *Pee-wee* to *Batman* to Two Films a Year," part 2, *Film Score Monthly*, December 1995, p. 11. Quoted in Halfyard, *Danny Elfman's Batman*, p. 14.

33. Lukas Kendall, "Interview: Steve Bartek," part 1, *Film Score Monthly*, December 1995, pp. 15–16. Quoted in Halfyard, *Danny Elfman's Batman*, p. 14.

34. Halyard, *Danny Elfman's Batman*, pp. 16–17.

35. Bernard Holland, "Loudspeakers Complicate Effort to Span Sonic Divide," *New York Times*, February 28, 2005.

36. The recording process consists of recording individual elements of a score one at a time. For example, Elfman records his percussion tracks before he goes into the studio

recording session with the rest of the orchestra. What he means here by "laying down tracks" is that when he is in the note-taking stage, he records ideas for the melody for each group of instruments one after the other, using his own voice, in order to have a record of his idea when he is not in a position to write.

37. Elfman, commentary on *Planet of the Apes* DVD.

38. Greg Pederson, "Danny's Big Adventure: Danny Elfman Embraces the Dark Rites of Film Composition," *Electronic Musician*, February 1997, p. 106. Quoted in Halfyard, *Danny Elfman's Batman*, p. 27.

39. Toward the middle of the editing process (post-production) the director will ask the music editor to prepare a temporary music track, or temp track, in order to give studio executives and test audiences an idea of what the film will be like once the final score is completed. The music for the temp track can come from anywhere, as no royalties need to be paid for this kind of private use. The only problem with temp tracks is that directors (and studio executives) sometimes get attached to them, forcing the composer to compose in imitation of the temp track instead of writing new work.

40. Lanser and Monahan, "Danny Elfman's Big Adventure Continues in Sleepy Hollow," E-mu, ca. 1999 (unverified). Source: http://www.emu.com/artist/d_elfman/elfman intrview.html (no longer available), now found at: http://www.bluntinstrument.org.uk/elfman/archive/Emu99.htm.

41. Elfman, commentary on the *Edward Scissorhands* DVD.

42. Jesse Green, "Matthew Bourne Does the Horizontal Ballet," *New York Times,* March 13, 2005.

43. In some ways, *Scissorhands* can be seen as a remake of *Pinocchio.*

44. From the liner notes for the *Nightmare* DVD.

45. From the "making of" featurette on the *Nightmare* DVD.

46. Frank Thompson, *Tim Burton's The Nightmare Before Christmas: The Film, the Art, the Vision* (New York: Hyperion, 1993), pp. 159.

47. Ibid., p. 160.

48. Halfyard, *Danny Elfman's Batman,* pp. 28–29.

49. Ibid., pp. 34–35.

50. Before the music is mixed down to one soundtrack, which is added to the film print, the different parts exist on separate tracks. With today's digital technology, these tracks can be adjusted individually up to the last minute. See also note 34.

51. Elfman, commentary on *Planet of the Apes* DVD.

52. Ibid.

53. Ibid.

54. Halfyard, *Danny Elfman's Batman*, p. 32.

55. Paul Ottoson, Kevin O'Connell, Gary Hecker, and Danny Elfman were all interviewed in the featurette "Making the Amazing: Sound and Music" on the *Spider-Man 2* DVD.

$$7$$

OTHER PATAPHYSICAL DIRECTORS

This book has posited Tim Burton as a trendsetter for contemporary pataphysical directors. However, other directors, in search of new forms to replace the aesthetically drained classical Hollywood genres, have taken up the banner. Some of them have imitated Burton outright, and others have struck out on their own, but all of the directors I discuss here (admittedly only a small sample of the directors I could have included)[1] have built on Burton's pataphysical foundation and followed his lead in looking to the past to project the future. Below I discuss the pataphysical films of Barry Sonnenfeld, Stephen Sommers, and Roland Emmerich.

Barry Sonnenfeld

Barry Sonnenfeld graduated from New York University's film school in 1978 and directed porn films until he shot *Blood Simple* (1984) for Joel and Ethan Coen, who also went to NYU. He then shot several more films for the Coen brothers, among others, before directing his first film, *The Addams Family*.

The Addams Family (1991)

This film is a cinematic version of the 1960s television series, which itself was based on the cartoons of Charles Addams. With a budget of $38 million, it eventually earned $192 million at the U.S. box office. The Addams family is composed of Gomez (Raul Julia); his wife, Morticia (Anjelica Huston); Uncle Fester (Christopher Lloyd); Wednesday (Christina Ricci in a star-making turn) and her brother, Pugsley (Jimmy Workman); Grandma (Judith Malina); Lurch, the butler (Carel Struycken); and disembodied hand called Thing (Christopher Hart); and villains Tully Alford (Dan Hedaya) and Abigail Craven/Dr. Pinder Schloss (Elizabeth Wilson). This is a fairy tale where everything is turned upside down: an imposter (Lloyd) pretends to be Gomez's long-lost older brother (and therefore heir) Fester, only to find out that he *is* Fester, that he had amnesia and was taken over by Craven. In this family it is the parents who misbehave, cause vandalism, and make out at every opportunity. They also indulge in an extreme level of S&M, which they are teaching to their children, though in true cartoon style we never see the results of the torture, and everyone always survives intact. They are cannibals as well (Morticia repeatedly voices a fondness for eating children). All the women are witches, and the men are loafers and ne'er-do-wells. They can only get away with this because they have a vaultful of doubloons (clearly Gomez and Fester are descended from pirates), which smoothes away any social upheaval they might cause. For most of the movie they seem to be socially isolated, but when they throw a party in Fester's honor, there is a ballroom full of eccentrics just like them, most of them related. In addition to the strangeness of their own behavior, they have a houseful of strange things, from the disembodied hand, who is a kind of highly intelligent pet, to the giant, speechless butler, Lurch.

Sonnenfeld has positioned the Addamses as noveau riche Euro-trash, and most of the humor comes from their encounters with average American suburbanites, who cater to them because of their wealth but find them repulsive and incomprehensible. The sequence where the family is forced to live in a motel and earn their own living after Fester has locked them out of their house has all the best laughs.

In his debut effort, Sonnenfeld has entered Burton territory, especially *Scissorhands,* and not just because Caroline Thompson wrote both screenplays. The score is a clear imitation of Danny Elfman's work, though mostly arrangements of songs (for example, the movie opens with a classic Christmas carol sung in a minor key by carol singers in front of the Addams mansion). The long traveling camera shot chasing Thing around the house is reminiscent of Burton's shots through various environments, and the conflict between the monstrous, outsider family and bland suburbanites is a clear retake of the Burton formula. The differences with Burton's approach are also of interest: there are more female characters, and they have more to do (in fact, in many ways Morticia is the center of the film, and Christina Ricci simply steals the show), and the family here is cohesive if weird.

The important thing is that *The Addams Family*, like *Edward Scissorhands*, combines a fairy-tale narrative structure with the comedy and transformations-without-consequences of animation. The characters are all one-note but well-known types from the TV show, animation series, and the original cartoons of Charles Addams. Most of the gags needed in-camera effects as well as CGI.

The plot is thin and relatively unimportant—what really matters is Sonnenfeld's take on European-American relations, which can be summed up as "we hate them because we envy them, and like Fester we would join them and be like them if we could." The new twist in the development of pataphysical films is the outsider-family plot, as compared to the lone outsider. This would up the stakes for Burton. Thompson made a point of putting Jack Skellington in a similarly eccentric but cohesive community in *Nightmare*, but Burton would later dismantle a family—and most of the community around it—head by head in *Sleepy Hollow*. With his first directorial outing, Sonnenfeld launched a franchise, which might have led to a third installment if Raul Julia, in many ways the comic lynchpin of the film, had not died suddenly after completing *Addams Family Values* (1993).

Men in Black (1997)

Based on the comic book series by Lowell Cunningham, *Men in Black* was another successful franchise. The first installment, budgeted at $90 million, grossed $250 million at the U.S. box office. The story focuses on K (Tommy Lee Jones), an experienced agent for a secret government program that helps alien refugees settle on Earth, appropriately disguised, and weeds out unwanted invaders. In the opening sequence, K's partner decides to retire, and K spends the rest of the first act finding a new one, settling on Agent J (Will Smith). Almost as soon as Smith dons the eponymous black suit Earth is threatened by a spaceship hovering over the planet, with a one-hour countdown prominently displayed, clearly an homage to *Independence Day* (see below) released the year before, which also starred Will Smith. These aliens communicate with

Earth, however, and what they want is a galaxy that fits into a glass bauble hanging on a cat's collar. The agents have to combat an intergalactic terrorist (a huge cockroach disguised as Vincent D'Onofrio) for the galaxy, with the help of pathologist Dr. Laurel Weaver (Linda Fiorentino). Once the struggle is over, Agent J discovers that Agent K has been training a replacement and not a partner. Once K retires, Dr. Weaver becomes his partner, Agent L.

Men in Black is a "textbook" pataphysical film: the characters are so flat, they have letter markers instead of names (the scene in which K deletes J's life history is played up to acknowledge this fact). Based on a comic book, the film has numerous special effects—all the aliens are CGI except for puppets needed for direct interaction (much as in *Jurassic Park*), and the interactions with the aliens are of a cartoon nature (the scene in which J struggles with a squidlike alien as she gives birth is typical). Again, the meta-discourse, and probably what really made the film a popular franchise (apart from Smith's elegance and the chemistry between Smith and Jones), is about American hypocrisy toward "aliens" or foreign immigrants—some get the royal treatment, and others are thrown back at the border, but clearly aliens are situated at every strata of our society ("Elvis isn't dead, he just went home") and the economy could not function without them. This time Sonnenfeld asked Elfman to write the score, rather than trying to find someone to imitate Elfman's sound, and the score was nominated for an Oscar.

Wild Wild West (1999)

Based on the 1960s television series, *Wild Wild West* depicts an American West filled with glass and metal architecture and futuristic devices right out of Jules Verne. Originally meant to star Mel Gibson and then George Clooney, the role of master-of-disguises Secret Agent Artemus Gordon went to Kevin Kline and the action role of Jim West to Will Smith. The agents are working to protect President Ulysses S. Grant (also Kline) from archvillain-in-a wheelchair Arliss Loveless (Kenneth Branagh), who is kidnapping scientists, one of which is the husband of Rita Escobar (Salma Hayek), who teams up with the agents in order to find him.

Most of the appeal of the film, as with the series, comes from the juxtaposition of the glass and metal architecture of Loveless's huge industrial complex, reminiscent of the Victorian factory area in Dortmund, Germany, which is contrasted to the tanklike locomotive that transports the agents. This train is crammed with futuristic devices such as the "skull master," a magic-lantern device that projects what is on a dead person's eyes, his final vision, instead of images from glass slides. Other devices include Loveless's amphibious tank (a stagecoach built like an armored tank) and various weapons, such as a Gatling gun. But the prize goes to the mechanical *Tarantula,* which the designers conceived as embodying all of Loveless's anger.[2] The *Tarantula* was clearly ILM's update of its own Imperial Walkers, designed for *The Empire Strikes Back* and *Return of the Jedi,* which were stop-motion, updated to CGI.

As is usual with pataphysical films, the critics were mostly negative. Janet Maslin in the *New York Times* suggests that box office is all that *Wild Wild West* is about. "It cares far more about herding audiences into theaters than about what they hear or see," she wrote. Stephen Hunter in the *Washington Post* goes further: "*Wild Wild West* is a rambling wreck from computer tech and a helluva souvenir—that is, for those interested in artifacts representing the American movie at its worst." Rod Dreher in the *New York Post* tops even that invective: "Nothing goes right in this empty-headed, extraordinarily dull and pointless exercise in throwing Warner Bros. money down a rat hole. It's a wild, wild waste of time."[3]

These critics are neglecting to discuss the meta-discourse in the film, the same as that of the TV series, that is, the American creation myth (the western), where problems are solved by action heroes carrying guns in large, open desert spaces and confronted by (European-originated) industrial technology. It is significant that Loveless is played by a British actor and that his *Tarantula,* a huge, corroded metal spider, destroys Monument Valley, the setting of many classic western scenes. At the level of technology the film contains a whole meta-discourse about the transition from stop-motion to CGI, from mechanical age to computer age, which can be followed simply by tracking the nature and uses of the various weapons, modes of transportation, and gadgets. There is also a layer of social commentary: Arliss's goal is to rekindle the Civil War by assassinating President Grant; the film posits the creation of the Secret Service as a response to such terrorism, embodied by a duo that combines action-movie heroics and elegant beauty with the wit and transformative abilities of an intellectual who is also a master of disguise. In spite of the distractions provided by Salma Hayek in all her exotic glory, the job of saving the world, as usual, is left to a homosocial government organization.

Stephen Sommers

A native of Minnesota, Sommers attended St. John's University and after spending some time managing rock bands in Europe earned a master's degree in film production from the University of Southern California. His short thesis film won an award, and from there he went to writing, directing, and producing his own films independently, starting with *Catch Me If You Can* (1989). He then went on to make films for Disney, which eventually led to his directing *The Mummy* (1999).

Van Helsing (2004)

Van Helsing is the mythical character from the book *Dracula* by Bram Stoker and almost all of the subsequent Dracula films, the gentleman-scientist with all the answers who leads the fight against Dracula and the other undead. Sommers brought a new twist to this character by making Van Helsing a virile action hero, as played by Hugh Jackman, fresh out of his role as Logan/Wolverine in *X-Men* (2000). The character's traditional intellectualism is now given to Carl (David Wenham), an inventor-scientist-researcher friar who travels with him.

The film opens with a black-and-white sequence that shows Victor Frankenstein (Samuel West) successfully bringing the Frankenstein monster (Shuler Hensley) to life in a lab provided by Dracula (Richard Roxburgh), who commissioned the research for his own nefarious ends. A mob has formed and is storming the castle. Dracula kills Frankenstein, but the creature takes Frankenstein's body and runs with it to a windmill. The mob sets the windmill on fire, and it burns to the ground; all assume that the creature has perished. We then meet Van Helsing, who is struggling with a large Hulk-like figure in the belfry of Paris's Notre Dame. At first, we think his enemy might be Jack the Ripper, then that it is the Hunchback of Notre Dame, but it turns out to be Mr. Hyde (Robbie Coltrane), of Jekyll and Hyde fame. This opening is incredibly weak, with its pastiche of various monstrous characters, and the digital rendering of the Hyde monster leaves a lot to be desired.

However, the film improves quite a bit after that, as Van Helsing travels to the Vatican, where we learn that he belongs to a secret order whose members are drawn from all the religions of the world to fight supernatural evil. Van Helsing came to them years ago with a case of total amnesia, the only clue to his past being a ring with the insignia of a dragon.

Van Helsing has a new mission: to go to Transylvania and save from Dracula the last two members of the Valerious royal family, Prince Velkan (Will Kemp) and Princess Anna (Kate Beckinsale), a family that has been harassed by Dracula for generations. An ancestor had vowed to kill Dracula or forgo heaven, and now nine generations have been unable to avenge their ancestor. Van Helsing's task is to kill Dracula and free the Valerious family from this limbo. Friar Carl equips him with an array of weapons, starting with the usual garlic, stake, and crucifix, and ending with a gas-powered crossbow and a fragment of an ancient document with the same insignia as the one on Van Helsing's ring.

Once they arrive in Transylvania, Van Helsing realizes that in addition to Dracula, there are Dracula's three brides (Elena Anaya, Silvia Colloca, and Josie Maran) to contend with. They can come out in daylight (as long as it is cloudy), and because they can fly, they represent a formidable threat. Van Helsing, Carl, and Princess Anna work together to eliminate the brides and then Dracula. In the process of rescuing Frankenstein's monster from Dracula (Dracula wanted to use the monster as a catalyst to bring life to his progeny), they succeed in destroying an army of vampires (Dracula's offspring) with a nuclear weapon that Carl has invented. They eventually rescue the monster, but fail to save Prince Velkan, who is turned into a werewolf. Velkan passes the werewolf curse onto Van Helsing, but it is precisely this that enables Van Helsing to kill Dracula, as only a werewolf can kill the undead. Anna reverses the curse after Van Helsing has killed Dracula but before it takes hold permanently, with an antidote of Dracula's. However, Van Helsing unwittingly kills her before the cure is complete.

In his confrontation with Dracula, Van Helsing finds that they have been enemies for centuries and that his actual name is Gabriel; the implication is that both are angels, one the fallen Lucifer, the other having taken human form to stop him from committing evil.

The film has serious problems. The division of the lead role into two characters (Van Helsing and Carl) hurts it. It would have been better to have an edgier, riskier combination of intellectualism and action in one character, as Burton did with Johnny Depp's Ichabod Crane in *Sleepy Hollow*, which would have left more room for a meatier interaction between Van Helsing and Anna. Anna's death should have been one of the most powerful scenes in the film, but it is thrown away, partly because of the way Anna's body is blocked (we don't see her die), and because

Anna's character and leadership ability are undercut throughout by her ridiculous dominatrix-style outfit, with six-inch stiletto heels and a leather corset that pushes her breasts up to her chin. Under the corset she is wearing a white linen blouse with an embroidered pattern of red cross-hatching, which makes her look topless during certain sequences. It was probably this bizarre costuming that led to a series of articles claiming that Beckinsale had had plastic surgery to enlarge her breasts, surgery that was not entirely successful.[4] (Beckinsale's representatives deny she has had any surgical work, and Beckinsale herself pointed out that her body had changed after her pregnancy.)

Also, when we later discover that Van Helsing is the angel Gabriel and that Dracula is Lucifer, we are left with too many unanswered questions: Why is Van Helsing human then? Did he choose to be human in order to better pursue Dracula, or was his humanity imposed on him as a punishment, and in either case, why does he have amnesia? In fact, the film does not fully commit to the both-of-them-used-to-be-angels scenario, though it is hard to understand how else Van Helsing can have memories of being at Masada with Dracula (even Dracula wasn't alive in 72 C.E.).

The movie is a visual spectacular, but some of the visuals are not well thought out. For example, the opening sequence matches the opening of *Frankenstein* (1931), and the windmill burning refers to that film as well. However, it is not enough to repeat a previous film; it needs to be creatively commented on, as Burton did in both *Frankenweenie* and *Sleepy Hollow*. Since the potential fans for *Van Helsing* are likely to be familiar with Burton's work, the opening must have fallen flat for them, and the idea of Dracula paying for the Frankenstein research seems forced. Sommers also quotes *Sleepy Hollow* in the carriage chase scene. This quotation works much better, because it adds enemies that can fly, and the emotional relationships between the Frankenstein monster, Carl, Anna, and Van Helsing change significantly as a result of what happens during the chase. And, of course, the film pays homage to the Universal monster films featuring the Wolfman, Frankenstein, and Dracula, of the 1930s and '40s (though Mr. Hyde has sneaked over from MGM). This is part of what we expect from a myth-cycle film, and fans appreciate such moments as when Dracula grasps a crucifix and it bursts into flames (a direct quotation of the original *Dracula*). The only problem here is too many monsters; one wishes that Sommers had insisted on a franchise and remade the Universal monster films one at a time, more in keeping with his reimagining of *The Mummy* (1999).

The biggest problem is one of tone. IMDB lists the film's genre as action/adventure/horror/fantasy/thriller, as compared to Sommers's *The Mummy* which was listed as adventure/action/fantasy/horror. Blending all of these genres is a challenge the movie fails to meet; on the DVD commentary, Sommers notes the difficulty in finding the right tone, and said he didn't feel he had found it until the first time Jackman and Beckinsale acted together. He also noted that he had wanted to cut the "butt-crack" moment, when the digital Hyde character pulls up his pants, but it tested well with audiences, so he left it in. Though moments like this may work individually for particular audiences, the movie is left with the issue of conflicting tones.

Reviewers said the following about *Van Helsing:* "Too camp to be kitsch, too kitsch to be camp, too big to be good, too good to be dull. That is to say, it's a modern, effects-insane, big-studio American summer movie, 17 or so hours long and one-fifth of an inch deep" (Stephen Hunter in the *Washington Post*); "A clattering, hectic spectacle that, by the end, has almost completely run out of ideas and inspiration" (A. O. Scott in the *New York Times*); and "*Van Helsing* is silly and spectacular, and fun" (Roger Ebert).[5]

Given the roundly negative reviews and the poor box office ($120 million U.S. box office for a film budgeted at $160 million), no sequel appears to be in the works. There was an earlier discussion of keeping the Transylvanian village set to use for an NBC television series,[6] an idea that was later dropped because the box office returns for the movie did not meet expectations, though the set will still be kept for some other use.[7]

Like cartoons such as Chuck Jones's *Chariots of Fur* or *Duck Dodgers and the Return of the 2412th Century* (1980), Sommers's films beginning with *The Mummy* combine parody, tongue-in-cheek humor, and homage. The difference between *Van Helsing* and *The Mummy* is that this film focuses on one mythical figure (the mummy), and the action is more coherent, which enables the character relationships to develop more fully. The female lead is not treated as another spectacular effect; in fact, she is that rare thing, a female intellectual, and the combination of Brendan Fraser's action hero and Rachel Weisz's specialist in the languages and lore of ancient Egypt works much better than the Jackman–Wenham combination.

The difference also can be seen in the reviews. For *The Mummy,* the reviews were mixed: "fast and furious, shallow, empty, casually racist, merry, jaunty, silly and utterly weightless" (Stephen Hunter in the *Washington Post*); "a gaudy comic video game splashed onto the screen. Think *Raiders of the Lost Ark* (1981) with cartoon characters, no coherent story line and lavish but cheesy special effects" (Stephen Holden in the *New York Times*). Roger Ebert in the *Chicago Sun-Times* pays the movie this most left-handed of compliments: "There is hardly a thing I can say in its favor, except that I was cheered by nearly every minute of it. I cannot argue for the script, the direction, the acting or even the mummy, but I can say that I was not bored and sometimes I was unreasonably pleased."[8]

It seems clear that by the time *The Mummy* came out, some reviewers had adjusted their thinking and were no longer judging pataphysical films against classical Hollywood films, but rather against some new, as yet undefined standard, which did not free the films from being well made. In spite of the negative reviews, *The Mummy* did well at the U.S. box office, earning $155 million; the sequel, *The Mummy Returns* (2001), also did very well, earning $202 million. In addition to its sequel, which kept the key actors, *The Mummy* was successful as a franchise: a prequel, *The Scorpion King* (2002), scripted by Stephen Sommers, was basically an action/fantasy/adventure version of *The Mummy* that filled a desperate need for non-white audiences to see their own heroes up on the screen.

For our purposes here, the main thing to note is that Sommers often makes pataphysical films, most of which he scripts. *The Mummy, The Mummy Returns,* and *Van Helsing* are reimaginings of the original Universal monster films (which themselves were adaptations of novels and plays). Like all pataphysical films, the narrative of *Van Helsing* (as well as Sommers's *Mummy* films) makes some sense when the spectator is aware of additional texts or discourses outside of the film, and its meaning both plays on and harks back to that. These films, then, cannot be viewed in isolation, but must be understood in relation to other texts. The narrative makes no attempt to be realistic, but rather depends on being accepted by viewers because it follows, or slightly twists, established generic conventions, although the lack of acceptable scientific explanation is missing here, as already noted; instead of making fun of the scientific establishment, the film dispenses with it altogether.

This reliance on genre conventions can be taken too far, as it is in *Van Helsing*, but it can also work well, as it does in *The Mummy*, showing that there are good and bad pataphysical films. Closely tied to the lack of realism is the tongue-in-cheek humor, a quality of parody that reminds us at all times that the real narrative here is the meta-narrative, the narrative that relates the film we are watching to other texts, rather than the actual film plot, which is rather thin. As a result, the characters are also underdeveloped. As I have demonstrated earlier, all of these characteristics are closer to animation conventions than they are to classical Hollywood conventions.

Although *Van Helsing* is not an animated film, it certainly has enough extremely visible effects, many of them digital, some in camera. Already mentioned is the poor CGI depiction of Mr. Hyde; the CGI versions of the three Wolfmen in the film work much better, especially since Sommers tweaked the transformations from man to werewolf and back again. Less successful are Dracula's brides in their harpy form, though adding their real faces onto the digitized bodies makes them more acceptable than they would have been had they been entirely CGI. There are frequent switches from real actors flying on cables to digital actors flying and fighting, most of which are unnoticeable (though the DVD commentary points out many of them). There are also some invisible effects that work quite well, such as the matting of the scenery in various shots, especially the carriage chase scene, the digital fire, and the fire-breathing dancers in the Halloween ball scene (the church used as a location would not allow the film crew to light real fire, so those characters were shot on a stage elsewhere and blue-screened in). Director of photography Allan Daviau and special effects coordinator Scott R. Fisher deserve a lot of credit for making all of this work as well as it does, as do editor Bob Ducsay and composer Alan Silvestri, whose music helps tie everything together.

Roland Emmerich

Roland Emmerich, a German-born filmmaker, learned filmmaking while enrolled in the director's program at film school in Munich, where his student film, *The Noah's Ark Principle*, went on to open the 1984 Berlin Film Festival. However, his penchant for special effects and science fiction (garnering him the nickname "Little Spielberg from Sindelfingen") eventually led him to a career in Hollywood.

Independence Day (1996)

One day everyone wakes up to find huge alien spaceships parked over Earth's major cities. Ex-scientist-turned-cable-technician David Levinson (Jeff Goldblum) realizes they have taken over Earth's broadcast airwaves to synchronize a countdown. He tries to get this information through to the U.S. president (Bill Pullman), without success, because his ex-wife (Margaret Colin), the press secretary, won't take his call. So he drives from New York to Washington, D.C., to force her to pay attention; by then it is almost too late. Once Washington is destroyed, the people surrounding the president who were able to evacuate end up at Area 51 (yes, it does exist, and yes, they have a spaceship that crash-landed in 1948, along with the bodies of its alien pilots, watched over by a mad scientist, (Brent Spiner). Captain Steve Hiller (Will Smith), a hotshot pilot, has managed to shoot down one of the alien scout ships and brings an alien back. His girlfriend, a stripper (played by Vivica A. Fox), manages to save her little boy and the first lady (Mary McDonnell) too (though she later dies of her injuries) and rejoin Hiller, just in time to see him pilot the 1948 spaceship back to the mother ship with Levinson aboard. Before leaving, Levinson and his ex-wife make up, and Hiller marries the stripper, even though it will hurt his military career. Hiller pilots Levinson to the mother ship, where Levinson manages to implant a computer virus that destroys it. Everyone returns home safe and sound, though that doesn't help all of Earth's major cities that were destroyed with great special effects glee.

Although snidely derided by many critics, who were suffering from a summerful of special effects action extravaganzas, *Independence Day* managed to take in $306 million at the U.S. box office.

As with Sommers's *The Mummy*, the critics seemed to realize intuitively that they were dealing with a different kind of film, but rather than try to analyze why these films might make so much money (in other words, why the audiences liked them in spite of the bad press) they simply derided them. Here are some typical examples, starting with Roger Ebert:

"Independence Day" is not just an inheritor of the 1950s flying saucer genre, it's a virtual retread—right down to the panic in the streets, as terrified extras flee toward the camera and the skyscrapers frame a horrible sight behind them. Like those old B movies, the alien threat is intercut with lots of little stories involving colorful characters, who are chosen for their ethnic, occupational and sexual diversity. Representing the human race here are not only David the techhead and the president, but also assorted blacks, Jews, Arabs, Brits, exotic dancers, homosexuals, cute kids, generals, drunken cropdusters, tight-lipped defense secretaries and "The McLaughlin Group." There is not a single character in the movie who doesn't wear an invisible label.[9]

And James Berardinelli:

Worse still, Independence Day gets mired in syrupy, artificial character development, and this bogs down the entire middle act. Once the aliens have blasted their way through New York, Los Angeles, and Washington, this film doesn't offer much in the way of compelling viewing. With its hackneyed plot, feeble attempts at characterization, and predictable finale, the second half of Independence Day becomes an extremely dull and lifeless affair.[10]

And Judith Shulevitz:

It's the saucers that make Independence Day exactly what its director/producer/co-writer Roland Emmerich must have wanted it to be: a wholly satisfying Saturday-afternoon sci-fi/disaster/fighter-pilot/video-game experience. Craggy, heavy, impossibly airborne, the alien ships raise to the level of consciousness the pleasing weightlessness of everything else. Skyscrapers, automobiles, highways, heliports, humongous naval aircraft carriers? Tinker toys to be demolished as brightly and loudly as possible. Characters? Caricatures, more like it, who make no claim on your emotions. They're information-spewing cogs in the rush to victory, to be crushed, rescued, killed off, or married as the plot's triumphalist logic requires. Aliens? They're spiny, gooey, and possessed of whiplike tails; they jump out of one another's stomachs; in short, they're indistinguishable from their much scarier counterparts in the Alien series, with all the ballast of an undergraduate film-student reference. But the plot line is the most lightweight of all: Aliens invade the earth and plot to destroy every person on it; the president of the United States (Bill Pullman), a dysfunctional scientist (Jeff Goldblum), a young fighter pilot (Will Smith), and the air forces of every quasi-developed nation on earth overcome their differences and team up to free the world.[11]

As with Burton's pataphysical films, each of these critics recognizes that there is something different going on here. The plots are thin, the characters are types; the overall approach is openly borrowed from other films and even television series; the special effects, even if achieved with old-fashioned means, add up to a lot of spectacle. Strictly following the rules, their job is to denigrate these films. Yet these reviewers admit there is some enjoyment to be had; they know that no one will *not* go to the film because of what they have to say about it. For example, in the same review, Bardinelli noted: "It's useless to advise people not to see *Independence Day*, so I'll issue a warning instead: curb your enthusiasm and don't expect much." Ebert admitted that, in spite of everything, he liked the movie: "Still, *Independence Day* is in the tradition of silly summer fun, and on that level I kind of liked it, as, indeed, I kind of like any movie with the courage to use the line 'It's the end of the world as we know it.'"

Shulevitz manages to come up with a selling point:

> *Independence Day* already has more than its share of very large, very visible maternal superegos hovering just overhead, and it is one of the film's secret pleasures that it puts this apocalyptic thought across with irresistible immediacy: If the men of this planet don't clean up their act, overcome all divisions of nation, color, and creed, and steer their little war planes straight, extraterrestrial supermoms will blow them away.

As I've noted before, the fact that a film is pataphysical does not automatically mean it is good, or even that it will do well at the box office. It has to have a meta-discourse that hits a nerve, as Shulevitz points out. So part of its appeal is that it comes out at the right time, that the movie's obsessions match those of the audience. In Emmerich's next pataphysical film, *Godzilla* (1998), that did not happen, and the film, which cost $200 million, ended up bringing in only $136 million at the U.S. box office.

Godzilla (1998)

In this film, French nuclear tests in the South Pacific have led to changes in various irradiated life forms, one of them being Godzilla, a huge amphibious reptile that carelessly destroys fishing boats and decides to make a nest in Manhattan. A worm scientist, Dr. Niko Tatopoulos (Matthew Broderick), is called in by the government to figure out what has happened here, and in classical pataphysical style he seems too shy and bumbling to be competent, so one can almost forgive government officials for not believing him. However, a French government agent (played by Jean Reno) does. Broderick's quest for the truth brings him back into the world of his ex-girlfriend, Audrey Timmonds (Maria Pitillo), who has been struggling to become a television reporter but has been hindered at every turn by her lecherous and controlling boss (played by Harry Shearer). Although Audrey steals a story from Niko, in the end she helps him find the nest and redeems herself, so the couple is reformed as Godzilla dies a horrible death that involves the complete destruction of the Brooklyn Bridge.

The film suffered from being too close a copy of *Jurassic Park,* and Godzilla lacked the personality (apart from his dying moment) of the Jurassic Park dinosaurs, as can be seen from one reviewer's remarks: "[*Godzilla* is] like . . . a shadowy, two-dimensional photographic image blown up and inserted into an enlarged tourist postcard" (Stephen Holden in the *New York Times*).[12] It didn't help that Godzilla's size in relation to the New York landmarks kept varying, or that Godzilla's footsteps shook cars but not people or that sometimes he could fit his head through a tunnel and other times not. If all these inconsistencies were homages to the original low-budget *Godzilla*s, they didn't work.

Then there was the issue of matching a public concern or obsession. As Shulevitz noted in her review of *Independence Day,* Emmerich's block-busters tend to foreground the misogyny of the genre, whether for commentary or for emphasis is hard to say. In *Godzilla,* this takes the form of the monster being, to all appearances, male (all the mayhem is certainly of the type that blockbusters associate with masculinity)—and pregnant. When we first see the nest full of huge eggs à la *Alien,* it reminds us of nothing so much as ovum-laden ovaries, but once all the eggs hatch, the newborn Godzillas roaming around Madison Square Garden look like nothing so much as sperm in a petri dish. There is something here about mutation and identity, but the theme is not carried over to the subplots, and as a result the whole movie slips away.

Emmerich's trademark destruction of landmarks was not missed by some, as the film was referred to cryptically by al-Qaeda prisoner Abu Zubaydah during FBI questioning, leading agents to put New York's Statue of Liberty and Brooklyn Bridge on full alert in May 2002.[13]

The Day After Tomorrow (2004)

The movie begins on one of the ice shelfs off Antarctica, with three climatologists collecting core samples. The shelf breaks away, cutting their camp in half, but Jack Hall (Dennis Quaid) manages to rescue some of his samples, which he uses in presenting his findings that global warming is taking place faster than predicted and could lead to a new ice age in less than a hundred years. The vice president, a Dick Cheney look-alike, dismisses all of Hall's findings and similar calls to take action to prevent global warming from international scientists and politicians, even though, as they leave the conference in New Delhi, it is snowing. Hall returns home to Washington, D.C., to deal with his estranged wife and son as the weather continues to worsen worldwide. His son, Sam (Jake Gyllenhaal), flies to New York with a couple of friends, while his father is suddenly called in by the U.S. government to help figure out what is happening, as tornadoes have destroyed Los Angeles and ice storms have buried other parts of the world. Hall concludes that the global warming predicted for next century will actually arrive in the next forty-eight hours and that everyone north of the Mason-Dixon line will be killed. While we are treated to more footage of landmarks around the world being destroyed, Hall finally convinces government officials to evacuate the southern states, then heads north to try to rescue his son, who has holed up with a few others in the New York Public Library. Along the way we are treated to a vision of the Statue of Liberty encased in ice. Hall, of course, makes it to the library and rescues his son, they are airlifted to Mexico, and the family is reunited.

The reviews were predictable: "[The Day After Tomorrow has] a trite plot, banal dialogue, clunky sentimentality and, worst of all, a sort of narrative arbitrariness by which [Emmerich is] shunting his paper-thin characters this way and that to shoehorn in as many effects as possible" (Stephen Hunter in the Washington Post); "Global warming may be one of the great dangers facing our planet. But clichéd scripts are still the No. 1 peril for the big Hollywood blockbuster" (Michael Wilmington in the Chicago Tribune).[14]

Nonetheless, the film sparked a huge debate in the press, which shows that this time Emmerich succeeded in tapping into a social anxiety (timing the release with an election year probably helped). Although the timing of the advent of the ice age in the film is impossibly quick, enough of the ice age events are based on those predicted by scientists, especially the breaking off of the Antarctic shelf, which actually occurred a few months after the movie was released. Serious environmentalists at first complained that the movie was unrealistic,[15] but they changed their attitude when the film raised consciousness about global warming[16] to such an extent that the Web activist organization MoveOn.org designed an environmental awareness campaign, with former vice president Al Gore as a key speaker.[17] On the Republican side, some claimed the movie had helped John Kerry's presidential campaign,[18] and NASA barred its scientists from giving interviews in which they were asked to separate fact from fiction in the film.[19]

The Day After Tomorrow is an example of the pataphysical film at its best: filled with jokes at the expense of U.S. environmental and foreign policies, delighting in the (mostly digital) destruction of world landmarks, in which American and British sites are singled out, the film is clearly playing on both American and non-American anxieties about U.S. involvement in Iraq and Bush's wholesale reversal of previous administrations' environmental policies. The environmentalists who criticized the film wished that Emmerich had given more information on global warming, but Emmerich knew something that they did not—that we already know, we already feel anxious, and that a film like this both gives play to our anxieties and, with the elaborate destruction, allows for some catharsis. It's hard to say if the film raised awareness about the dangers of global warming, but it did show that, at least abroad, where *Day* made 61 percent of its $528 million box office take (on a budget of $125 million), these concerns are paramount.

Notes

1. A more complete list of directors who make pataphysical films can be found in the introduction to this book.

2. Kevin H. Martin, "A Walk on the Wild Side," *Cinefex* 79 (October 1999): 31.

3. Movie reviews of *Wild Wild West*, June 30, 1999 (StudioBriefing.com), http://pro.imdb.com/news/sb/1999–06–30#film2.

4. "Beckinsale Hurt by 'Worst Boobs' Headlines," November 5, 2004; and "Guillory Slams 'Surgically-Enhanced' Beckinsale," October 5, 2004 (wenn.com), http://pro.imdb.com/news/sb/1999–06–30#film2.

5. All quotations from StudioBriefing.com, May 7, 2004, http://pro.imdb.com/news/sb/2004–05–07#film1.

6. "Set Gives Rise to the Series," April 27, 2004 (StudioBriefing) http://pro.imdb.com/news/sb/2004–04–27#tv3.

7. "NBC Kills the Dead," May 24, 2004 (StudioBriefing), http://pro.imdb.com/news/sb/2004–05–24#tv2.

8. All quotations from StudioBriefing.com, May 7, 1999. http://pro.imdb.com/news/sb/1999–05–07#film1.

9. Roger Ebert, review of *Independence Day,* http://rogerebert.suntimes.com/apps/pbcs .dll/article?AID=/19960702/REVIEWS/607020301/1023.

10. James Berardinelli, review of *Independence Day,* http://movie-reviews.colossus.net/ movies/i/id4.html.

11. Judith Shulevitz, review of *Independence Day,* http://slate.msn.com/id/3189.

12. Stephen Holden, "So, How Big Is It Again?" *New York Times,* May 19, 1998.

13. "Godzilla Links to New Terrorist Attack," May 30, 2002, http://www.imdb.com/ news/wenn/2002–05–30.

14. Movie Reviews: *The Day After Tomorrow,* May 28, 2004 (StudioBriefing.com), http:// pro.imdb.com/news/sb/2004–05–28#film1.

15. "Disaster Film Has Environmentalists Up in Arms," May 12, 2004 (StudioBriefing .com) http://pro.imdb.com/news/sb/2004–05–12#film4.

16. "Gore Adds Voice to 'Day' Chorus," *Hollywood Reporter,* May 12, 2004, p. 6.

17. " 'Tomorrow' Gets Free PR: Environmentalists Aid Marketing," *Hollywood Reporter,* May 7, 2004, p. 1.

18. This claim was taken seriously enough by the Republican Party to criticize the U.S. Army for allowing the filmmakers to use Blackhawk helicopters. See "Army Unwittingly Aided Democrats, Says Report," May 24, 2004 (StudioBriefing.com), http://pro.imdb .com/news/sb/2004–05–24#film5.

19. "NASA Orders Scientists Not to Discuss Global-Warming Movie," April 26, 2004 (StudioBriefing.com) http://pro.imdb.com/news/sb/2004–04–26#film3.

Conclusion

I n *The Classical Hollywood Cinema: Film Style and Mode of Production to 1960,* David Bordwell, Janet Staiger, and Kristin Thompson conclude with a chapter called "The Persistence of Hollywood Practice," in which they say:

> [E]ven the most ambitious directors cannot escape genres. New Hollywood cinema consists of gangster and outlaw films, thrillers, westerns, musicals, science-fiction films, comedies, and an occasional melodrama. *Apocalypse Now* is primarily and almost entirely a war movie. *Blue Collar,* a film of putative social significance, includes fight scenes . . . a caper intrigue, and even a car chase. Classical film style and codified genres swallow up art-film borrowings, taming the (already limited) disruptiveness of the art cinema.[1]

Even at the time their book was written, filmmakers, screenwriters, and screenwriting teachers were bemoaning the "aesthetic bankruptcy"[2] of the classical Hollywood film genres. It was clear that those who cared were searching for some kind of alternative, and screenwriting gurus like John Truby predicted that new forms were just beyond the horizon, as the need to find them was acute.

What happened instead was that Hollywood films began to combine genres in individual films, to produce hybrids. It was no longer good enough to make a science-fiction film; one had to combine sci-fi and horror (*Alien,* 1979). Soon after that it wasn't enough to combine sci-fi and horror, but action had to be added; soon it was sci-fi, horror, action, thriller, fantasy, and comedy—all in one film. (*Jaws,* 1975, represents an early example of this multigenre blending, for it combines features of action, thriller, monster, slasher, and buddy movies.[3] For other examples, see the films I discussed in Chapter 7.) Such long lists of genre combinations are typical of current films and are an absolute requirement for pataphysical films.

Instead of developing new genre forms, what has occurred is that the use and meaning of genre conventions has changed. Genres have become like musical keys in an Elfman composition: a contemporary Hollywood film will switch smoothly and naturally from one key to another in short order. So will a pataphysical film or almost any Hollywood film change genre "register," moving from an action sequence to a horror sequence to a sequence that combines several genres at once. Genres, instead of being umbrella classifications, are now more like colors that writers and directors mix on a single palette.

For purposes of discussion, film scholars have reverted to the three main categories that have underlined storytelling in the Western world for millennia: myth, fairy tale, and what I have called pataphysical films, which are parodic or satiric treatments of myth and fairy tales that use an alternative system of narration, closer to animation narration conventions than anything else. Like myths and fairy tales, pataphysical films have existed since the beginning of film history, but they were not necessarily recognized as such (I felt the need to come up with a "new" term because it is a classification that is applied retroactively, like the term *film noir* once was). New technological developments such as the advent of CGI and the rise in stylistic importance of special effects facilitated the development of a meta-narration style, in which the diegesis is of secondary importance, and the extradiegetic level of narration is where everything that is interesting is really going on. These kinds of films work best with audiences that are steeped in contemporary pop culture and often play on cultural anxieties that are widely felt but rarely acknowledged by mainstream media, such as fears about the environment, American imperialist policies, reactions to such polices from other nations and from terrorists, or, on a more personal level, shifts in the battle of the sexes or anxiety about sexual identity.

If we adopt this new understanding of genre in Hollywood, then Tim Burton becomes a figure of key importance, because his early pataphysical films set new standards that many others have imitated.

Burton's status as a film auteur is complex. Film scholars have recognized for some time now that the category of "film auteur" is really an untenable one today, when studios dominate and the final film is the product of the efforts of large numbers of people. However, the mainstream media still use the auteur concept to describe what is really better understood as a "brand," and filmmakers themselves, especially filmmakers who stand out for their aesthetic choices, find it essential to construct an artistic persona for themselves that becomes a hook on which the media can hang their auteur status. In Burton's case, this persona is carefully constructed by carefully repeating certain stories about his past (such as the anecdote about his parents' bricking up the windows of his room) and repeatedly allying his film work with Hammer and Roger Corman films, monster movies, and so on. Finally, a carefully maintained Goth appearance, especially in his early professional career, completed the picture, all of this supported by his truncated way of speaking and natural introversion. Such strategies are typical of art house/independent filmmakers; what is unusual about Burton is that he has used these strategies to carve out a niche for himself in Hollywood. Although he has made films for Fox and Disney, his "home" is Warner Bros., with whom he now has a long-term contract; his company develops projects like *The Corpse Bride,* but their eventual production is always a result of Burton's "clout," which shifts slightly from film to film but which is very resilient overall. One way that Burton has maintained his position has been by keeping tight control over any idea, sketch, or concept that originated with him—so *Nightmare* became *Tim Burton's Nightmare Before Christmas,* and he is listed as a producer on the *Family Dog* series. He has taken a different approach than Steven Spielberg, a director only a few years his senior. Spielberg has aggressively asserted a more vertical-integration style of control from almost the beginning of his career, and today is regarded more as a studio mogul and industry head than as a director, though he continues to produce a film every year.

Filmmakers whose reputation is based more on their auteur status, like Burton, Terry Gilliam, Alfonso Cuarón, and Guillermo del Toro, have particular styles and thematic concerns that are associated with their name. Once this association takes place (often with their very first commercial film), it is very hard to break away from. In Burton's case, as this book has made clear, his brand consists of a certain kind of narrative that often features a more reactive than active hero, a more episodic narrative structure, and a layer of comedy, often black comedy or satire, that works primarily at the level of extradiegetic narration (that is, based on references in the story world but not really a part of it, such as inside jokes).

Whether you like Burton's films or not, the most important lesson to be drawn from a study of Burton's career is that our current genre categories no longer hold; we can still use these terms as labels for aesthetic approaches within individual films, but a new umbrella categorization system is already in place, with a continuum that can be summed up with the terms

Myth ↔ fairy tale ↔ drama ↔ pataphysical film

This system categorizes Tim Burton's films, but it also applies to every film coming out of Hollywood today.

Notes

1. David Bordwell, Janet Staiger, and Kristin Thompson, *The Classical Hollywood Cinema: Film Style and Mode of Production to 1960* (New York: Columbia University Press, 1985), p. 375.
2. As a film student, I heard this phrase used repeatedly in various screenwriting courses.
3. See Thomas Schatz, "The New Hollywood," in *Movie Blockbusters,* ed. Julian Stringer (London: Routledge, 2003), p. 25.

Filmography

Film Work[1]

The Corpse Bride (director, producer) 2005
Charlie and the Chocolate Factory (director) 2005
Big Fish (director) 2003
Planet of the Apes (director) 2001
Stainboy (animated short) (director, producer, writer) 2000
Sleepy Hollow (director) 1999
Mars Attacks! (director, producer) 1996
James and the Giant Peach (producer) 1996
Batman Forever (producer) 1995
Ed Wood (director, producer) 1994
Cabin Boy (producer) 1994
The Nightmare Before Christmas (producer, writer, story and characters) 1993
Batman Returns (director, producer) 1992
Edward Scissorhands (director, producer, writer, story) 1990
Batman (director) 1989
Beetlejuice (director, writer, story, uncredited) 1988
The Black Cauldron (conceptual artist, uncredited) 1985
Pee-wee's Big Adventure (director) 1985
Frankenweenie (live-action short) (director, writer, idea, storyboard artist, uncredited) 1984
Luau (director, producer, The Supreme Being/Mortie, writer) 1982
Vincent (animated short) (director, writer, production designer) 1982
Tron (animator, uncredited) 1982
The Fox and the Hound (animator, uncredited) 1981

Stalk of the Celery Monster (animated short) (director, producer, writer, animator) 1979

The Lord of the Rings (animated) (in-between artist, uncredited) 1978[2]

The Island of Doctor Agor (live-action short) (director, writer, animator, uncredited) 1971

Television

Tim Burton's Lost in Oz (TV movie) (executive producer, writer, story, pilot) 2000

Family Dog (animated TV series) (executive producer, character designer, uncredited, design consultant) 1993

Beetlejuice (animated TV series) (executive producer, writer, creator, developed by) 1989

Alfred Hitchcock Presents (TV series) (director, episode "The Jar") 1985

Amazing Stories (TV series) (character designer, animated episode "Family Dog") 1985

Hansel and Gretel (TV movie) (director, writer, idea) 1982

Shelley Duvall's Faerie Tale Theatre (TV series) (director, episode "Aladdin and His Wonderful Lamp") 1982

Notes

1. Salisbury, Mark, *Burton on Burton*, London and Boston: Faber and Faber, 2000. Smith, Jim and J. Clive Matthews, *Tim Burton*, London: Virgin Film, 2002.

2. Tim Burton's flmography on imdb.com is the only source for this.

Bibliography

Abel, Richard. *The Ciné Goes to Town: French Cinema 1896–1914*. Berkeley: University of California Press, 1994.

Aldiss, Brian. Introduction. In *The Planet of the Apes*, by Pierre Boulle. London and New York: Penguin, 2001.

Altman, Rick, ed. *Sound Theory/Sound Practice*. New York: Routledge/AFI Film Readers, 1992.

Arijon, Daniel. *Grammar of the Film Language*. London: Focal Press, 1982.

Patricia Aufderheide, Erik Barnouw, Richard M. Cohen, Thomas Frank, Todd Gitlin, DAvid Lieberman, Mark Crispin Miller, Gene Roberts, Thomas Schatz. *Conglomerates and the Media*. New York: New Press, 1997.

Braun, Marta. *Picturing Time: The Work of Etienne-Jules Marey (1830–1904)*. Chicago: University of Chicago Press, 1992.

Breese, Keith. *Clowns of Death: A History of Oingo Boingo*. Philadephia, PA: Xlibris, 2001.

Brodrowski, Steve. "Edward Scissorhands." *Cinefantastique,* February 1991. Reprinted in Paul A. Woods, *Tim Burton: A Child's Garden of Nightmares*. (Ultrascreen series, London: Plexus, 2002), pp. 70–71.

Brooker, Will. *Batman Unmasked: Analyzing a Cultural Icon*. London and New York: Continuum, 2000.

Brotchie, Alastair, ed. *A True History of the College of Pataphysics*. London: Atlas Press, 1995.

Burton, Tim. *The Melancholy Death of Oyster Boy & Other Stories*. New York: Rob Weisbach Books, 1997.

Canby, Vincent. " 'Beetlejuice' Is Pap for the Eyes." *New York Times,* May 8, 1988.

Carvin, Andy. "An Interview with Tim Burton." *EdWeb,* http://sujnsite.ust.hk/edweb/nightmare.burton.html.

Cavell, Stanley. *Contesting Tears: The Hollywood Melodrama of the Unknown Woman*. Chicago: University of Chicago Press, 1996.

Cerone, Daniel. "Reigning Bats and Dogs: Tim Burton Rides High with 'Batman' Sequel, 'Frankenweenie.'" *Los Angeles Times*, March 12, 1992.

Coleman, David. "Vincent." *Cinefantastique* 13.4 (April–May 1983). Reprinted in Wood, p. 13.

Clark, Rick. "Danny Elfman." *Mix Magazine*, http://mixonline.com/ar/audio_danny_elfman/.

Clarke, James. *Animated Films*. London: Virgin Film, 2004.

Crafton, Donald. *Emile Cohl, Caricature, and Film*. Princeton, NJ: Princeton University Press, 1990.

Crafton, Donald, *Before Mickey: The Animated Film 1898–1928*. Chicago and London: The University of Chicago Press, 1993.

Cubitt, Sean. *The Cinema Effect*. Cambridge: MIT Press, 2004.

Daniels, Les. *Batman: The Complete History*. San Francisco: Chronicle Books, 1999.

Deneroff, Harvey. "In the Matter of Writers and Animation Story Persons." In *Storytelling in Animation: The Art of the Animated Image, Vol. 2*, ed. John Canemaker, published in conjunction with the Second Annual Walter Lantz Conference on Animation. Los Angeles: American Film Institute, 1988.

Ebert, Roger. "Edward Scissorhands." *Chicago Sun-Times,* December 14, 1990.

Edelstein, David. "Mixing Beetlejuice." *Rolling Stone*, June 2, 1988, pp. 51, 53, 76.

———. "Tim Burton's Hollywood Nightmare." *Vanity Fair*, November 1994, pp. 124, 129–34.

Eisner, Michael, with Tony Schwartz. *Work in Progress*. London: Penguin Books, 1998.

Felperin, Leslie. "Animated Dreams" (an interview with Henry Selick). *Sight and Sound*, December 1994. Reprinted in Woods, pp. 102–107.

Fielding, Raymond. *The Technique of Special Effects Cinematography*, 4th ed. London and Boston: Focal Press, 1985.

Furniss, Maureen. *Art in Motion: Animation Aesthetics*. London: John Libbery, 1998.

Gabler, Neal. *Life: The Movie: How Entertainment Conquered Reality*. New York: Vintage Books, 2000.

Garsault, Alain. "Méliès retrouvé." *Positif* 336 (February 1989), pp. 61–63.

Greene, Eric. *Planet of the Apes as American Myth: Race and Politics in the Films and Television Series*. Jefferson, NC, and London: McFarland & Co., 1996.

Halfyard, Janet K. *Danny Elfman's Batman: A Film Score Guide*, Scarecrow Film Score Guides, No. 2. Lanham, MD: Scarecrow Press, 2004.

Handelman, David. "Heart and Darkness: Even as the New, Improved *Batman* Sequel Continues His Unbroken String of Hits, Tim Burton Insists He's Not Cut Out to Be a Director." *Vogue,* July 1992, pp. 142–194.

Hanke Ken. *Tim Burton: An Unauthorized Biography of the Filmmaker*. Los Angeles: Renaissance Books, 1999.

Hirschberg, Lynn. "Drawn to Narrative." *New York Times Sunday Magazine,* November 9, 2003.

Hirshey, Gerri. "Welcome to His Nightmare: Weird Genius Tim Burton Goes Back to His Roots in Animation—and to Disney, His Old Employer—to Put a Creepy-Crawly Spin on the Kiddie Christmas Movie." *GQ,* November 1993. From the Margeret Herrick Library Clipping Fil, page numbers not available.

Hoberman, J. "Ed Wood . . . Not," *Sight and Sound,* May 1995, pp. 10–12.

Katz, Steven D. *Film Directing: Shot by Shot*. Studio City, CA: Michael Wiese Productions, 1991.

———. *Film Directing: Cinematic Motion*. Studio City, CA: Michael Wiese Productions, 1992.

Kendall, Lukas. "Danny Elfman: From *Pee-wee* to *Batman* to Two Films a Year," part 2. *Film Score Monthly,* December 1995, pp. 11–14.

———. "Interview: Steve Bartek," part 1. *Film Score Monthly,* December 1995, pp. 14–16.

Kieskowski, Ellie. "Tim Burton's Animated Series 'Stainboy' Premieres: Shockwave.com Announces New Fall Line-up and Online Store," September 26, 2000. http://www.streamingmedia.com/r/printerfriendly .asp?id = 6231.

King, Geoff. *Spectacular Narratives: Hollywood in the Age of the Blockbuster*. London and New York: IB Tauris Publishers, 2000.

Lanser, Bryan, and Kevin Monahan. "Danny Elfman's Big Adventure Continues in Sleepy Hollow." *E-mu*, http://www.emu.com/artist/

d_elfman/elfman_intrview.html (no longer available). Now at: http://
www.bluntinstrument.org.uk/elfman/archive/Emu99.htm.

Lloyd, Anne. "Pee-wee's Big Adventure." *Films and Filming* 394 (July
1987). From the clipping file at Margeret Herrick Library, page numbers not available.

Lutz, E. G., *Animated Cartoons: How They Are Made, Their Origin, and Development*. Bedford, MA: Applewood Books, 1998 (originally published
in 1920).

Mannoni, Laurent. *The Great Arts of Light and Shadow: Archeology of the
Cinema*, trans. and ed. Richard Crangle. Exeter: University of Exeter
Press, 2000.

Martin, Kevin H. "A Walk on the Wild Side." *Cinefex* 79 (October
1999), pp. 15–44.

McMahan, Alison. "The Quest for Motion: Moving Pictures and Flight."
In *Visual Delights: Essays on the Popular and Projected Image in the Nineteenth Century*, ed. S. Popple and V. Toulmin. Trowbridge: Flicks Books,
2000, pp. 93–104.

————. *Alice Guy Blaché: Lost Visionary of the Cinema*. New York: Continuum, 2002.

McMillan, Sam. "Flinch Studios Makes Its Mark with Tim Burton's Stain
Boy." http://www.designinteract.com/features/stainboy/.

Miller, Greg. "Tim Burton to Animate Cartoons for Shockwave." *Los
Angeles Times*, January 28, 2000.

Mills, David. "One on One—Tim Burton." *Empire*, February 2000. Reprinted in Woods, pp. 147–150.

Moore, Booth. "Social Confidential" *Los Angeles Times*, February 10,
2000.

Morales, Juan. "A Stain on Humanity: Director Tim Burton Brings His
Brilliantly Bizarre Artistic Vision to the Web." *Detour*, April 2000.

Neale, Steve, and Murray Smith, eds. *Batman, Batman Returns* and Post-
Classical Film Music." In *Contemporary Hollywood Cinema*. London:
Routledge, 1998.

Newman, Kim. "Beetlejuice." *Monthly Film Bulletin*, August 1988. Reprinted in Woods, pp. 32–34.

Pearson, Roberta E., and William Uricchio. *The Many Lives of the Batman:
Critical Approaches to a Superhero and His Media*. New York: Routledge,
1991.

Pendreigh, Brian. *The Legend of the Planet of the Apes, or How Hollywood Turned Darwin Upside Down*. London: Boxtree, 2001.

Pettigrew, Neil. *The Stop-Motion Filmography: A Critical Guidet to 297 Features Using Puppet Animation*. Jefferson, NC, and London: McFarland & Co., 1999.

Pierson, Michele. *Special Effects: Still in Search of Wonder*, Film and Culture Series, ed. John Belton. New York: Columbia University Press, 2002.

Poole, Steven. *Trigger Happy: Videogames and the Entertainment Revolution*. New York: Arcade Publishing, 2001.

Randall, Laura. "Burton's Shorting Shockwave: Director Brings 'Stain Boy' to the Net, Takes Stake in Company." *Hollywood Reporter*, January 28, 2000.

Rayn, James. "Oyster Boy and Other Misfits." *New York Times*, November 2, 1997.

Rose, Frank. "Tim Cuts Up." *Premiere*, January 1991, pp. 96–102.

Russo, Joe, and Larry Landsman, with Edward Gross. *Planet of the Apes Revisited: The Behind-the-Scenes Story of the Classic Science Fiction Saga*, foreword by Charlton Heston. New York: St. Martin's Press, 2001.

Salen, Katie, and Tommy Pullotta. "Shoot First, Play Later: Filmmaking with Gaming Engines." *RES* 3.2 (2000): 48–53.

Salisbury, Mark. *Burton on Burton*. London and Boston: Faber & Faber, 2000.

———, "A Head of the Game." *Fangoria* 189 (January 2000).

Shannon, Jody Duncan. "Cheap and Cheesy and Off-the-Cuff: The Effects of *Beetlejuice*." *Cinefex*, 34 (May 1988), pp. 4–43.

Shay, Don, and Jody Duncan. *The Making of Jurassic Park: An Adventure 65 Million Years in the Making*. New York: Ballantine Books, 1993.

Smith, Jim, and J. Clive Matthews. *Tim Burton*. London: Virgin Films, 2002.

Smith, Scott, "Tim Burton: Dark Prince of the Web," *Res* 3.2 (2000).

Sobchak, Vivian, ed. *Meta-Morphing: Visual Transformation and the Culture of Quick-Change*. Minneapolis and London: University of Minnesota Press, 2000.

Solomon, Matthew. "Twenty-Five Heads under One Hat: Quick Change in the 1890s." In *Meta-morphing: Visual Transformation and the Culture of Quick Change*, ed. Vivian Sobchak. Minneapolis and London: University of Minnesota Press, 2000.

Stuart, Mel, with Josh Young. *Pure Imagination: The Making of Willy Wonka and the Chocolate Factory.* New York: St. Martin's Press, 2002.

Svehla, Gary J., and Susan Svehla, eds. *Vincent Price.* Baltimore: Midnight Marquee Press, 1998.

Talbot, Frederick A. *Moving Pictures.* New York: Arno Press, 1970 (originally published in 1912).

Thompson, Anne. "Tim Burton's Tasty *Beetlejuice.*" *Movieline,* April 8, 1988.

Thompson, Frank. *Tim Burton's Nightmare Before Christmas: The Film, the Art, the Vision.* New York: Hyperion, 1993.

Vaz, Mark Cotta. "A Region of Shadows." *Cinefex* 80 (January 2000), pp. 86–113.

Well, Paul. *Animation: Genre and Authorship,* Short Cut Series. London and New York: Wallflower Press, 2002.

White, Taylor L. "Aladdin's Lamp." *Cinefantastique,* November 1989, p. 77.

————. "Hansel and Gretel." *Cinefantastique,* November 1989, p. 69.

————. "Other Weirdness." *Cinefantastique,* November 1989, p. 85.

Williams, Alex. "Vanishing Act." *NYMetro.com,* http://www.newyorkmetro .com/nymetro/news/features/n_9787/index.html.

Williamson, Colin. "This Is Quake II: What Are You Going to Do About It?" *PC Gamer* 4.10 (October 1997): 98–122.

Wood, Aylish. *Technosicence in Contemporary American Film: Beyond Science Fiction.* Manchester: Manchester University Press, 2002.

Woods, Paul A. *The Planet of the Apes Chronicles,* London: Plexus, 2001.

————, ed. *Tim Burton: A Child's Garden of Nightmares.* London: Plexus, 2002.

Wyatt, Justin. *High Concept: Movies and Marketing in Hollywood.* Austin: University of Texas Press, 1994.

Zahed, Ramin. "Stainboy." *Variety,* November 13, 2000.

Index

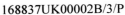
Lightning Source UK Ltd.
Milton Keynes UK
07 March 2011

168837UK00002B/3/P

9 780826 415677